Don Green.

SUCCESSFUL LANDLORDING

SUCCESSFUL LANDLORDING

Kathleen S. Abrams
Lawrence F. Abrams

Structures Publishing Company
Farmington, Michigan 48024

Manufactured in the United States of America

Edited by Virginia A. Case

Produced by Carey J. Ferchland

Text design by Linda A. Zitzewitz

Photography is by the authors unless
otherwise indicated.

Technical Editor—Jack Zimmerman, Builder and
Apartment Developer

Current Printing (last digit)

10 9 8 7 6 5 4 3 2 1

Structures Publishing Co.
24277 Indoplex Circle
Box 1002, Farmington, Mich. 48024
Cover design by Linda A. Zitzewitz.

Library of Congress Cataloging in Publication Data

Abrams, Kathleen S.
Successful landlording.
Includes index.
1. Real estate management. 2. Real estate investment. I. Abrams, Lawrence F., joint author. II. Title.
HD1394.A27 332.63'24'068 80-36678
ISBN 0-89999-006-1
ISBN 0-89999-007-X (pbk.)

Contents

Preface

Successful Landlording is written from our experiences with landlording. The advice we offer in the following pages comes from continual evaluation of our successes and failures as landlord and lady of "Abrams Apartments."

When we purchased our first duplex, we knew nothing about the art—or science—of landlording. We had heard real estate was a good investment. We did not know why, exactly, but we accepted the logic of friends and relatives who either had invested in real estate or wished they had invested in real estate. "You buy the property, rent it out and take the tax break," was the general consensus of the experienced and inexperienced people with whom we discussed our venture into the world of finance.

Over the years we have learned landlording is more complicated than this general statement implies. We made our first mistake with our very first purchase. We anxiously asked the lender if we could put 25 percent down instead of the required 20 percent so we could be sure we would "come out" each month on the expenses. His willingness to take our money started us thinking and soon we formulated our first rule as landlords: "Never part with more money than is required of you to complete the deal." Although there are exceptions to this rule and they are discussed in the book, the wise landlord generally adheres to this policy.

After our first mistake, we made many more, but from each error we learned a valuable lesson. We learned how to use financing and tax laws to our advantage. We learned how to find and keep good tenants. We learned how to spot exceptional deals, when to buy and when to sell. We learned how to increase the value of our properties. All of our lessons are recorded for others to read in *Successful Landlording.*

We discovered our individual strengths and weaknesses as landlords and we learned to work as an effective team. We found we enjoyed the challenge of acquiring and managing a string of well-paying rental units. We are not realtors or accountants. Our educational backgrounds are unrelated to the world of finance. We think that makes our book different from many of the other books available on the subject of real estate investment. We are writing for the layman from the layman's point of view. Those who read this book should remember it is intended as a guide. We share down-to-earth advice on all aspects of landlording. Every successful investor, however, knows his limitations and consults an expert on certain legal, financial and maintenance problems.

We wish we had read this book long ago. For those of you who are reading it now, we wish you a prosperous and rewarding landlording career.

The authors enjoy some time at home with their dog, Gabriel, who—if she could have her way—would ban cats from all their apartments.

Introduction

From the time the first colonists arrived in America with the hope of becoming property owners, real estate has been a popular investment. The lure of choice lands contributed to the westward expansion and continues today as people invest in speculative property. Although property in the United States has been bought and sold many times since the first settlers, it has not lost its investment appeal. In fact, real estate is one of the largest industries in the United States. In 1977, real estate accounted for $125.8 billion in revenue in the United States. According to *Business Week*, (August 1, 1977), "...prime U.S. real estate is probably the most sought after investment target in the industrial world."

Most of the millionaires in the United States did, indeed, make their first millions through real estate investments. According to Andrew Carnegie, "Ninety percent of all millionaires became so through owning real estate. More money has been made in real estate than in all industrial investments combined. The wise young man or wage earner invests his money in real estate."

Perhaps the greatest appeal of real estate investment lies in the last sentence of Carnegie's statement. Any "wise young man"—or woman—can invest in and profit from real estate. Despite the large amount of capital it draws, real estate is a small business. Ninety percent of all the firms connected in some way with real estate employ ten or fewer people. A prudent investor can build a string of well-paying rental units in a short period of time entirely independent of all firms or corporations. He need not share his profit with anyone—except the federal government—and he can enjoy the sense of accomplishment which comes from achieving on his own.

There are some pitfalls in real estate investment, however. Contrary to popular opinion, one can lose money through real estate investments. There are some problems with ownership of rental properties the beginning investor may not anticipate. This book explores some of those problems. It is written for the private investor who intends to manage his investments himself. The book is for both those who want to get started in real estate and for those who want to manage their existing units more efficiently. It speaks to investors of varying goals, from those who want to secure a retirement income to those who want to earn a substantial income—now—from their units. The book also discusses problems and rewards of the rental business and gives tips on financing and selecting properties.

One is never too old nor too young to invest in real estate. Hopefully, this book will provide the incentive and the insight for those who want to give this investment a try.

1
Choosing the Right Property

One of the first considerations for both the beginning investor and the veteran speculator is the type of rental property in which to invest. Every investor should remember to invest in individual properties rather than generally in real estate. Any property, from a single-family dwelling to an apartment complex, may be an ideal investment. When choosing a property you should consider:

1. your future goals as an investor;
2. amount of cash or equity you have available for the investment;
3. the degree of risk you can comfortably tolerate;
4. the amount of time you are willing to devote to real estate;
5. location;
6. present condition of the building;
7. future potential of the building.

FUTURE GOALS

Your future goals help to determine the type of property you purchase. If your purpose is a hedge against inflation, a tax break for a substantial income, or a retirement income, you may decide to buy a well-kept, relatively new multi-unit property. Although you may show an actual loss on the property during the first few years, it is a worthwhile investment because you intend to keep it as a long range investment.

If, on the other hand, you want some quick cash, you may find an older unit showing a good return or a unit which can be remodeled or redecorated and sold quickly for a profit to be the best buy for you. If you want to earn a living from rental units, you will probably start with older units and "buy up", (purchase more and better units as quickly as you can), until you have reached the return you need to live comfortably.

AMOUNT OF MONEY AVAILABLE

The amount of money available for the investor helps to determine the type of property he purchases. If you want to start in real estate but have very little money available, you may choose a single-family dwelling or you may join with several other people and purchase a multi-unit as a partnership. The various ways to finance rentals are discussed in detail in the chapter *Financing Rental Units.* Each type of investment has specific advantages and disadvantages which are discussed later in this chapter.

RISK

Whatever your goal as an investor, you must realize there is an element of risk in the real estate business. Contrary to popular opinion, people can lose money in real estate. A population shift may cause the property to depreciate rather than appreciate. Renters may all move out at a slow renting period. The apartments may remain vacant for several months, and you may have to feed your own money into the building to keep your investment alive. You may need to sell when the market for property is sluggish or investment money is tight. Before buying, you should decide how much risk you can comfortably tolerate, then buy accordingly. If you must re-finance your home to purchase a rental, for example, you are assuming greater risk to your personal security than if you use cash savings, an insurance policy or equity in other rental units. If you are just beginning to invest in real estate, you may feel more comfortable with a duplex you own yourself than if you purchase a multi-unit in partnership with other investors.

Before buying rentals, you should know your emotional limitations as well as your financial limitations. Will you be irritated when tenants call you about minor problems? Will you fret about the loss of income each time you have a vacancy in an apartment building? Do financial obligations frighten you? If you must answer "yes" to these questions, you should choose your investments carefully. In other words, do not buy several duplexes or one expensive multi-unit for starters. If you really want to try landlording, start with one well-kept, fully rented duplex in a good neighborhood. If you enjoy the experience with that building, you may want to purchase additional properties. If you do not enjoy the experience, your financial commitment is not great and you can sell one building more easily than you can sell many.

TIME

You must also know how much time you are willing to spend managing your investments. Rentals need repairs, they must be shown to prospective renters and they require accurate record keeping. While work necessary to manage one rental unit may not be a noticeable infringement on your leisure, ten units may be impossible to manage properly if you also hold a demanding full time job. If your goal is to earn your living from rentals, then you should be willing to put in the extra time until you have built a large enough chain to warrant a manager.

When you have your goals and limitations firmly in mind, you are ready to consider specific types of rental properties in which to invest.

LOCATION

In the selection of rental properties, location is as important as it is in the selection of a personal residence. Before buying, you should investigate the neighborhood. Ask yourself these questions:

1. Are the other properties in the neighborhood well-kept?
2. Is the building close to a bus line, shopping center, and employment opportunities?
3. If the building lacks laundry facilities for the tenants, is there a laundromat near by?
4. What kind of renters will be attracted to the location?
5. What is the zoning history of the neighborhood?

If the property you choose is close to a university, for example, the building will probably rent easily, but it may have a high turnover rate. This necessitates frequent trips to show the apartments and results in more bookkeeping for the landlord. If your time is limited, you may prefer to purchase a rental unit in a residential section which would attract a long-term renter.

The stability of the neighborhood should be another consideration. Consider population shifts, main roads and school enrollments which will help to determine if the building will have the same (or better) potential as a rental unit five years from the date of purchase. With the high price of transportation, renters consider location carefully and the landlord should also.

Related to the stability of the neighborhood is its zoning history. Property may be zoned residential, commercial or industrial. In older neighborhoods, the zoning may vary from block to block. It may even vary from lot to lot. One property, for example, may be zoned for business while the property next to it is zoned residential. There are also variations in zoning within the three categories. A neighborhood zoned residential may include zoning for single-family, duplex and multi-family dwellings.

An investor should check the zoning of the property he is considering. The property should be zoned for the use the investor intends. If the investor intends to use the property as a duplex, the property should be zoned for use as a duplex. An owner who wants to change the zoning of a property after he has purchased it will find this is a time-consuming, complicated and often impossible task.

When the zoning of a neighborhood changes, normally the zoning regulations are not retroactive. If the zoning of a neighborhood has changed from multi-family to single family, for example, any buildings in use as multi-family dwellings at the time of the change may remain in use as multi-family dwellings. Often this is referred to as a guarantee under a "Grandfather Clause."

The problem for an investor who buys property covered under a "Grandfather Clause" is that the building is actually considered to be a "non-conforming use" according to the current zoning regulations. This means if the property's present use is discontinued for a time (usually one year), the property changes to the present zoning at the end of the time period. For example, let's say that an investor buys a property in a residential area with office space. He is allowed to rent out the space as offices because the building is covered by a "Grandfather Clause." For some reason, he decides not to use the building as office space for more than a year. Then he decides that he wants to use the building again as office space. He may not be allowed to do so because the privilege granted him under the "Grandfather Clause" has expired and the building has reverted to residential zoning. An investor should check carefully into the zoning of the property before he purchases it so he knows exactly the conditions under which he may use the building.

An investor should also check the zoning of the neighborhood in which the property is located. Have there been changes in the zoning of surrounding properties? Perhaps an older residential neighborhood is slowly being converted to commercial or even industrial property. Can a restaurant, bar or office complex be built next to your duplex? Will your unimposing frame duplex be sandwiched in between two department stores? If so, this would probably decrease the value of your property as a residential rental. On the other hand, gradual re-zoning of a property may actually work for the investor. If you purchase an older rental in a neighborhood that is becoming a commercial center, you may find your property appreciates rapidly because it is valuable for use other than a residential rental. When checking the zoning be sure to check zoning patterns for several blocks around your property. This will help you make sound long-term or speculative purchases.

Another aspect of location which may be overlooked in the fervor of finding a "good buy" is the location of the rental in relation to the buyer's private residence. If you plan to manage the rental yourself, (and most landlords must at least initially manage their own buildings), you will probably be happier with a property which is conveniently located to your home or place of employment. When you have to drive to another town to answer a late night maintenance call, landlording loses some of its appeal.

PRESENT CONDITION OF THE BUILDING

The building you are planning to purchase should be examined carefully. Walk around the outside of the rental. Start your scrutiny at the ground line. Is the foundation solid? Do not be pacified by the statement, "The basement needs a little cement work." A crumbling or cracked foundation may indicate other problems which could be expensive to repair.

Examine the exterior of the building. If the siding is old but has been painted recently, check the ends of the siding for rot. If the building has been recently painted and is beginning to peel, this may indicate paint will not adhere to the siding. You may have to plan to repaint every couple of years or cover the building with aluminum siding. Either of these situations is costly. Before making an offer on the building, secure an estimate on the cost of painting it or covering it with aluminum siding. If the building already has care-free exterior, it is a plus in its favor.

Next check the windows. Are there storms and screens for all the windows? Actually count the number of storms or screens stored. Especially in older buildings which have numerous windows and large windows, the cost of replacing lost storms or screens is significant. It is best to calculate this cost when making your offer rather than be surprised by the additional cost after you have bought the building.

Self-storing storms and screens, especially on second and third stories of older buildings, make a building more desirable than individual storms and screens which have to be removed with the changing seasons. Self-storing storms and screens save the landlord numerous hours if he maintains the building himself. If he hires someone for the exterior maintenance of the building, self-storing storms and screens save him a lot of money in maintenance costs.

One of the buildings we bought had two large sunporches, an attractive feature until you think of the windows. A person who would put the storms on in the fall and take them off in the spring was recommended to us. He charged one dollar per window. That seemed to be a reasonable price. Then we counted the windows. Since the cost of having the windows changed each season cut substantially into our profit, we decided to do the work ourselves. Then we found we had to give up two Saturdays, one on a beautiful fall day and one on a beautiful spring day. Even if you have a lot of time or a maintenance person on a salary, self-storing storms and screens are desirable for a rental unit. Most successful landlording begins as a part-time job, and time is always at a premium.

Next check the roof. How old is it? Has it been kept in good condition? Will it need replacing soon? How many times have new shingles been nailed over the old shingles? Check in the attic for leaks which may not be visible from the outside. If the roof is old, secure an estimate for replacing it.

Another aspect of the roof to consider is the pitch. If you live in the northern states, snow could be a problem. Will snow build up on the roof? Is the roof accessible to you so you can remove the snow? Also look for crevices in the roof where ice may build up and cause water damage to the interior of the building. Many times older buildings with a number of additions have crevices where ice can build up. Although this may not prevent you from buying the building, you should plan to make provisions for the problem either by hooking up electrical heating tape to the roof (which melts the snow) or by frequent manual snow removal.

Inside the building, check for water in the basement. Water may seep in either through the walls or through the floor. Rate the seriousness of the problem and determine what you will have to do to correct it. If the problem is serious enough to require digging around the foundation, you should secure an estimate for this work before making an offer on the building.

Next, consider the furnace. Today the landlord has more to think about than the age of the furnace. The first thing you should consider is the type of heating presently used and the types of heating available to the building. Current statistics show natural gas is the most reasonable way to heat. If the building already has a natural gas furnace or can be hooked up to a natural gas line, this is a desirable feature. Since the recent hikes in oil prices, electricity ranks second to natural gas in cost with oil being the most expensive of the three. When purchasing a rental unit, you will want to consider the type of fuel used to heat the building.

You will also want to consider the number of heating units in the building and the type of heating system in each apartment. Because of the high cost of heating, separate furnaces or heating units are more desirable than one heating system for the entire building. When each tenant is responsible for his own heating cost, there is less waste. When the landlord does not have to calculate heating cost into the rent, he also has a more predictable income. Heating costs change so rapidly that it is difficult to estimate them over a year's period. From an aesthetic view, furnaces are preferred over space heaters. An apartment will probably rent faster if the unit is heated by a furnace than if a space heater fills the living room or kitchen.

Take a critical look at the kitchen and bathroom. Are the fixtures modern or antiquated? A unit is usually easier to rent when the kitchen and bathroom have modern fixtures. Check for rotten boards wherever water may be spilled such as around the sinks, toilet and bathtub or shower. Carpeting may camouflage this so do not be fooled by an attractive facelift. If you suspect rotten floor boards, ask to check the floor more carefully.

The floors and doors of a building may tell you some things about the general condition of the building. Does the floor tilt or squeak? Do you have difficulty shutting the doors properly? This may mean the building has shifted on the foundation. If you are suspicious about the construction of the building, ask a contractor to evaluate the construction.

The wiring of older buildings may also present a problem. Some older buildings are not adequately wired for the number of appliances used by tenants today. Blown fuses are a nuisance; running in additional service is expensive. Make sure the wiring is adequate before you purchase the building.

Also make certain the building conforms to fire safety standards. In some cities these standards vary depending upon the number of units in the building. Check on the required number of exits for each apartment and make certain the building you are considering conforms to the code. It is also a good idea to have the insurance company which will be insuring the building check it before you make an offer. Occasionally, a building will conform to city ordinance, but it will not conform to the more rigid requirements of the insurance company. If you know repairs will have to be made to the building to make it conform to the insurance company's restrictions, you can use these as a bargaining factor when making your first offer on the building. For example, if the insurance company requires railings on outside entrances but the city does not, you can include a statement that the present owner will install a railing before you purchase the building.

If you have any doubts or questions about the building conforming to city code, call the building inspector and request he check the building. Occasionally, a qualified lender may require that a property be surveyed, and he may check on things such as easements to the property, but the buyer should not depend on the lender to require these checks. If you have any doubts about the property, you should request the necessary checks be made. If you are buying the building on a land contract, you should take the initiative to see the property conforms to all city standards.

Lastly, check the amount of insulation in the building. Do not make the mistake of thinking insulation does not matter unless you are paying the utilities. Today, renters ask if the building is insulated before they rent. They do not want to pay for the utilities in an uninsulated building any more than the landlord does. They are also not willing to absorb the extra cost of heating an uninsulated building even when the landlord pays the utilities. Unless you rent to a very naive renter, you cannot charge him more for an uninsulated building than for an insulated building. If your building is not insulated, the extra cost of heating it will come out of your pocket.

When all the physical characteristics of the building have been considered, you should turn your attention to the aesthetic qualities of the rental. Although attractive buildings rent easier, the aesthetics of a building mean more than the pleasing appearance of the grounds and the building. Actually, the prospective landlord should look at the building from a negative point of view. What are the features of the building which may make it difficult to rent? What features would make the rental you are considering bring in lower rents than a comparable building? What features would make it expensive to maintain?

Some features which may make an apartment more difficult to rent or lower the rent the unit will bring are:

1. **Bedrooms which open off other rooms,** especially off other bedrooms, rather than a common hallway. When the renter must walk through one bedroom to reach another bedroom, the apartment is usually limited to families. Single roommates need more privacy than this feature allows them.

2. **A bathroom which opens off a bedroom.** If this is the only bathroom in the apartment, many renters will shy away from the apartment because of the inconvenience and lack of privacy this feature causes.

3. **A bathroom which must be shared by two apartments.** Many renters object to this lack of privacy and

inconvenience. Usually the bathroom is located between the two apartments and the tenants must leave their own apartments to use the bathroom. A shared bathroom is also an inconvenience for the landlord since he must screen his tenants more carefully. If women are renting one apartment, he should look for women to rent the second apartment. Apartments with shared bathrooms will also bring less rent as a general rule than apartments with private bathrooms.

4. **A first floor apartment without basement facilities.** Generally, this apartment will bring less money than a first floor apartment with basement facilities. People willing to pay the added cost for a first floor apartment want the added convenience of basement storage and washer-dryer hook-ups.

5. **Apartments without a garage.** Garages are a plus in renting apartments so consider that when you look for buildings to buy. A building with a garage should bring better rent than a comparable building without a garage.

6. **Outdated kitchen or bathroom.** New kitchen cupboards and fixtures for kitchens and bathrooms are expensive. Replacing sinks and toilets to make the apartment more attractive or convenient will add significantly to any facelifting you plan to do. You should not make the mistake of thinking "anything is good enough for renters." While you would probably not remodel an apartment with the most expensive material available, the apartment you offer for rent should be attractive. Generally, an unattractive apartment will have a higher turn-over rate and bring in less rent per month than an attractive apartment.

7. **Fireplaces.** A fireplace is an attractive feature to many tenants, but it may actually detract from the desirability for the landlord. If you pay the heat, you will find your heat bill increases in direct proportion to the tenant's use of the fireplace. When the tenant uses the fireplace, you do not have any control over the care he takes with closing the glass door as the fire cools or the damper when he is not using the fireplace. The use of a fireplace may also cause problems in heating the remainder of the building, especially if the thermostat is located in the apartment with the fireplace. Additional expense in maintaining the building is also a factor because the fireplace chimney must be cleaned periodically. Although the landlord may smile when tenants say, "A fireplace! We'll take it!" because he is pleased to rent the unit so easily, the additional cost of maintaining a building with a fireplace is a detracting feature for many landlords.

These disadvantages may be overlooked because the physical condition of the building is more obvious. But the aesthetic features of the building may determine whether or not the landlord rents the units consistently for top rents, and if he subsequently makes a profit the first few years he owns the building.

FUTURE POTENTIAL OF THE BUILDING

Another factor to consider when choosing a rental is the future potential of the building. The creative ways you can envision to increase the productivity of the building will help distinguish a good buy from an exceptional deal.

The first thing you should consider is the zoning of the building. If the building is zoned for duplex, but is presently used as a single-family dwelling, or if the building is zoned for multi-unit but is presently used as a duplex, you may be considering an exceptional deal. Can the upstairs be converted into an apartment? Is one unit large enough to be divided into two apartments? Can you remodel the basement or attic into a third or fourth apartment?

Even when a building looks large enough for additional units, be sure to check the building code before you purchase the building. Codes may restrict your remodeling of the building. Remember, not every old building can be converted to a multi-unit apartment house. Check the zoning regulations and building codes before you buy.

Another exceptional deal may be a building that is zoned for business but is presently being rented as a residential apartment house. If there is a need for office space in your town, you may be able to convert the building to office rentals. Office rentals usually carry longer leases than residential housing; thus you will have less turnover in the building. You may also be able to increase the rents and, therefore, the income of your building.

Another thing to look for when buying income property is additional land. Will an extra lot be sold with the building? Although savings-and-loans do not give loans for vacant land, they will finance land attached to the property occupied by the rental. Later, you can have the lot released from the original mortgage for a nominal fee and sell it, thereby putting cash in your pocket. Another alternative is to keep the lot and build on it, increasing your number of income properties.

Lastly, do not avoid a property because it needs a facelift. Fixing up property is one of the surest ways to make a profit in real estate, especially if you do most of the work yourself.

If you consider the building a good buy, look beyond its present state to its future potential. Maybe you will discover it is an exceptional deal.

The Single-Family Unit

The single-family rental unit is usually a small or older home in a residential neighborhood. As a rental, the single-family has several advantages. First, the tenants are responsible for all of their own utilities. This means the investor does not have to figure the fluctuating costs of utilities into the rent payment.

Another advantage of a single-family rental is the lack of "tenant-tenant" problems. Since the tenants are not having late parties upstairs or using too much hot water downstairs, the landlord is not called to mediate these grievances. The single-family, therefore, can be rather trouble-free.

A single-family rental is usually easy to sell. The building appeals to buyers who want it as a private residence or as a rental. In tight money situations when investment money is scarce, the single-family dwelling is easier to sell because it can be sold to someone wanting an owner-occupied residence. Even in tight money times, loans are usually available for owner-occupied dwellings.

There are also some disadvantages to owning a single-family rental. Single-family rentals appeal to a limited clientele. They are usually quite a bit more expensive to rent than a duplex of comparable space, and the landlord may have to wait longer to rent this type of unit. However, he will probably attract a long-term renter when he does rent it.

The Duplex Unit

The next type of rental unit to consider is the duplex. A duplex is two rental units in the same building. These apartments may be arranged one above the other or side-by-side. Duplexes are often large older homes which have been converted to an upper and a lower apartment. The popularity of duplexes with both renters and investors has resulted in building many new side-by-side units. These units are often divided by a double garage and feature individual basements and yards. Many are very fine buildings and appeal to the investor who plans to live in one part of the duplex and rent the other half as a means of helping with the mortgage. These duplexes are proportionately more expensive than other rentals and may show an actual loss for several years. They usually appeal to an investor with particular goals, such as help with the mortgage or a retirement income.

Just as duplexes are popular investments, they are also easy to rent. Most renters prefer duplexes because there are fewer tenants in the building. Duplexes can also be relatively trouble-free for the landlord. Usually one of the tenants will assume responsibility for the lawn or snow shoveling which might be a considerable expense for the landlord. Although most older buildings have one furnace and one electric meter, arrangements can usually be made so the tenants are responsible for at least some of the utilities.

Like single-family rentals, duplexes appeal to long-term renters. In a tight money market they are easier to sell than multi-units because they appeal to someone wanting an owner-occupied property. The duplex, especially the well-kept older unit, is one of the best investments in real estate.

The 3-Plex and 4-Plex

The 3-plex and 4-plex are rentals with three and four units respectively. Especially in the case of a 3-plex, this type of rental is often an older building that has been converted to apartments. The units may or may not be identical in size and facilities. If the units are of varying sizes, they will probably bring varying amounts of rent.

One advantage of a 3-plex or 4-plex is that it usually costs less to heat such a unit than it does to heat two duplexes or four single-family homes. If the 3-plex or 4-plex does not have laundry facilities for the tenants, the water and sewer bill will also be less than for a building which provides these facilities.

Another advantage is the landlord may find it more convenient to have a number of apartments in one location. There may be just one furnace to have serviced, one fuse box to check, one stop to make to collect rent. When a number of apartments are grouped under one roof, you have one bill to write out for water and sewer, one insurance payment to make, one tax bill to remember to pay.

Although a 3-plex or 4-plex may be more convenient in many ways and more reasonable for some utilities, it does require more expenditures than a duplex, for example. If you live in an area where winter means snow, you will have to have the snow removed from the parking lot and common sidewalks. Usually the tenants in a single-family or duplex remove the snow from the sidewalks and parking areas connected to their units.

Also in an older 3-or 4-plex, if the units are of varying sizes and bring varying rents, they may attract people of varying economic and social backgrounds. If a downstairs unit, for example, attracts a middle income professional couple and a third floor "garret" apartment attracts lower income roommates, you may have a personality conflict in the building which causes tension. You may find you have to mediate more "tenant-tenant" conflicts in a 3-or 4-plex than you do in a duplex.

Another factor to consider when buying any property with more than two rental units, is that they may be more difficult to sell than single-family units or duplexes. Lenders do not readily advance money for investment property during times of tight money.

Multi-Units

A multi-unit is a building that has more than four units. A multi-unit may be a large older house that has been converted or a new apartment complex.

The older multi-unit buildings have the same advantages and disadvantages of older 3- and 4-plexes. They are usually more economical to heat and they provide better leverage for the investor than does the single-family or duplex.

One disadvantage is that they may have only one furnace which is costly to repair and an outdated electrical system which is inadequate for the number of families living in the building. The investor should have sufficient capital to see him through a major repair problem if he owns an older multi-unit.

There may be more tenant problems because so many different people live in a relatively small space. Another disadvantage of the older multi-unit is it may have several very small apartments. These apartments usually have a high turnover rate.

The newer multi-units eliminate many problems of older buildings converted to multi-units. These buildings usually have separate utilities for which the tenant is responsible. They also often have separate entrances, parking areas and yards. This provides more privacy, keeps the noise level at a minimum and eliminates many personality clashes among the tenants. The units are usually similar if not identical. This also helps to eliminate personality conflicts among the tenants because they are all of similar economic and social backgrounds.

One disadvantage of the newer multi-units is they are usually very expensive and it is difficult to "come out" on the rents for the first few years. The investor who purchases a new multi-unit should be very sure he can afford to maintain the building and keep the mortgage payments current.

Another disadvantage is it usually takes longer to find a buyer for such a building than it does to find a buyer for a rental with fewer units. Often you will need to coordinate the sale among several individuals who are purchasing the building together. You have to time your sale for a period when money is readily available for investment properties. These buildings are more difficult to sell without the help of a realtor because you may have to attract out-of-town investors, investment groups or an investor who can pay a large down payment. Multi-units should not be counted on if you are forced to sell.

Business Rentals

Another type of rental you may consider is commercial property. Business rentals vary from buildings with a storefront downstairs and apartment upstairs to modern office complexes. Business rentals may be neighborhood groceries or doctors' offices.

Before purchasing commercial rentals you should consider the type of business which will be attracted to the rental and the potential for success of that business. Location is also very important for the commercial rental. Will a prosperous business be attracted to your rental? Although the income may be greater from commercial property, the risk is also greater than many other types of rentals. Before you invest in commercial properties, you should consider the advantages and disadvantages carefully.

The advantages of a commercial rental are that you may be able to tie your renter to a longer lease than you could expect from residential property. You may also be able to charge a higher rent per square foot than you could for residential property.

On the other hand, commercial property is usually more difficult to sell in time of tight money because money for business property is usually the first to be cut. Also in times of recession, your business property may be vacant for long periods of time because new businesses will not be opening as readily as they do in good times.

Although you may be able to charge more for a commercial rental, you may find you have additional costs because the property is commercial rather than residential. You may have to do extensive remodeling to attract a renter.

You should remember also that the success of your rental depends on attracting a successful business. Especially in the case of the beginning investor, the type of property you can afford may attract only marginal or beginning businesses.

SUMMARY

When choosing rental property consider:

- your future goals as an investor;
- the amount of cash or equity you have available for the investment;
- the degree of risk you can comfortably tolerate;
- the amount of time you are willing to spend managing your investment;

- the location of the building;
- the present condition of the building;
- the future potential of the building.

When considering the location of the building evaluate the neighborhood in which the rental is located. Also consider the proximity of the rental to your home. Rentals in towns other than the town in which you live are often more difficult to manage yourself.

When evaluating the present condition of the building, be sure to consider aesthetic factors, such as placement of the bathrooms and bedrooms and general appearance of the units, as well as the construction of the building.

Different types of rental properties have varying assets. Single-family rentals, for example, can usually be sold even in tight money situations. Multi-units usually offer the best leverage. The landlord should have his goals as an investor firmly in mind when he shops for property.

2
Financing Rental Units

Just as there are numerous types of rental properties from which to choose, there are also numerous methods of financing rental properties. The way in which a rental is financed affects its immediate and long term yield. A careful investor gives as much thought to the financing of the investment as he does to the buildings he chooses to buy. Each method of financing has advantages and disadvantages. When seeking financing, you should consider:

1. the type of rental unit being purchased;
2. the purpose for buying a particular building;
3. how the purchase of that building will affect other properties you already own;
4. current interest rates and the availability of investment money;
5. cash flow of the building being purchased;
6. personal finances.

With your goals for a particular investment firmly in mind, you should explore various types of financing. Whether this is a first investment or one of a long line of rental properties, the wise investor shops for money just as he shops for a building. Banks and savings-and-loans (in some parts of the country called cooperative banks or homestead associations) offer varying interest rates, mortgage lengths and costs for closing on the loan. If you are known at a particular lending institution, you may be able to negotiate better terms there than at a place where you are not as well-known. Banks and savings and loans also have varying amounts of available money. While one savings-and-loan, for example, may be considering applications for single-family dwellings only, the one across the street may still have money for duplexes.

You should not be discouraged if you are denied a loan at one institution. Because a bank, savings-and-loan or credit union is often more willing to discuss loans with people who are presently using their banking facilities, it is a good idea for an investor to keep accounts with several lending institutions. Even for a person just beginning in the rental business, small savings accounts or loans at several banks or savings-and-loans are helpful in securing financing. Usually the first question asked a prospective borrower is, "Do you have an account with us?" If you can answer "Yes," and your credit is good, your chances of getting the money you need are probably better than if you do not have an account with the lender. If you are turned down by one lender, you can request the money from another lender with whom you have an account. Then you can hope the second lender has more money currently available.

There are numerous ways to finance a rental. These methods vary in convenience, cost and availability. You should consider all means available to you before selecting a particular method of financing.

THE CONVENTIONAL MORTGAGE

Secured through a savings-and-loan, individual or a bank, the conventional mortgage is one of the most common means of financing real estate, especially for the home buyer or beginning investor. The conventional mortgage usually requires between 20-30 percent down payment. The loan is written for 15 to 30 years with 20 to 25 being the most common. A variety of closing costs, one of which is often a fee for initiating the loan, are charged above the amount of the mortgage.

Today, the conventional mortgage is usually amortized. This means the payments are divided equally over the term of the mortgage. As the loan matures, the amount applied to interest decreases and the amount applied to the principal increases. For this type of loan, monthly payments are usually required. By the time the loan matures, the principal is also paid in full.

If the loan is not fully amortized, the loan matures before the principal has been paid in full. The balance is due when the loan matures. This is called a balloon payment. When the loan matures, the borrower is expected to pay the balance in full. If the borrower does not have cash, he will have to re-finance with the same or another lender.

During the Great Depression, many people lost their properties because their loans matured and they could not re-finance or pay with cash within the available time. Since that time, fully amortized loans are generally written for real estate. However, balloon payments are becoming more common again for investment property financing. In some cases, an investor prefers the balloon payment because he may have more ready money during the life of the loan. Fluctuations in the money market which may make cash or refinancing possibilities tight add risk to this type of mortgage.

With conventional loans, the yearly property tax payment often is divided into 12 installments and included with the mortgage payment. Representatives of these institutions reason if the investor should encounter financial problems, he may allow the insurance to lapse and endanger the safety of the investment. Usually these additional charges for taxes and insurance are held in an escrow account for the mortgagee and paid for him on the dates they come due. Occasionally, however, these payments are deposited in a savings account in the borrower's name and draw interest for him while the money remains in the account.

Even when the lending institution does not include the cost of fire and hazard insurance in the monthly payment, they do require the buyer to produce proof at the time of closing he has secured adequate insurance for the building. Usually, an insurance binder is sufficient to complete the closing.

Another stipulation usually attached to a conventional mortgage is a prepayment clause. This clause states that if the mortgage is paid up before the due date—say in two years rather than 25—a fee will be charged the borrower. This fee is usually a percentage of the amount remaining on the loan. While some loans give no date for prepayment, others state the loan may be prepaid at a specific rate each year or within a certain time period short of the expiration date of the mortgage,

Although a lender may say he has never charged for prepayment, the borrower must realize if a prepayment clause is included in the contract he signs, the lender may charge it should the loan be prepaid. This is especially important for the investor who plans to buy and sell. If you sign a contract with a lender which includes a prepayment clause, you must add this to the price of selling the building or assume the loss. The present cost of real estate makes the prepayment clause a significant consideration in buying and selling rental properties.

Variations of the real estate mortgage are available for owner-occupied buildings. For example, if you plan to buy a duplex and live in one of the units, you may qualify for a FHA-insured loan or a VA-guaranteed loan. The FHA loan is backed by the federal government. The VA loan is backed by the Veterans Administration. Both types of loans are available with no or small down payments at lower interest rates than conventional mortgages. Veterans and people within certain income brackets qualify for these loans. Since the requirements change periodically, you should inquire about the current regulations regarding these loans.

In summary, the advantages of the conventional mortgage are:

1. It is offered through a reliable institution which is regulated and legally required to inform the borrower of all the costs charged to him.
2. The inexperienced investor is protected because the lender checks out the purchase and advises him of the requirements involved in a purchase of property.
3. It is convenient.

The disadvantages of the conventional mortgage for the investor are:

1. Usually a large cash down payment is required.
2. Prepayment clause adds additional costs to selling the property at a future date.
3. The escrow account often brings no interest.
4. The investor is dependent on the economy and the lender's appraisal of the property before he can buy and sell property.

STRAIGHT-TERM MORTGAGE

A straight-term mortgage is short term. The loan is usually made for one to five years. The loan principal is paid when the loan matures. Until the loan matures, the borrower pays only the interest on the loan. Investors who know they will be able to sell the mortgaged property before the loan expires may profit from a straight-term loan. During the term of the loan, the borrower's required payments are low.

If you finance a property with a straight-term mortgage, you will have more money (from the income of the property) to improve the property or to invest in other ways. You do run more risk of losing the property than you would with a conventional loan, however. Fluctuations in the money market may cause a decrease in money available for real property mortgages. This condition slows investments in rental properties. Lenders stop giving loans for business and rental properties. They attempt to save the mortgage money available to them for single family homes. If the market is sluggish when your straight-term mortgage is due, you may find you cannot sell your property even though you must pay off the loan. Those who are new to real estate investment will probably want to secure financing by means other than the straight-term mortgage until they have had practice in predicting the market.

The advantage of a straight-term mortgage is:

1. The person who intends to buy and sell within a short time can put his monthly income from the property into other investments.

The disadvantages of a straight-term mortgage are:

1. The investor may be caught in a tight money situation and not be able to repay the mortgage on time.
2. The straight-term mortgage has a greater risk factor than the conventional mortgage.

THE BLANKET MORTGAGE

Another type of mortgage which is secured through a lending institution is the blanket mortgage. This type of mortgage allows the buyer to use equity in another building which he owns as the down payment on a building he wishes to purchase. Usually the borrower is allowed 80 percent of the equity in a building he already owns toward the down payment on another building. Both buildings are then included in the same loan.

Because the existing loan is re-financed, a loan initiation fee may be charged on the combined properties. The investor is borrowing the down payment, using a building he already owns as collateral; thus the down payment is considered part of the loan. The loan initiation fee will be greater than if the investor used a cash down payment, which would be subtracted from the amount of the loan.

Another way the blanket mortgage costs the buyer money is in interest rates. Although this can work in reverse, the building being re-financed usually was secured at a lesser interest rate than the present rate. When the loan is re-written to include the second purchase, the interest rate is usually raised. One way to make this practice work for you is to watch the fluctuation in interest rates closely and apply for a blanket mortgage when interest rates drop below the rate of a current mortgage.

Another problem which may occur with a blanket mortgage is the release of property should the investor wish to sell. If more than one property is included in the loan, the investor may have to obtain appraisals on all the properties included in the loan before the lender will release one. Usually the interest rate on the remaining properties included in the mortgage is also increased to current levels. Although these charges may seem minimal in view of the larger transaction, you should be aware of them and include them in the selling price of your property.

Advantages of the blanket mortgage are:

1. If his equity is sufficient, he can purchase additional rental property with no cash down.
2. It is an excellent way to use the equity in a building.
3. It may be possible to lower his interest rate on the existing loan.

Disadvantages of this type of loan are:

1. This can be a costly way of financing.
2. Interest rates on the original mortgage are usually raised when the loan is re-written to include the second purchase.
3. Several properties are tied up in one loan.

SECOND MORTGAGE

Another way to get equity from a building is to secure a second mortgage. Some lenders (such as some savings-and-loans) do not offer second mortgages during tight money times, but they may be available through banks, credit unions and other lending institutions. When an investor obtains a second mortgage, he pledges the equity or market value above his existing mortgage as collateral for a cash loan. A second mortgage usually carries a higher interest rate and a shorter term than a conventional mortgage.

A second mortgage may also be obtained through a private lender. A seller, for example, may offer a second mortgage to a buyer when the buyer cannot obtain the entire amount of the sale price through a conventional lender. In a second mortgage deal, the seller retains the right to a certain interest in the building. In effect, he simply defers his profit until a later date. The buyer pays the seller interest on the second mortgage and makes payments to the seller as stipulated in a private contract. While the seller may find this to his advantage for tax purposes, the buyer must remember the entire payment is usually expected upon expiration of the loan. The buyer must then find another lender to secure a second mortgage or put a sizable amount of cash into the building. A second mortgage is a means of obtaining property when money for conventional loans is tight or the buyer's credit is marginal.

Advantages of a second mortgage are:

1. A second mortgage allows the owner to use his equity in a building to secure other types of investments.
2. The second mortgage allows the buyer to purchase a particular property when the bank or savings-and-loan will not lend the full amount of the purchase price.

The disadvantages of a second mortgage are:

1. The interest rates are high.
2. The principal may be due all at one time.

ASSUMING A MORTGAGE

Another way to finance real estate is to assume the seller's mortgage. When a buyer assumes the seller's mortgage, he assumes primary responsibility for the debt. The seller, however, may be held responsible if the buyer defaults on the mortgage. When a mortgage is assumed, the seller should negotiate with the lender to be released from further responsibility toward the loan.

Assuming a mortgage has several advantages for the buyer:

1. The mortgage he is assuming usually has a lower interest rate than he could negotiate if he were to take out a new mortgage.
2. Assuming the mortgage allows him to buy a building during a tight money market.

Disadvantages of assuming the mortgage are:

1. The buyer may need a lot of money down to assume the mortgage because he will have to use cash to pay the difference between the purchase price and the seller's existing loan.
2. The interest rate on the mortgage is usually raised to an average between the original interest rate and the current interest rate.

ADDITIONAL WAYS OF OBTAINING MONEY

Other types of loans are available to help the investor purchase property. Although these loans may not provide the entire amount needed for the purchase, they may make enough money available to the investor so he can make the down payment on the property or save a property when he cannot sell it quickly.

When the lender insists upon a cash down payment, the borrower can usually raise the money from a combination of sources. One way to acquire investment capital is to borrow on your signature or with collateral. Credit union members, for example, can obtain a certain amount on their signatures. If both you and your spouse are members, you have a good start toward a cash down payment. Other lending institutions may also offer this type of loan to their customers. Lenders will also issue loans using cars, boats or land as collateral. Many investors do get a start by borrowing on their signatures or with collateral, but this does have one significant disadvantage; the interest rate is high and will consume much of the initial profit on a building partially financed this way.

A less expensive way to borrow the down payment is through life insurance companies. Investors who have paid into a life insurance policy for a number of years can borrow on the dividends in their policies at low interest rates. This borrowing plan has two advantages. First, the interest rate is low. Secondly, the borrower may be able to set the conditions of re-payment. If you borrow on a life insurance policy, you may be able to defer the payments for a year until you have recovered your investment in closing costs and other initial expenses. Or you may decide to pay only the interest on the loan for a few months. If you do decide to finance a rental partially with money borrowed on a life insurance policy, you should check with your agent before proceeding too far with negotiations for the property. Insurance plans vary. Find out how much you can borrow on the policy, what the interest rate will be, and what re-payment plan you can negotiate. The money available through these policies is usually minimal unless you have held the policy for a number of years.

Another way to acquire money at a low interest rate is to borrow on a savings certificate. This is called acquiring a shared loan and has the same advantages as borrowing on life insurance policies. The interest rate is usually 1-1½ percent above the interest rate earned by the savings account, and payments can be negotiated by the borrower. This method of borrowing can be used during a tight money market when you cannot use your equity in buildings you already own to purchase another rental. When investment monies loosen up, you can remortgage the equity in one or more buildings and pay up the shared loan. Although these alternatives may be sought more often in tight money situations, they should be considered at all times.

THE LAND CONTRACT

The most popular non-banking method of finance is probably the land contract (also referred to as contract for a deed, contract of sale, or installment sales contract). This arrangement is entered into between the buyer and the seller without a lending institution as a third party. In a land contract, the seller acts as the bank. Because the seller retains his interest in the building, he also continues to assume responsibility for any loans he has on the building. The buyer makes payments to the seller under the conditions of the contract.

The advantages of a land contract are:

1. Usually this type of financing is less costly to initiate than the conventional mortgage. Attorney's fees in negotiating the contract, an appraisal of the property and filing the land contract are usually the only expenses.
2. Often a building can be obtained for a lower down payment under a land contract. To reduce taxes on his income from the sale, the seller may choose to take a 10 or 15 percent down payment.
3. A land contract is a means of buying or selling in a tight money market because whenever two people can agree on the terms of a contract the property can be sold.
4. The seller makes the money usually reserved for the bank. The seller charges interest on the loan in the same manner as a bank. He must record this income and should remember to keep the payments within one-third of the entire amount of the sale per year allowed him by the Internal Revenue Service for maximum tax advantage.
5. The buyer may be able to negotiate a lower interest rate than that offered by the bank. The seller could have a loan on the property which carries a lower than current interest rate. As part of the negotiated terms, he may be willing to pass that savings on to the buyer.

Disadvantages of the land contract are:

1. It is usually short-term with the entire amount coming due at once. The buyer must plan to sell the property before the loan is due or re-finance through some other source in order to pay the loan to the holder of the land contract mortgage. If the loan matures during a tight money market or when the buyer has marginal credit, he could have a difficult time re-financing.
2. The seller assumes the risk of the bank or savings and loan. If the buyer defaults on payments and the seller is still responsible to another lender for payments on the building, he must put his own money into the building to keep the investment current. If the buyer defaults on the building, he may also have allowed the property to deteriorate. The seller may find himself with a property which has depreciated rather than appreciated during the time the buyer held the building. On the other hand, if the buyer is in a financial squeeze for a few months, he may find the seller unsympathetic and lose the property.
3. The seller may find his mortgage contract stipulates if he sells the property on a land contract or otherwise sells or reassigns the mortgage, the lender may raise his interest rate on the mortgage to the current amount or demand the mortgage be paid in full. The seller should check with the lender holding his mortgage to make sure of any restrictions before he agrees to a land contract. **Read every contract thoroughly.**

Many of these disadvantages can be eliminated with the proper contract. Some of the things for the buyer and seller to include in a land contract are:

1. The buyer should insist he be allowed to pre-pay the loan at any time. Then he is free to sell the property before the loan expires. The seller, on the other hand, may insist the loan be paid in three installments of one-third each year. This allows the seller a special tax advantage.
2. The buyer should seek a renewal clause. If the contract matures during a tight money market or when the buyer cannot re-finance he has the option to renew the contract if such a clause is inserted.
3. If a renewal clause is included in the contract, it should stipulate the interest rate is re-negotiable. This protects the buyer if the interest rate from area lenders drops during the term of the contract. It protects the seller if the interest rate should increase during the term.
4. The exact amount the buyer must pay toward the principal and the exact amount he must pay toward the interest should be spelled out clearly. This protects the buyer from discovering his entire monthly payment is going to interest.
5. The seller should specify what may be done to the property by the buyer during the term of the contract. If the buyer has to default on the loan and has removed several hundred dollars worth of shrubs or fencing, the seller loses.
6. The seller should check the buyer's credit rating before signing the land contract. This can be done through the credit bureau in the region where the seller lives. For a nominal fee, the credit bureau will check the credit of the buyer. If the buyer does not live in the same region as the seller, the seller's credit bureau will charge an additional fee to check the buyer's references. This fee covers long distance calls and payment of the second credit bureau's fee.
7. The buyer should make sure all owners of the property agree to the deal. If a husband and wife own the property jointly and only the husband signs the contract, the wife could decide not to honor the terms of the contract.

Because land contracts vary from state to state and among individuals, an attorney should be hired to help negotiate the deal.

RENTING WITH AN OPTION TO BUY

One way for the first-time investor to buy property with little or no money down is to rent with the option to buy. This agreement is between the landlord and the tenant, and it should be a legal, witnessed document for the protection of both parties.

This agreement simply states that at the end of a certain period, usually one to two years, the tenant has the option to buy the property he has been renting. Should he decide to purchase the property, a previously specified portion of his rent money will be applied to the down payment. Both this amount and the purchase price should be specifically stated in the signed agreement. As with the land contract, these agreements vary with individuals. They should be entered into cautiously and with legal advice.

TRADING

Trading is another means of acquiring income property. Trading, or exchanging properties, is becoming an increasingly popular means of building equity and establishing a well-paying chain of rental units.

In simplest terms, a trade is an exchange of one property for another. If the properties are of "like kind," meaning both are held as investments rather than one as a private residence, the profit is wholly or partially tax-free. When income property is sold, the profit is subject to a capital gains tax. When income property is traded, this tax can often be delayed until the final sale of the new property. This additional tax break is the reason why trading is an increasingly popular means of acquiring property.

Although trading sounds simple—one property exchanged for another—it is usually not that easy. Although two people may trade their properties, it is usually difficult to find two people who will receive mutual benefit from such a trade. Usually trading occurs among three parties. This means the person initiating the trade must have numerous contacts among investors in real estate. Trading is also complicated because it means exchanging comparable equities. Since equity is a figure on paper rather than a tangible object, a person must be skilled in juggling figures. Although two or three investors may initiate and accomplish a trade on their own, often a broker or consultant negotiates the deal. Some real estate firms belong to trading clubs and advertise their expertise in the area of trading as a way of attracting customers. Usually a trade is made easier with the help of a broker or other informed consultant.

To clarify the concept of trading, consider the following example:

Investor Jones owns a single-family dwelling which he is now renting. The property is valued at $25,000. He owns the property free of encumbrances. He wants to buy a multi-family unit. To protect his entire $25,000 as investment capital, he looks for someone to trade properties with him. Investor Jones wants to exchange his property for one with more income potential. He wants a property which will give him greater leverage.

Investor Smith, on the other hand, is nearing retirement and he wants to reduce his rentals so he can manage them more easily. Money for investment in income property is tight so he is willing to consider a trade. He has $25,000 equity (not necessarily cash) in his property. Investor Jones trades his single-family dwelling as the down payment for Investor Smith's multi-family unit.

Complications in trading result when the equities are not equal. Usually one party must accept some cash which is called "boot." This boot is taxable because it is not property of "like kind."

The advantage of a trade is that the profit is wholly or partially tax free.

The disadvantage of a trade is trading often involves a complicated juggling of figures and complicated methods of finance. A good trade requires expertise and numerous hours of negotiation. The beginning investor who wants to trade properties should consult a recognized broker or investment consultant.

INVESTING WITH PARTNERS

When an investor lacks capital, he can pool his resources with other investors to buy real estate. This may be a rather informal and private agreement between two friends or a formal agreement handled by an investment agency between individuals who often do not know and do not come in contact with each other.

Investing with partners does have several advantages. Investors with limited capital can buy well-paying income properties by pooling their investment capital. Sometimes investors use this method as a means of getting started in real estate. Another type of investor who finds the partnership approach satisfactory is the person who does not want to manage the building himself. If he invests through an investment corporation or finds a partner who is willing to manage the property, he is relieved of some management concerns.

There are some problems with investing with partners, however. It can be the surest way to ruin a beautiful friendship. Each investor's responsibilities should be carefully drawn up in writing before the property is purchased.

SUMMARY

Rental property may be acquired through an outright sale. An outright sale may be financed in various ways such as the conventional mortgage, the FHA-insured loan or the VA-guaranteed loan. These loans are obtained through a legal lending institution. An outright sale may also be financed through private individuals acting in place of a bank or savings and loan, such as in the case of a land contract and some second mortgages. Rental properties may also be acquired through trading or in partnership with other investors. Various alternatives are available to investors as a means of acquiring a down payment, a home improvement loan, or additional cash needed to sustain the investment.

The importance of financing cannot be overemphasized. Creative financing of income property is one of the surest and swiftest ways to financial independence. On the other hand, rash or hasty financing can break the back of even the established investor.

The beginning investor should proceed with caution. He should read all he can find on the subject of finance and consult experts before he deviates from the more usual and acceptable means of financing.

Please remember this chapter is meant to introduce you to various methods of financing. It is not intended as a definitive discussion which will make you an expert in this highly complicated field. Only when you are well informed about the basics of real estate transactions should you attempt tradings and complicated buying and selling which will add substantially to your profit. Even when you feel confident of your knowledge, you should consult an attorney whose expertise is real estate and financing real estate for help in negotiating the transactions.

3 Renting Apartments

Renting units is one of the landlord's most important jobs. Vacant units cost time and money. While the apartment is unrented, you must answer telephone calls about it, and you must be willing to show it often (usually at the prospective tenant's convenience). Although the revenue is not collected while the unit remains unrented, the expenses continue to accumulate. The unit must be heated (at least to the minimum required to keep the pipes from freezing if you live in a cold climate), and the utilities must be paid. If there is a mortgage on the building, it comes due whether or not all the units in the building are rented. Property taxes and other maintenance costs must be paid also. Advertising is another expense of an unrented apartment. The apartment should be advertised daily until it is rented. The landlord's goal is to rent the apartment as quickly as possible. Ideally, the unit should be rented on a long term basis to reliable people. Renters are often transient by nature, and even the most reliable people encounter financial or personal difficulties. But there are some approaches you can take to successfully rent vacant apartments.

ADVERTISING

Advertising is a subtle art. Universities and trade schools recognize this and offer degree programs to prepare people for careers in advertising. Businesses and industries also recognize the importance of advertising. They pay large amounts of money to professionals who will promote their products in a manner most appealing to the public. Most landlords neglect to think of owning and managing rental properties as a business which also requires proper advertising. Rentals are a business, however, and successful management of rental properties requires some knowledge about advertising.

Writing the Advertisement

The purpose of advertising an apartment is two-fold: to entice people to inquire about the unit, and to do a preliminary elimination of people who are not interested in the particular apartment you have available. The wording of the ad, therefore, is very important. The ad should tell enough about the unit to appeal to interested tenants, but it should not give every detail about the apartment. For example, running an advertisement which reads: "APARTMENT FOR RENT" has several disadvantages. First, you will receive calls from people who want every kind of apartment from an efficiency to a townhouse. But you may also miss hearing from people who simply will not take the time to call on an advertisement which lacks pertinent details.

On the other hand, if you place an advertisement which gives every detail about the apartment, including the price and the location, you may miss the opportunity to do some selling over the telephone. Sometimes prospective tenants think they do not want an apartment for a certain price, in a particular location or without a special feature. But when they discuss the unit with the landlord or actually see the apartment, they are often willing to overlook one drawback in favor of the unit's other features. Something the tenant at first considered a drawback diminishes in importance.

We have witnessed this "change of heart" often. One case in point is that of a young man who insisted he would not look at an apartment we were renting because it was close to a busy street. We assured him it was a very nice apartment and surprisingly quiet, and he finally agreed to look at it. He liked the apartment as much as we thought he would, and he has continued to live in the unit for more than a year. He is also one of our best tenants, so persuading him to look at the unit was advantageous to us as well as to him. If we had printed the location, he most likely would not have called about the apartment, and we would have lost a chance to interest a very good tenant.

Another disadvantage of a long advertisement is that it can be confusing. Many people also may not take the time to read it carefully. For this reason, a long advertisement may not accomplish its intended purpose, namely, eliminating anyone who is not really interested. You may receive many calls from people who have not read the advertisement carefully.

Finally, a long advertisement is expensive because rates for classified advertisements are determined by the word. Cost is another reason to keep the advertisement brief and to choose words carefully.

Even a brief advertisement can be confusing. Again, word choice is important. Once we listed an *unfurnished* apartment with an advertisement which read:

> One-bedroom upper apartment, stove and refrigerator furnished, all utilities provided.

We received many calls from people who wanted a *furnished* apartment. Since we had not listed the apartment as furnished, we wondered why there was so much confusion. When we looked at the advertisement carefully, we realized people were interpreting "stove and refrigerator furnished" as "stove and refrigerator, furnished." We now write, "appliances" or "stove and refrigerator" without the "furnished" when we place an advertisement. It saves us money and our readers confusion.

Special instructions about contacting the landlord should be included in the advertisement. If you are home after five only, be sure to state that information in the advertisement. If this is not stated and tenants call several times without receiving an answer, they become tired of calling and cross that number off their list.

When preparing the advertisement it is tempting to use words such as "attractive," "nice," and "charming," in combination with the facts about the apartment. Examples of this wording are: "Attractive one-bedroom," "Nice neighborhood," "Charmingly furnished." Although these terms may be true for the apartment you are advertising, they are often used incorrectly to entice people into looking at a unit. These descriptive words often have an effect on prospective renters which is just the opposite of the intended purpose. When you pay by the word, these terms add cost to your advertisement without adding pertinent details. A better choice would be : "Large, carpeted one-bedroom," "Residential neighborhood," "Downtown, near bus line," "Newly redecorated."

Putting all these considerations together, you might compose an ad which reads:

> Newly redecorated, one-bedroom upper apartment with separate entrance, heated, carpeted, garage, phone 725-8244 after 5 p.m.

Another example of an effective advertisement is:

> Large, two-bedroom lower apartment, near bus line, separate utilities, washer/dryer hook-ups, new appliances, double garage, phone 559-8762 after 3 p.m.

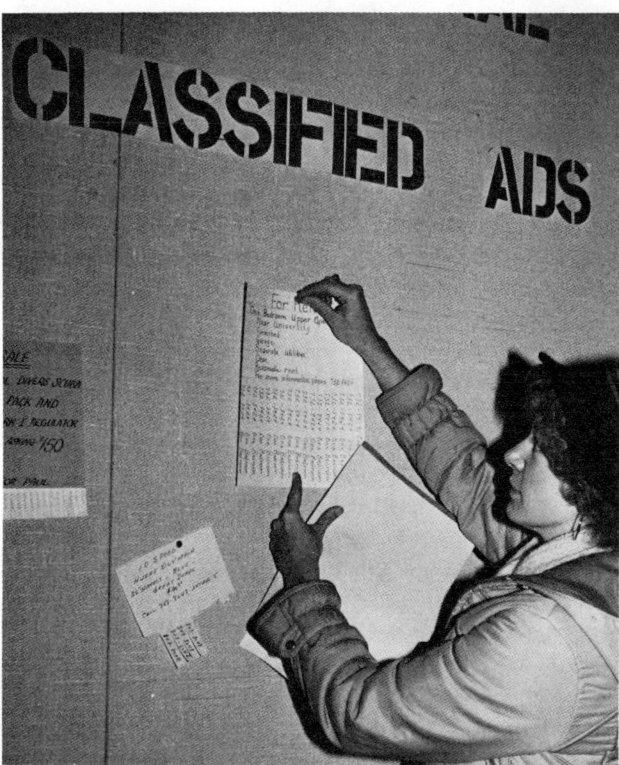

Make use of all advertising opportunities available to you.

Placing the Advertisement

Placing the advertisement can be as important as the wording. The "Apartments for Rent" section of the daily newspaper provides a good source for advertising the unit. Most prospective tenants consult the newspaper first when they begin shopping for an apartment.

Area shopping guides provide another good advertising source. Like daily newspapers, they are distributed to a large number of people and are often consulted by people looking for apartments. Placing an advertisement in a local shopper usually seems less expensive than placing the same advertisement in a daily newspaper. Unlike the newspaper which is distributed daily, however, the shopper is usually distributed once each week. Although you may receive many calls from an advertisement placed in the local shopper, it does not remain in front of people daily. A shopper, therefore, should not be the only source you use for advertising a vacant apartment.

There are also several sources of free advertising which the wise landlord can use to his advantage. One source is bulletin boards in grocery stores, shopping centers, universities and trade schools. If these boards are located in trade schools, universities or near neighborhoods which contain many rentals, they offer excellent contact with prospective tenants. There is one problem with posting an ad on one of these boards, however. The advertisement may be removed without your knowledge by someone interested in calling about the apartment. Then, although you think the apartment is being advertised, it is actually not available to anyone except the person who removed the advertisement. One way to help prevent this is to list your telephone number numerous times beneath the description of the apartment and design the advertisement so the telephone numbers can be taken without removing the description of the unit. This is not a foolproof way of insuring your advertisement stays on the board, but it does help. If you are placing an advertisement on a bulletin board, you should check with the proper authorities before posting it. There may be restrictions for posting advertisements which must be followed.

Another free source for advertising a vacant apartment is the office of the local school board. This is an especially good source in the fall and again in January when new teachers are hired into the district. Usually the secretary for the superintendent or the assistant to the superintendent (depending upon the size of the district) takes the listing. The best procedure is to call the board office, explain the situation and inquire about the procedure.

A rental service is another source for advertising apartments. Rental services are agencies which list available apartments. Usually this service is free to landlords. People shopping for an apartment pay a fee to consult the agency's listings. The prospective tenants make direct contact with the landlord and he shows the apartment. Rental services should not be confused with management agencies which manage apartments. Management agencies charge the landlord for listing and showing the apartments he owns. Clients of a rental service are people who are interested in finding an apartment. The rental service's only function is to make information available to the client. One advantage of listing with a rental service is that usually people who are willing to pay a fee to consult the listings from an agency are seriously looking for an apartment. The landlord who lists vacant apartments with an agency may also advertise the apartment with other sources available to him. Listing a vacancy with a rental service is a good additional advertising outlet.

Whatever source or sources you choose for advertising your vacant apartment, be sure to check your advertisement periodically. Make sure the advertisement appears on the day it is scheduled and the information—especially the telephone number—is correct. If the telephone number is incorrect, for example, you may miss your chance to rent the apartment. We experienced this situation once. When we advertised the apartment, we listed two telephone numbers. When the newspaper printed the advertisement, they listed one telephone number which was a combination of the two numbers we had listed. The advertisement read "845-7344" rather than "845-6532" or "842-7344." The first three numbers of one number and the last four of another number were combined into a useless number. We did not check the advertisement for several days and wondered why we were not receiving any calls. When the advertisement was finally corrected, we had lost most of the people who were interested in an apartment for that month. Now we conscientiously check each advertisement on the day it appears. Also, be sure to check the bulletin boards and call the listing agencies to make sure they are promoting your apartment. If you do not receive calls on your apartment, the first thing you should consider is your ad may be incorrect or unavailable to interested people.

Timing the Advertisement

Equally important as the wording and the outlets for the ad is the timing for placing the advertisement. Peak rental periods are usually near the first of the month and the fifteenth of the month. Advertisements placed just after the first or the fifteenth will draw numerous shoppers. You may find yourself showing the apartment often to people who are not in a hurry to rent any unit. If you place the advertisement a few days before the first or fifteenth, you will probably draw a greater percentage of people who are seriously looking for an apartment. They will be more inclined to rent immediately if they like the unit. Timely placement of the advertisement saves the landlord both time and money.

SCHEDULING APPOINTMENTS

Because most landlording is conducted in addition to a regular full time job, saving time is as important as saving money. One of the most time-consuming jobs of landlording is showing apartments. There are ways, however, to cut the time spent in showing a vacant apartment.

When we first started landlording, we carefully spaced the appointments 15 minutes apart. We thought this would give each person time to look at the unit and talk with us without feeling rushed. On busy nights, we would have as many as eight appointments spaced over a two hour period. Usually the apartment was still occupied by current tenants, and we found ourselves sitting in the car in front of the building in all kinds of weather. Every 15 minutes we would pop out of the car, meet the arriving client and disturb the current tenant again. This is not the most exciting way to spend an evening. Then we found that while we had arranged the appointments 15 minutes apart because we thought this was the most courteous method, not all people were as concerned with politeness. Many times prospective tenants neglected to keep their appointments. Sometimes this left us waiting for 30 to 40 minutes between appointments.

Finally, we decided to make all of the appointments for the same time. At first we were apprehensive this practice would create a mob atmosphere and might prove unpleasant, but this has not happened to us. By scheduling all of the appointments at one or two times, we cut our showing time from two hours to 30 minutes. Occasionally a client complains about the procedure, but most people accept it and many landlords we know also use a similar method of scheduling apartment showings.

Scheduling more than one appointment for the same time has another advantage besides saving time. One question prospective tenants invariably ask is, "How many people have seen the apartment?" By asking this question, they hope to determine how much longer they can wait before deciding about the unit. When several people arrive at the same time and express an interest in the unit, this has the psychological effect of forcing a decision more rapidly. You will often rent the apartment immediately.

The third advantage is if several people neglect to keep the appointment, you are not inconvenienced. You are still able to show it to a number of people who have kept the appointment.

People who neglect to keep appointments for apartment showings are one of the greatest irritations of landlording. When you make an appointment, there are several things you can do to insure the appointment will be kept. First, ask for the person's complete name—"Sue" or "Bob" is not enough. Be sure to get the last name, too. When a person gives his full name, he tends to feel more committed to the appointment. If he is unwilling to give you his full name, he may not be a very good prospect and you may be better off not renting to him, anyway. Also, ask for a telephone number so you can call him if you cannot keep the appointment. If he thinks you can contact him, he tends to keep the appointment. When you have his telephone number, say something like this:

> I'll see you at 102 Scott Street at 7 p.m. unless I call you by 6:30 p.m. If you can't make the appointment, I'd appreciate your calling me before 6:30 p.m.

This indicates to the client you are committed to the appointment. It also indicates you will not waste his time if the apartment is rented before his appointment or if you cannot keep the appointment. Many people will naturally return your courtesy. If the person does not keep the appointment, you have the option of calling to ask why he did not meet you. Although you will probably not take the time to do this, the option is worth having.

Another way to prevent neglected appointments is to refuse to schedule showings more than one-half day in advance. Often people call early in the week and request an appointment on the weekend. Appointments made this far in advance are seldom kept. The best response to such a request is to say pleasantly,

> I'm sorry, but I do not make appointments that far in advance. Too many things can happen in the meantime. The apartment may be rented or you may change your mind. Why don't you call back Saturday morning and we'll set up an appointment then.

If the client is interested he will call back. If he loses interest, your Saturday afternoon is not wasted waiting for him.

As you become more experienced in scheduling appointments, you will begin to listen for hesitancy in the client's manner. Whenever possible let the client choose the approximate time: morning, afternoon or evening. If you still sense a hesitancy about the appointment, do not be afraid to ask, "Are you sure you can keep this appointment?" Usually if he is having second thoughts, that question will prompt him to say he will call you back. Although you might be disappointed in losing the contact, remember you have probably saved yourself a long wait in front of the apartment.

Do not try to second guess the client. If he says he will keep the appointment, but you have doubts about his sincerity, you should still keep the appointment. Remember, you need to have the apartment rented as quickly as possible to save yourself time and money. You cannot afford to show the apartment only when you have nothing better to do or when you especially like the sound of the client's voice.

When you have scheduled the appointment and are waiting for the client to arrive, you should not be disappointed if he is late. You must remember everyone is not as familiar with the area as you are. The client may have difficulty in finding the building or some other problem may detain him. You should plan to allow at least 15 minutes after the scheduled time for late-comers.

These procedures are not foolproof. You may still occasionally find the clients neglect to keep their appointments, and you are left waiting in front of the building. But when adapted to your situation, you should find these hints make landlording duty easier and less time-consuming.

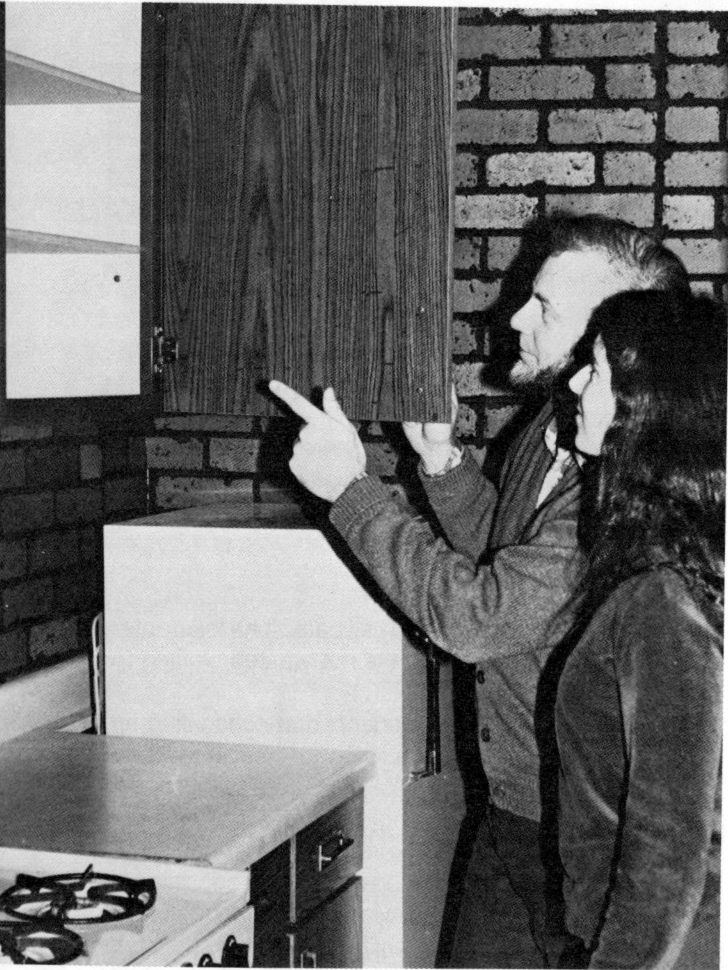

Show the tenant through the apartment. Highlight the good features. Remember the unit is strange to the client and he may feel uncomfortable. Try to put the client at ease as you show the unit.

SHOWING THE APARTMENT

Showing the apartment requires as much skill as advertising it. Realtors, for example, are trained in the techniques of showing buildings. A landlord should also be skilled in showing apartments.

When you have an apartment showing, begin by greeting the prospective tenant cordially. Introduce yourself as the landlord. Ask for the client's name and compare it mentally with the name given to you on the telephone so you know you are meeting the right person. Shake hands with the client if he seems inclined to do so. Remember some people shop as carefully for the landlord as they do for the apartment. They want to be assured the landlord is friendly and sincere. They will be concerned they can approach you with problems about the building and that maintenance problems will be corrected within a reasonable time. When you are showing an apartment, you sell yourself as well as the unit.

Once inside the apartment, show the client around the unit. Do not stand in the middle of the floor of the first room and expect him to see the apartment himself. Remember the unit is strange to him and he may feel uncomfortable. Name each room as you walk through it and highlight the good features. For example, you might say:

- This is the living room. Both the drapes and the carpet are included with the apartment.
- This is the kitchen. The appliances are included but the dining room table and chairs belong to the current tenant.
- This is the second bedroom. I see the current tenant is using it for a sewing room.
- In the bathroom there is both a shower and a tub.
- There's a large closet in the hall and extra storage space in the basement.

Show the client where he can park his car. Outline his responsibilities for snow shoveling, lawn care, garbage pick up and any other tasks connected with the apartment. Be sure to go over with him what utilities are included in the rent and what utilities he is expected to pay. Although your advertisement may have stated this clearly and you may have repeated the information when you talked to him on the telephone, face to face contact is always the best way to make the situation clear.

Tenants respond in a variety of ways to an available apartment. Some say almost nothing as they look at the unit. Others seem very excited about the place and tell you it is just what they have been looking for. Some clients are very critical of the apartment. Do not be insulted by a prospective tenant's criticism of the apartment. He may hope, through his criticism of the apartment, to make you reduce the rent. He also may be trying to talk himself out of an apartment he knows he cannot afford. He may be unacquainted with the prices in your area and need to shop around before he can appreciate the unit you are showing him.

Do not be drawn into an argument with the client. He may not be able to find another one-bedroom apartment with more storage space than the unit you have available, for example. After he looks around, he may decide to rent the unit you have shown him after all. On the other hand, if you were defensive when he originally criticized the storage space in the apartment, you may find you have lost a tenant. The best response to criticism is to quietly and politely point out the positive aspects of the apartment and to accept the criticism in a manner which says, "You are entitled to your opinion." (Criticism in this instance means aesthetic concerns. Actual physical defects in the structure such as leaking roofs or broken stairs should not be overlooked by you. See the chapter on *Tenants' Rights* for a discussion of this concern.)

Although you have the responsibility to treat even troublesome clients with respect, you also have a responsibility to rent to pleasant, reliable people. You want to rent to someone who can get along with the other tenants already living in the building, and you want to rent to someone with whom you can communicate. While you are showing the unit, you should try to learn as much about the client as possible so you can make a fair judgment if he decides to rent the unit. Pleasant conversation is usually the best way to learn what you need to know without appearing to pry into the client's personal life and establishing yourself as the stereotype nosey landlord.

A good opener is: "Are you just moving into town?" If he says, "Yes," but does not volunteer any information you can follow up with a question such as: "Where are you from?" or "Where will you be working?" We consider work references vital in our decision to rent to a prospective tenant. If your client says he is looking for a job in the area, you may decide to check further references before you rent to him. (For more information on the legal implications in refusing to rent to prospective tenants, see the chapter on *Tenants' Rights*.)

Another important piece of information to acquire before you rent to a client is the number of people who will be living in the apartment. If you pay the utilities, the number of people in the unit will affect the electric and water bills. Do not assume the people who come to see the apartment are the ones who will be renting it. Often one person will rent an apartment for another or a couple will leave their four children with a sitter while they shop for an apartment. Unless you ask who will be living in the apartment, they will probably not volunteer the information.

We once rented to a couple who were very concerned if they could keep two dogs on the premises. After they had rented the apartment, we discovered four children and a grandpa also came with the dogs. The renters paid the utilities so extra people did not mean extra cost to us. They proved to be excellent renters. They had been so careful to mention their dogs that we assumed they had not deliberately hidden the size of their family from us. We were surprised, however, the first time we stopped at the building after we had rented the unit to them. Although there was no problem in this case, in another situation a problem might have developed.

Consider, for instance, this hypothetical example. A sweet, young woman carrying a pleasant baby appears at the door of the two-bedroom apartment you are showing. You like her and her references are in order, so you rent the apartment to her. You think she wants the unit for herself and her child. Actually she intends to share the apartment with a girlfriend who has two children. After they move in, you find the utilities you pay have doubled and the wear and tear on the unit is increased. You also think the apartment is too small for five people. Now you are faced with raising the rent, evicting the women or telling the first woman her friend cannot share the apartment with her. All three alternatives are unpleasant. The entire situation could have been avoided by asking the woman who would be living in the apartment with her.

Remember, this is your property and you have the right to screen renters as long as you do not violate the law. If a client seems surly or reluctant to answer your questions, you may decide to check his references carefully before renting to him.

You should also ask how long the client expects to remain in the apartment. If he plans to be in the area only for the summer or until a short term construction job is completed, he may not be willing to sign the six or 12 month lease you require.

Skillful showing of the apartment is an important aspect of landlording. A few appropriate questions and comments can prevent problems from arising after the client has rented the apartment.

RENTING THE APARTMENT

If the client likes the apartment, he may ask you if he can rent it immediately. But he may also decide to bargain with you. He may want to paint the walls or do other minor facelifting jobs. He may also want you to do major repairs to the apartment such as installing new carpeting or a shower. You should decide what changes you are willing to make to the apartment. Painting the walls is a usual request and many landlords have this done each time a tenant moves out of the apartment. Remember some people are more careful with painting than others. Although allowing the tenant to paint the apartment is probably the least expensive choice, you may decide to do it yourself or to hire a professional. You can usually decide this as you talk with the prospective tenant.

Major alterations to the apartment, such as showers, or large redecorating projects, such as new carpeting, should be given careful thought. Perhaps you have been planning to install a shower or new carpeting. The tenant expresses a desire to help with the project and convinces you he has the skill required. You may find this a good arrangement for you both. Perhaps you have been trying unsuccessfully to rent the apartment and you realize the tenant's request is reasonable if you are to rent the apartment.

Whatever you decide, you should prepare a written agreement stating exactly what repairs are to be made and the responsibilities of both the landlord and the tenant in making the repairs. This can be attached to the information sheet (discussed later in this chapter) you require each tenant to sign before you rent the apartment. If you do not prepare a written statement, confusion and negative feelings may result later. Consider, for example, the problem of a landlord who paints and carpets an apartment before he rents it. The new tenants want to redecorate the unit to suit their tastes, but the landlord refuses saying the apartment has just been painted and carpeted. Finally, he agrees the tenants can paint the walls of the unit if they wish. However, he says he will not be responsible for paying for the paint. The tenants paint the apartment and send the landlord the bill. A written statement prepared at the time of renting will prevent this problem.

The current condition of the apartment should also be noted and recorded in a formal statement. Some states may require check-in sheets be used. List broken windows, torn carpet, damaged furniture and other items. Beside each item note if and when you will repair it. This protects the tenant from paying damage done by a previous renter. It also protects the landlord against tenants who claim the damage they have done to the apartment was done before they moved in. A list signed by both the landlord and the tenant when the apartment is rented prevents misunderstandings later.

When all the business has been satisfactorily agreed upon, you should have the tenant complete an information sheet (see illustration) before you agree to rent to him. This sheet includes several important details. You may decide to rephrase the questions, but each item is included for a particular reason.

First, the questions about residence are important. The client's previous address may indicate a reference you want to check. His length of time at that address and his reason for moving may indicate a pattern in his moving habits. Is this a person who moves every six months as an alternative to cleaning his closets? Or is this a person who finds a place he likes and settles into it?

The emergency number is important in case you rent to a client who does not intend to have a telephone installed. Few things are more annoying than to need to talk to a tenant and be unable to reach him. An emergency number gives you a guarantee of contact with the renter.

The question referring to income is also important. This will indicate whether or not the client can afford the apartment you are considering renting to him. We once discussed renting an apartment with a young lady whose income would have left her $50 a month after she had paid her rent. Even though the rent payment included utilities, we doubted she could meet the rent payments and feed and clothe herself with the remaining money. After thinking about it, she decided the apartment she was considering was too expensive for her budget. Sometimes the landlord must do a little financial counseling in a polite manner. This can save problems later.

The questions about pets and children will clarify conditions of the rental and assure you of how many people will be occupying the apartment. The importance of this detail has already been discussed.

The questions about references is one of the most important items on this questionnaire. Even if you do not plan to call each reference listed, you should ask for several references. Note the relationship of the reference to the applicant. Does he list a best friend or a relative instead of an employer or a previous landlord? If so, you should request work references from him.

As you become more experienced in talking with prospective tenants, you will probably find you actually check references less often than you did when you first started landlording. You will probably become quite skilled at determining which people will be reliable tenants. Occasionally, however, something will make you hesitate about renting the apartment to a particular prospect. Then it is helpful to have references so you can check them and call the client. As a general rule, it is always wise to check at least one reference before renting to the client even if you feel confident about him.

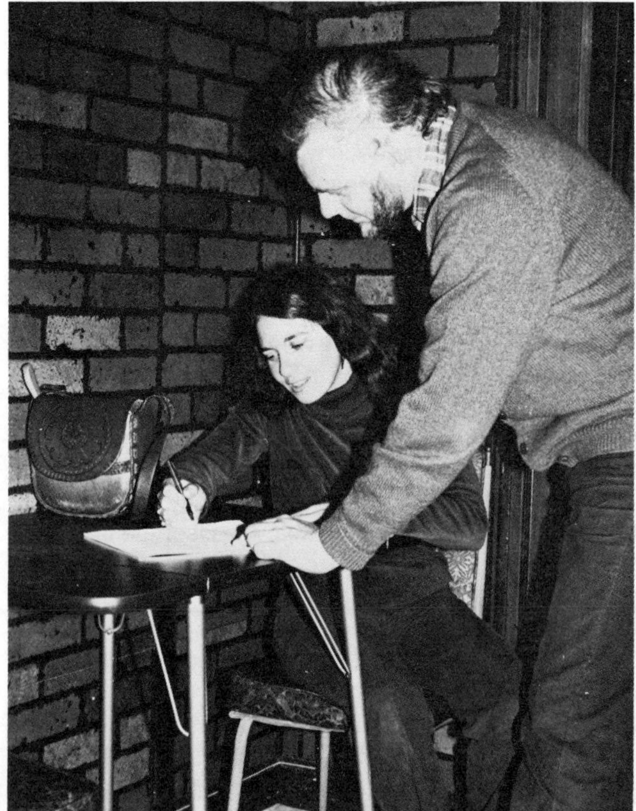

Go over the terms of the rental carefully with the client. Discuss the responsibilities as a tenant and explain the written lease if there is one. Have the tenant fill out an information sheet.

TENANT INFORMATION SHEET

Address of the apartment the tenant is renting____________________

____

Date apartment is rented____________________

Tenant's name____________________

Previous address____________________

Length of time at that address____________________

Reason for leaving____________________

Place of employment____________________

Length of time at that job____________________

Income____________________

Home phone number____________________

Business phone number____________________

Emergency contact:

Name____________________

Phone____________________

Address____________________

Names and ages of people who will be living in apartment:

____

____

____

References:

Character references____________________

____

Credit reference____________________

(cont.)

Repairs/remodeling landlord agrees to make:

____

____

____

Security deposit receipt:

Amount due: ______________________________

Amount paid: ______________________________

Balance due: ______________________________

(This deposit is general monies and may be used by the landlord to cover the costs of damages to the apartment by the tenant or his/her guests or as delinquent rent.)

Security deposit paid by: ______________________________

Security deposit paid for pet: ______________________________

Signed: ____

(Date) (Tenant)

____

(Date) (Tenant)

____

(Date) (Landlord)

Although the client will usually receive a favorable reference, occasionally you may find the reference is completely invalid. We experienced this situation one time. The prospective tenant gave us a work reference with a long distance number. The client said he had been laid off of work and he had come to our town to find work in another line. Evidently, he did not expect us to call the reference because of the long distance number and the late hour. However we did call the reference and learned the employer had not laid off anyone in the last year. In fact, the opposite was true. The employer was constantly looking for people to work for him. In addition, the employer did not know the person about whom we were inquiring. This was a lesson to us that even when a reference looks acceptable, it may be invalid.

When calling a reference, it is best to state your name and explain your reason for calling. Say something like this:

> Mr. Jones, my name is Mary Smith. Your name was given as a reference to me by Jon Anderson. He would like to rent an apartment from me. In your opinion, would he be a reliable renter?

Usually, the person is willing to discuss the client with you.

As a landlord, you will often be asked to supply a reference for a previous tenant. When you give a reference, be sure you limit your statement to the facts. Although it is tempting to make value judgements, this is unwise.

For example, if the tenant was consistently late with his rent, do not say, "He never paid his rent." State, instead, "In the last three months the tenant rented from me, he paid his rent on the 20th of each month rather than the first of each month when it was due."

Do not say the tenant was a troublemaker while he lived in your building. Instead you should state the facts: "The other tenants in the building complained about him. The police were called to his apartment three times last month."

By stating the facts you can warn the prospective landlord about troublesome tenants without risking legal problems.

As a precaution, you should always request an information sheet from each single adult renting the apartment. If you are renting to two men, two women or an unmarried couple, it is important to establish who is responsible for the rent. Record the name of the responsible party or parties on all the information sheets pertaining to the rental. Usually when women or men decide to rent an apartment together, they intend to split the rent. This means you will receive an equal portion of the total rent from each party. It also means each party is responsible only for his share of the rent. If two people share an apartment and one disappears, you—not his roommate—lose his share of the rent. You can help prevent this problem by declaring each tenant equally responsible for 100 percent of the rent.

It is tempting to treat unmarried couples like married couples by having them fill out one information sheet and collecting the first month's rent. Since they are not married and thus, they are not responsible for each other's debts, it is wise to treat them as you would two women or men sharing an apartment. If you assign the responsibility to both parties equally before you rent the unit to them, you eliminate most problems.

SECURITY DEPOSITS

Although some landlords prefer not to bother with collecting a security deposit at the time of rental, most landlords consider a security deposit essential. A security deposit is a sum of money in addition to the rent money collected from the tenant at the time of rental. This money is held in the tenant's name and can be used by the landlord to pay for damage done to the apartment during the tenant's occupancy. In some states it may also be used as rent money should the tenant terminate his occupancy without paying rent due to the landlord. However, some states require this money to *only* be used as a deposit for damage, and in some cases this money *must* be put into escrow. Check your state's legislation. Security deposits should be at least the sum of one month's rent. Often landlords require more than one month's rent, especially if children or pets will be staying in the unit. Collecting more than one month's rent also protects you from the tenant who tries to use the security deposit as the last month's rent.

It is not uncommon for a tenant to call the landlord and say, "I will be moving on the first of next month. You can keep my security deposit for this month's rent." If you agree to this, you may have trouble later. If the security deposit is used as the last month's rent, you do not have money to pay for any damage to the apartment or for cleaning. For that reason, some landlords (and states) require the first and last month's rent in advance plus a deposit for cleaning and repairs.

The entire security deposit should be collected before you agree to rent the apartment to the client. Some landlords agree to take the deposit in two installments. The first installment is due when the client rents the apartment. The second installment is due with the second month's rent. It has been our experience, however, that if you do not receive the entire amount with the first month's rent, you will probably not receive the second installment.

The first month's rent plus the security deposit often total a considerable amount of money. It is tempting to accept a tenant's excuse he is new in town, just beginning a new job, or that for a variety of other reasons he cannot pay the security deposit now. Before you sympathize too much with reasons why the tenant cannot pay the security deposit, you should remember how much he would need if he were planning to buy housing. When thought of in that way, a security deposit does not seem unreasonable. If the tenant cannot afford to pay the security deposit, perhaps the apartment he is considering is too expensive for him.

There are several good reasons for insisting on a security deposit. The most obvious, of course, is that this obligates the tenant to maintain the apartment in the condition in which it was rented to him. If he wants his money refunded to him when he vacates the unit, he must take care of the apartment and give you the agreed upon notice. The security deposit also serves as a financial reference. If the tenant cannot afford to pay you a security deposit, he probably cannot afford the apartment you are offering him, and you should discourage him from renting.

Make sure that you write out a separate receipt for the security deposit and credit it to the person who has paid it. If you do not do this, you may find yourself in the middle of a fight over the security deposit when roommates separate and vacate the apartment. Make sure the tenant understands what the security deposit is meant to cover and the terms by which it will and will not be refunded. Some landlords, for instance, refund the security deposit in person on the day the tenant vacates the unit. Other landlords require a forwarding address and send the deposit within a previously specified time. Again, consult your state's laws as some require deposits returned within a specific amount of time.

State laws differ in their stipulations concerning the security deposit. In some states landlords are required to pay interest on the deposit or put it in escrow. In Wisconsin, for example, the security deposit is considered general monies. It may be used as rent or as compensation for damage to the apartment. If the tenant fails to give 30 days notice before vacating the apartment, the landlord may deduct daily rent from the tenant's security deposit until the apartment is rented to someone else. He may also deduct any expenses accrued in the renting process, such as advertising, mileage accumulated in showing the apartment or the cost of hiring someone else to show the apartment.

Security deposits should be deposited in a collective savings account and used for its intended purpose. They should not be used for paying monthly bills, for investments, or for maintaining the rental units.

Collecting security deposits requires more bookkeeping, but it is well worth any inconvenience it causes. Without a security deposit, you are vulnerable for several kinds of monetary losses.

A Deposit to Hold the Apartment

Another problem occasionally encountered is the prospective tenant's request to deposit a certain amount of money to hold the apartment until a later date.

Consider the following hypothetical example. You are showing an apartment which will be available in 10 days. A client likes the apartment, and he wants to rent it. He does not have the full amount necessary to rent the apartment. He asks you if he may put down a small amount of money to hold the apartment until the first of the month. He reasons he cannot move in until the first of the month, anyway. He also admits all his money is tied up in the security deposit held by his present landlord. He assures you the money is his when he moves from the apartment.

It is tempting to take $25 from him and consider the unit rented, but this is not a good idea. You may find requiring the total security deposit from him is a safer practice. Agree that unless you have the month's rent by the first, you will consider the apartment available and will treat the situation as though he had given 30 days notice. You will use his security deposit to pay the daily rent until the unit has been rented. (Check your state statutes to assure that this is an acceptable practice.)

Before bargaining with the prospective tenant, remember you still have ten days remaining before you begin to lose money on the unit. Actually, it is to your advantage not to rent the apartment to someone who seems short of money. While it is convenient to stop showing the apartment, you may find your haste causes you problems later.

LEASES

Recent court decisions have changed the tenant-landlord relationship. (See the chapter *Tenants' Rights*.) Because of this change, an increasing number of landlords find it helpful to define the terms of tenant occupancy with a written lease.

Legally, a lease may be written or oral. Most people, however, think of a lease as a written agreement, so this section is limited to a discussion of the written lease.

A lease is a written agreement between the landlord (lessor) and the tenant (lessee) which states the specific terms of the rental agreement. Included in any lease should be:

1. A complete description of the property the tenant is renting.
2. The exact date the lease will expire.
3. The amount of rent due each month.
4. The date the rent is due.

Residential Lease Form

THIS AGREEMENT for the lease of premises, made this ________ day of ________________ A. D., 19______

Between ____

Address ______________________________ hereinafter called the "LESSOR."

Parties

and ____

____

______________________________ hereinafter called the "LESSEE."

WITNESSETH:

Description of Premises

FIRST: The LESSOR for and in consideration of the rents to be paid and the covenants to be performed by the LESSEE, does hereby Let and Lease the premises commonly known as

____

____

____

in the City of Ann Arbor, County of Washtenaw, State of Michigan, for the term of ______________________

____

from the ________ day of ________________ 19______ to and including the ________ day of ________________

19______, to be used and occupied by the LESSEE for residential purposes.

Rent

SECOND: The LESSEE does hereby hire the above premises for the full term above stated and does hereby covenant and agree as follows:

To pay as rent for the use of said premises the sum of ______________________

______________________ Dollars ($______________)

in monthly installments in advance, payable as follows: (a) On or prior to the signing of this lease ______________

______________________ Dollars ($______________)

(b) On the ________ day of ________________ 19______; ______________________

______________________ Dollars ($______________)

(c) On the first day of ________________ 19______; ______________________

______________________ Dollars ($______________)

and a like sum on the first day of each and every month thereafter, to and including the first day of

________________ 19______.

Advance Rent

THIRD: The LESSEE further agrees to pay the sum of ______________________________ Dollars ($______________) to be applied to the rent then owing for the last month of occupancy by the LESSEE in the demised premises. It is agreed and understood that this payment of the last month's rent does not void or nullify any of the provisions herein made relating to the requirement of at least (30) thirty days advance written notice when terminating occupancy and shall not in the event of a hold-over tenancy be used as rent for any period except the last month of said hold-over term.

Damage and Security Deposit

FOURTH: (a) The LESSEE further agrees to pay $______________ in advance to be held by the LESSOR. This sum is to be applied to the LESSOR'S claim for damages to the premises including all parts of the entire building and grounds, by the LESSEE, his co-lessees, family, servants or guests, also including his moving in or moving out, over and above normal wear and tear. The LESSOR'S decision on the matter of damages to the premises shall be final.

(b) The LESSOR shall repay to the LESSEE, within 30 days after vacating the premises, all or whatever part of said deposit that may be remaining, if any, after reimbursement of the LESSOR from this fund for any claims including his cost to place it in as clean condition as when taken.

(c) The LESSEE further agrees to pay any sum above and beyond this security deposit claimed by the LESSOR for damages within ten days after receiving his "Statement of Damage and Security Deposit Account."

Delay of Possession

FIFTH: It is agreed and understood that if the LESSEE shall be unable to enter into and occupy the premises hereby leased at the time above provided, by reason of the said premises not being ready for occupancy, or by reason of the holding over of any previous occupant, or as a result of any cause or reason beyond the direct control of the LESSOR, the LESSOR shall not be liable in damages to the LESSEE. In order to prevent a delay of possession the LESSEE may, at his option, accept the premises in an "as is" condition. If this option is exercised, it is agreed and understood that the tenant will NOT surrender the premises at the termination of this lease, or any extention thereof, in the same condition as when taken, but shall deliver the premises in reasonably clean and tenantable condition, and it is further agreed that the LESSOR may assess damages and cleaning charges against the LESSEE or against the LESSEE'S damage deposit or advance rent without considering the condition of the premises when taken by the LESSEE.

Condition of Premises

SIXTH: The LESSEE further covenants and agrees that by the acceptance of possession of said premises, he is acknowledging that the condition of said premises are acceptable to him and that upon the expiration of said term of this Lease or any extension thereof, he will deliver up possession of said premises to the LESSOR, in as good order and repair as when delivered to him, damage by fire, casualty, war or insurrection, riot or public disorder, or act upon the part of any governmental authority, ordinary wear and tear and damage by the elements excepted.

Lessee's Utilities

SEVENTH: The LESSEE shall furnish for his own______________electricity,__________and telephone service, and shall pay all charges for the same.

Service by Lessor

EIGHTH: The Lessor agrees to furnish LESSEE with the use of a stove, refrigerator, heating plant or facilities and hot water heater or facilities, air conditioning if any, garbage disposal if any, to supply hot and cold water for laundry use, cold water to the apartment, and some janitor services outside the apartment. LESSOR shall not be liable for any stoppage or interruption of any of said services caused by riot, strike, labor disputes or neglect, inevitable accident, or other causes beyond the immediate control of the LESSOR, or for stoppage or interruptions of any of such services for the purpose of making needful repairs, provided the LESSOR shall use reasonable diligence to cause such services to be resumed.

Lawful Use

NINTH: The LESSEE agrees that he, his co-lessee's, family, servants, or guests, shall use and occupy said demised premises for residential purposes only and maintain the same in accordance with all police, sanitary or other regulations imposed by any municipal or governmental authority and to observe all reasonable regulations and requirements of any insurance underwriters concerning the use and condition of the premises, tending to reduce fire hazards and insurance rates, and not to permit or allow any rubbish, waste materials or products to accumulate upon said premises, or to permit any use thereof to interfere with the lawful and proper use and enjoyment of said building or any part thereof by the LESSOR, its agents, servants or any of its' other tenants in said building.

Non-Assignment

TENTH: The LESSEE agrees not to lease, sublet or assign any part of the said premises without the written consent of the LESSOR (the Lessor in most cases will NOT grant such permission) nor to allow any other persons to occupy said premises hereby rented, excepting casual visits of friends or guests, limited to a two week stay. It is further agreed that the number of permanent occupants, including occupying LESSEES and family, shall not be more than__________ except with the written consent of the LESSOR.

Quiet Possession

ELEVENTH: The LESSOR covenants that the LESSEE, on paying the rent and performing the covenants aforesaid shall and may peacefully and quietly have, hold and enjoy the demised premises for the term aforesaid.

Rules and Regulations

TWELFTH: The LESSEE agrees to abide by and to see that his guests abide by and conform to rules and regulations of this tenancy, which are attached hereto and made a part hereof. Any violation of said rules and regulations will constitute a breach of this lease agreement, and will automatically give the LESSOR the right to evict the LESSEE from the premises thirty (30) days after serving the LESSEE with written notice of such termination of tenancy.

Alterations

THIRTEENTH: The LESSEE shall make no structural alterations, additions, or improvements in or about said premises, do no painting or decorating, nor make any other changes in the interior of said premises, including the equipment therein, without the written consent of the LESSOR in each and every instance, and then only under his supervision. This includes such work as: installation of additional locks, picture hooks or fixtures; placing nails, bolts or screws in the walls, doors, trim or sills; tacking or cementing carpets, rugs or linoleum on the floor; removing and replacing shoe mold when laying carpet; providing additional electrical wiring, and erecting television aerial or connections on the premises. LESSEE shall reimburse LESSOR for any damages resulting therefrom. The LESSEE shall not receive credit towards rental payments for any repairs, alterations, additions or improvements of any description undertaken by him. All repairs, alterations, additions or improvements shall immediately become the property of the LESSOR.

Repairs

FOURTEENTH: The LESSOR agrees to make all necessary exterior and structural repairs to the demised premises, and also to include as his obligation any necessary repairs to the roofs of the said building and any necessary decorating or painting at times which are mutually agreed to by the parties to this lease. The LESSOR agrees to make all repairs to the electric, gas, plumbing, heating and air conditioning systems, if any, which may from time to time become necessary. The LESSOR shall have the right to enter the leased premises at all reasonable hours to make such repairs or alterations as he may deem necessary.

Entry

FIFTEENTH: The LESSEE hereby agrees that for a period commencing 60 days prior to the termination of this lease, the LESSOR may show the premises to prospective tenants. The LESSOR shall have the right to enter the leased premises at all reasonable hours to examine or inspect the same.

Liability for Damage to Premises

SIXTEENTH: The LESSOR shall not be liable for any injuries to personal property, to said premises or to said LESSEE or other persons, arising from the building or any part or appurtenance thereof becoming out of repair, or resulting from accident, fire, windstorm, theft, explosion, freezing, bursting, leaking or backing up or overflowing of water, gas, sewer, steam pipes or any plumbing connected therewith, or from any damage caused by defective electric wiring, or from any acts or neglect of caretaker or co-tenants or other occupants of the building; nor shall the LESSOR be responsible for the loss of personal property from the above causes. Further the LESSEE shall reimburse the LESSOR for any damage to the demised premises or equipment therein during his tenancy, except damages from causes beyond his control, or from ordinary wear and tear and shall pay on demand the amount of such damage, which is hereby designated as additional rent. The LESSOR shall be entitled to all of the remedies provided in the lease for non-payment of rent in the event the LESSEE fails to pay such damages.

Damage by Fire

SEVENTEENTH: In case the buildings and improvements on said premises are injured or destroyed in whole or in part by fire or other catastrophe during the continuance of this lease, the LESSOR shall forthwith repair the same to good and tenantable condition so as to be substantially the same as they were prior to such fire or other castastrophe, and the rent herein provided for shall abate entirely in case the entire premises are so rendered untenantable, and pro-rata for the portion rendered untenantable in case a part only is untenantable, until the same shall be restored to a condition so as to be occupied again by the LESSEE; provided, however, that in case the building and improvements shall be destroyed to an extent of more than one-half their value, and it is inadvisable to restore the same, then the LESSOR, may at its' option, terminate this lease forthwith by written notice to the LESSEE. There shall be no abatement of rent if such fire or other cause damaging the leased premises shall result from the negligence or willful act of the LESSEE, his family, servants, or guests.

Eminent Domain

EIGHTEENTH: If the demised premises or any portion thereof which includes a substantial part of the premises shall be taken or condemned by any public authority under power of eminent domain for any public use or purpose, the term of this lease shall end upon, and not before, the date when the possession of the part so taken shall be required for such use or purpose, and without apportionment of the condemnation award or settlement. Current rent shall be apportioned as of the date of such termination of possession on a day to day basis.

Bankruptcy and Insolvency

NINETEENTH: The LESSEE or any one of the LESSEES' signed to this agreement agree that if the estate created hereby shall be taken in execution, or by other process of law, or if the LESSEE shall be declared bankrupt or insolvent, according to law, or any receiver be appointed for the business and property of the LESSEE, or if any assignment shall be made of the LESSEE'S property for the benefit of creditors, then and in such event this lease may be cancelled upon 30 days written notice from the LESSOR.

Re-Entry TWENTIETH: If the LESSEE shall neglect or fail to pay rent, perform, or observe any of the covenants herein contained on his part to be observed and performed, then the LESSOR shall have the right upon seven (7) days written notice to re-enter into, re-possess the said premises, and forceably remove the LESSEE and his effects, if necessary, without being deemed guilty of any manner of trespass. The LESSEE further agrees to indemnify and reimburse the LESSOR for all expenses incurred in obtaining possession of said premises, all commissions and expenses which may be incurred in re-renting the same, and all loss of rent which the LESSOR may incur by reason of such repossession, during the residue of the term above specified. Such indemnification and reimbursement may be taken from advance rent or damage deposit, or both, if needed.

Hold-over TWENTY-FIRST: It is agreed that a holding over upon the expiration of the term herein specified, shall operate as an extension of this lease from month to month only.

Termination TWENTY-SECOND: In the event the LESSEE desires to terminate tenancy on lease expiration date or at any time thereafter, the LESSEE agrees to notify the LESSOR in writing not less than thirty (30) days in advance of such vacating date.

Remedies Not Exclusive TWENTY-THIRD: It is agreed that each and every of the rights, remedies and benefits provided by this lease shall be separate and independent of each other, and shall not be exclusive of any other of said rights, remedies and benefits, or of any other rights, remedies and benefits allowed by law.

Capacity of the Parties TWENTY-FOURTH: By the execution of this said Lease, each of the persons who signs as LESSEE represents that he or she is of the full age of eighteen years, and signs this Lease fully and freely with knowledge of the contents thereof, and that he or she has full capacity to sign the said Lease and is under no undue influence, coercion or duress as to the execution thereof.

Rent As A Necessity TWENTY-FIFTH: The LESSEE undertakes and agrees that the rent due under the terms of this Lease is payment for the premises as a necessity to maintain shelter and refuge for the LESSEE and for the authorized occupants of the premises under this lease.

Notices TWENTY-SIXTH: All notices to be given hereunder by either party shall be in writing and given by personal delivery to the LESSOR or to the LESSEE, or shall be sent by the United States Post Office, addressed to the party intended to be notified, at the post office address of such party last known to the party giving notice, and notice given as aforesaid shall be a sufficient service thereof, and shall be deemed given as of the date when deposited in any post office or in any post office box regularly maintained by the Federal Government, with full address properly placed thereon, and with full postage prepaid.

Definitions TWENTY-SEVENTH: The word "LESSEE", wherever in this agreement mentioned shall be construed to mean either singular or plural, masculine or feminine, and the word "LESSOR" shall be construed to mean the LESSOR and his duly authorized agents, and this Lease shall be binding jointly and severally upon the parties hereto, and their respective heirs, executors, administrators, successors, legal representatives and assigns.

In witness whereof the parties hereto have set their respective hands and seals this ______ day of ________________ 19____

WITNESSES: LESSOR:

____

LESSEE:

____

______________________________ ______________________________ (L. S.)

______________________________ ______________________________ (L. S.)

______________________________ ______________________________ (L. S.)

Inflation has made the lease more desirable for the tenant than for the landlord. Interest rates and the cost of utilities and building repairs have risen sharply. Some landlords bound to a lease, especially a long-term lease with a stipulated amount of rent for the duration of the lease, have suffered financially as a result. To correct this problem, many landlords now insert an escalation clause in the lease. This clause provides for a periodic increase in the rent during the life of the lease.

Other clauses which should be inserted in the lease are conditions of rental, such as yard maintenance and utilities which are to be paid by the tenant. While most leases state the tenant has the right to the "quiet enjoyment" of the property he is renting, many landlords insert a clause which states they retain the right to inspect the property on a regular basis. This is an especially important clause for the landlord. If he suspects the apartment is not being maintained, he has the legal right to inspect it. If he decides to sell the property, the tenants must allow him to show their units.

Leases may present another problem for the landlord. When tenants wish to move before the lease expires, they may often try to sublet the property. If they are allowed to sublet, the landlord does not have control over who inhabits his apartment. It is best to stipulate in the lease the conditions under which the renter may sublet. Most landlords will want to approve the people to whom his original renters sublet the apartment.

Another way around the problem of subletting is to state when a renter is transferred, his lease may be automatically terminated. Landlords may also state the lease can be terminated by mutual agreement. When the landlord thinks it is to his benefit to terminate the lease rather than allow the tenant to sublet, he may do so.

Although lease forms may be purchased from most office supply shops, you may decide to have an attorney draw up a standard lease form for you which meets your specific requirements. The attorney's fees are usually reasonable for this service. He knows the state statutes thoroughly and may think of protective statements you may have neglected to include. After he has drawn up the lease, you can have the lease formally printed or you can take it to a quick print shop and have it duplicated from the typewritten copy.

Advantages of a lease are:

1. Anything written has more impact. We are a society of the written word. A signature is a symbol of an important commitment. "You signed it," is a statement meaning, "You are responsible."

2. The lease clearly defines the terms of the rental. It prevents misunderstanding later.

3. If you do have problems with the renters, a well-drawn lease is a good basis for court action.

Disadvantages of a lease are:

1. A lease may make a building more difficult to sell because the buyer is bound by the seller's leases.

2. A lease may make it more complicated for you to evict a tenant because you are bound by the conditions of the lease. For example, some leases require the tenant be sued each month for rent past due rather than for a lump sum spanning the life of the lease.

3. The landlord must be careful his interests are protected by the lease. An escalation clause and language covering the subletting situation, for example, are recommended.

When the terms of the rental have been agreed upon and the money collected, tell the tenant what day he can move into the apartment and acquaint him with the procedure for picking up the key. Give him a card on which you have printed your name, address and telephone number. Tell him where you can be reached during the day and where you will be in the evenings if these numbers are different. Tell him which time is best to reach you. Also on the card print the procedure for collecting the rent. Many tenants expect the landlord to stop by and pick up the rent each month. If you have numerous apartments, this becomes time-consuming. You may prefer to have the checks sent to you. Indicate to whom the check should be made payable. If both husband and wife are involved in managing the apartments, have the check made payable to the person who keeps the books even if this may not be the same person who has shown the apartment.

Depending on the number of tenants you will have you may wish to have these cards and the information sheet typed once and taken to a printer for duplication. Or they may be duplicated by a copier found in banks and some department stores and libraries. There is no need to make out an individual copy of the information sheet and card for each tenant.

If you cannot be present on the day the tenant moves into the apartment, make sure you stop by as soon as possible. An important part of landlording is public relations. The tenant should feel you are concerned about him and about your property. He should know you want everything to run smoothly.

If you follow these recommendations, you should have an easier time advertising, showing and renting your apartments. And your road to successful landlording should be well established.

Landlord's name ______________________________

Address ______________________________

Home phone number ______________________________

Best time to contact the landlord is ______________________________

In an emergency when the landlord cannot be reached contact:

Name ______________________________

Address ______________________________

Phone number ______________________________

Please send your rent in the form of a check or money order to the landlord's address promptly on the first of the month.

Information card given to the tenant at the time of rental.

SUMMARY

Renting apartments successfully begins with proper advertising. An effective advertisement will help screen clients and will save you time and money. One way to save money is to take advantage of sources of free advertising such as bulletin boards in schools and grocery stores.

Other factors which make this aspect of landlording easier are skill in scheduling and showing the rental units. When scheduling apartment showings, make sure you ask for the full name of the client making the appointment. When showing the apartment point out the attractive features of the unit.

If the tenant expresses an interest in the apartment, be sure you know exactly who will be living there and make sure the client knows the conditions under which he is renting the apartment. Whether you require a written lease or not, you should request an information sheet from each tenant. Security deposits are another form of insurance a landlord can request from a prospective tenant.

4 Managing Your Apartments

KEEPING THE BOOKS

Keeping careful financial records or books is one of the most important jobs of successful landlording. It is also one of the most time-consuming. Books are essential for your own records. They are a good indication of whether or not you are managing your landlording responsibilities successfully. Accurate books are also essential for your annual accounting to the IRS, and they are helpful if disputes over rents, security deposits or other monies should occur between you and your tenants. Remember that landlording is a business and should be conducted as you would any other business venture.

Even if you have only one rental you should have a separate checking and savings account for the apartment. The accounts should be listed under the title you choose for your business. Some people use their last name, such as in the case of Robert Olson who owns Olson's Apartments. Some people combine their first names to form a unique title, such as in the case of Robert and Anne who combined their first names and called their apartments ROAN Apartments. Some people name their apartments after a street on which the apartment is located, such as Maple Street Apartments. Whatever name you give to your apartment business, you will find thinking of it as a responsibility apart from your family budget is helpful. Only monies pertaining to the apartment business should be deposited in your apartment accounts. Besides making your bookkeeping easier, separate checking and saving accounts are an additional record of monetary transactions.

Organizing Your Records

There are numerous ways to organize records pertaining to your rental units. We have tried many different filing systems. On the following pages, we describe the way we have found to work best for us. You will probably want to test our method and modify it to your situation.

Each year we purchase a spiral notebook and a loose leaf folder for each apartment building. On the front of the notebook and the folder we print the address of the rental and the year. We place the spiral notebook in one pocket of the folder. In the other pocket of the folder we file information sheets for the tenants who are currently living in the building, insurance policies, closing statements and other written material pertaining to the apartment building for that year. We also place in that pocket a manila envelope which contains all the receipts connected with the apartment during the year.

The spiral notebook is divided into three sections labeled "Rents Collected," "Bills Paid," and "Diary of Tenant Contact." The first section, "Rents Collected," is divided into 12 months. Under each month the amount of the rent and the day it was collected is recorded. The name of the tenant from whom it was collected is also recorded.

The second section is also divided into 12 months. In this section each bill and the date it is paid is recorded. This is not as time-consuming as it sounds because all the bills are paid on one day of each month rather than individually as they come in. The bill is filed in the manila envelope and clipped to other bills for that month.

In the third section, special transactions with the tenants are noted. Examples of items worthy of noting are:

1. The date you informed a tenant his rent would be raised and the date you said he should begin paying the increase in the rent.

2. The date a tenant informed you he was moving and the date he said he would be moved from the apartment.

3. The date and check number of the security deposit which the tenant pays.

4. The date you sent an eviction notice and the date you told the tenant to be moved from the apartment.

RENT PAYMENT RECORD

TENANT'S NAME	JAN	FEB	MAR	APR	MAY	JUNE	JULY	AUG	SEPT	OCT	NOV	DEC
(120 State-Apt #1) BOB SMITH	200 R / S.D. 100	200 R. / S.D. 100	200 R	200 R	200 R	200 R	*220 R					
(120 State-Apt #2) DIANE OTT	200 R	200 R	200 R	200 R	200 R	200 R	*220 R					
(120 State-Apt #3) RAY BROWN	190 R	190 R	190 R	190 R	190 R	190 R	*200 R					
(120 State-Apt #4) KAREN OLSON	190 R	100 90 R	190 R	190 R	190 R	190 R	*200 R					
(26 Grand Ave.-Lower) DAVE JONES	250 R	250 R	200 50 R	250 R	250 R	200 50 R	200 R					
(26 Grand Ave.-Upper) MIKE GREEN	210 R	210 R	210 R	210 R	210 R	210 R	210 R					
(414 Elm-Lower) BARB PETERS	225 R	225 R	200 R	250 R	225 R	200 R	-0- R					
(414 Elm-Upper) RENEE BAUERS	195 R	195 R	195 R	195 R	195 R	195 R	195 R					
(202 Maple) PHIL JOHNSON	350 R / S.D. 350	350 R	350 R	350 R	350 R	350 R	350 R					
(14 Grant-Lower) JERRY PIERCE	VACANT	250 R / 250 S.D.	250 R.	250 R	250 R	250 R	250 R					
(14 Grant-Upper) ANDY KING	100 R / S.D. 100	200 R / S.D 100	200 R	200 R	200 R	200 R	200 R					

A schedule of rents paid.

This section is an important part of your records. As you build a string of rental units, you will find that you cannot keep track of all the people living in your buildings as easily as you could when you owned your first rental. But if you do keep careful records of the comings and goings of the tenants, you prevent problems in communication. You can refer to your diary for questions about security deposits or proper notice of intention to move. In this way you eliminate confusion and conflict.

Another essential aspect of record keeping is a record of the number of trips made to each rental. For this record, we use a calendar. We hang the calendar in a convenient place, preferably close to the back door. Each time we make a trip to an apartment we record the address in the box under the date. The total mileage for each trip to a rental unit, or to other places such as department stores or hardware stores on business for the apartment, is deductible as a business expense. You must keep accurate records of these trips, however, or you may find the deduction is denied to you at year's end. Inaccurate records may be a basis for refusing to allow you to deduct as many trips as you actually made during the year. These trips are a considerable deduction and you should protect your right to take the full deduction. There are many ways to record these trips, but we find the calendar method is the most convenient. It is always in view as we leave for one of the apartments. We do not have to go to a desk and search for the record book. At the end of each year, we can quickly total the trips made to each apartment. We then file the calendar away with the folders in case questions arise later about the business deduction.

MARCH

SUNDAY	MONDAY	TUESDAY	WEDNESDAY	THURSDAY	FRIDAY	SATURDAY
						1 ELM STATE
2 ELM	3 ELM	4 ELM	5 ELM	6 ELM	7 ELM GRANT	8
9	10	11	12	13	14 GRANT	15
16	17	18	19	20	21	22 GRANT
23 GRANT	24	25	26	27 GRANT	28 GRANT	29 GRANT
30	31					

Record the trips you make to the apartments on a calendar.

You should have a special place to work on apartment business. An area with a work table, bulletin board and file cabinets is the minimum necessary for organizing your bookkeeping responsibilities. You may decide to set a room aside in your home for this purpose. The home office is a questionable deduction, but a separate room in your house devoted to rental business is convenient.

BUILDING PUBLIC RELATIONS

There is more to managing apartments than keeping accurate records. A successful landlord must also manage the buildings he rents to tenants. Managing the buildings requires skill in two areas: building maintenance (discussed in detail in a separate section of this book) and building public relations.

A successful landlord must be able to recognize trouble brewing in his buildings. This trouble may be between:

1. tenants in the same building;
2. tenants and landlord;
3. tenants and other people in the neighborhood.

Without seeming to pry into his tenants' personal lives, the landlord must keep himself informed of the climate in the building. Indications of trouble may come to you directly or indirectly. Consider the following hypothetical example of an indirect indication of trouble.

APARTMENT REGULATIONS

Contained herein are the answers to questions most frequently asked upon leasing. All regulations have been established not only for the protection of the Lessor's property but for the benefit of all tenants alike. Your full cooperation will assist us in maintaining these apartments as a comfortable, pleasant and respectable place in which to live.

Decorating by tenant is not allowed.

Redecorating in our color group will be approved if paid by tenant.

No nails or screws shall be placed in any walls.

Picture hook tapes if properly installed and removed will not damage walls.

Drapery and curtain rods are to be screwed to steel window frames only.

Mirrors secured to walls subjects tenant to damage charges.

Control your children's noises—and don't allow them to annoy your neighbors.

Walk lightly—close doors quietly—it's easier on the nerves.

Turn down radio or TV volume to one room range.

Hold entertainment noises within limits—if you're going to have a big celebration, your neighbors won't object so much if you invite them too.

Do housework during the daytime if possible. Avoid late hour vacuuming, etc.

Close windows when leaving your apartment.

Use your kitchen vent fan often—air out cooking odors.

Never deposit sanitary napkins, baby diapers or similar objects in toilets.

Keep halls free of all personal belongings such as overshoes, baby carriages and toys. It may save someone from a bad fall and you from a law suit.

Laundry and storage rooms should be left tidy after using.

No pets are allowed in the apartment building at any time.

Provide a duplicate key outside your apartment as a precaution against being locked out.

Place requests for repairs with the Manager before noon for more prompt service.

Rent is due promptly on the first of the month. Please send the rent in the form of a check or money order to the landlord's home address.

No waterbeds are allowed in the apartments.

Do not allow your guests to block other tenants' parking areas. Please ask them to use the general parking area.

Sample of apartment rules.

One evening you receive a call from a young woman who lives in one of the upper apartments of a multi-unit you own. Her voice sounds strained as she tells you she will have to move immediately. She was happy with the apartment when she rented it four months earlier and her rent checks have arrived punctually on the first of each month. You consider her to be an ideal renter. In view of her reputation with you as an excellent renter, you should be concerned when she calls unexpectedly and neglects to give the required 30 days' notice. Her previous conduct as a renter indicates she will follow the proper procedure in notifying you of her intention to move. But you are new to the business and you assume she does not like you or the apartment, and you fear you will not rent the apartment again.

Soon after she leaves, you have a direct indication of trouble in the building. Another tenant begins to complain to you about late night parties of one of the other tenants. She reports personal harrassment and the police are called to the building several times.

Eventually, you realize you must evict the tenant who is causing the other tenants to complain, and the building settles into a peaceful routine. You could have prevented much of the trouble for yourself and other people in the building if you had been attuned to the indirect indication of trouble you first received. When a reliable tenant neglects to give proper notice, ask why.

Landlords walk a tightrope in their roles of maintaining an acceptable climate in the building. A landlord must know when to intervene in conflicts between tenants and when to allow the tenants to resolve their own problems.

You can, of course, also over-react to tenants' complaints. This can cause as much trouble for you as your previous failure to detect a problem. Consider the following situation. It is 10 p.m. and you receive a call from a tenant complaining of excessive noise in the building. The tenant describes a noisy party and says he called the police the previous evening about the same problem. The next day you confront the tenants about whom the complaint was made. They deny the accusation. You are unsympathetic to their side of the story because you remember your experience in the other building. The tenants move. You rent the apartment to another couple. The situation is repeated. Eventually you discover that the tenants who are complaining like to go to bed soon after their evening meal and they expect absolute quiet in the building from early evening through the night. Few other people can tolerate that life style. You have challenged the wrong tenants.

This type of situation does occur occasionally and it is extremely difficult to resolve. From the landlord's viewpoint, both tenants may be excellent renters. You may not want to lose either family as tenants. You cannot, however, continue to lose tenants in one half of the building

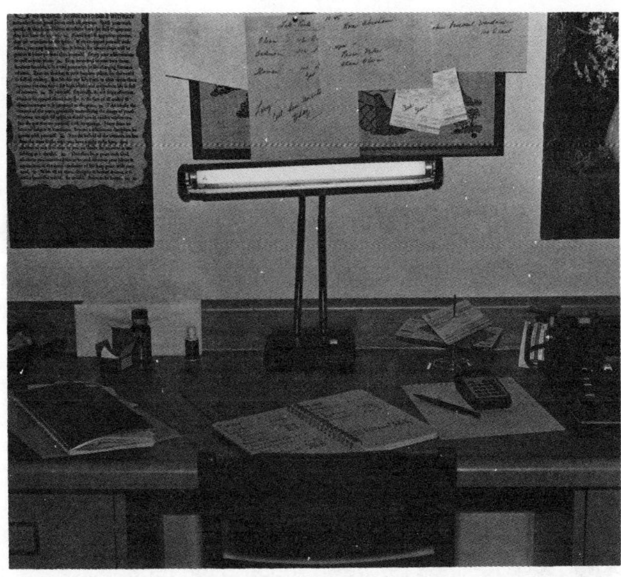

You should have a special place set aside to work on apartment business.

Post rules for your rental units where all the tenants can easily see them.

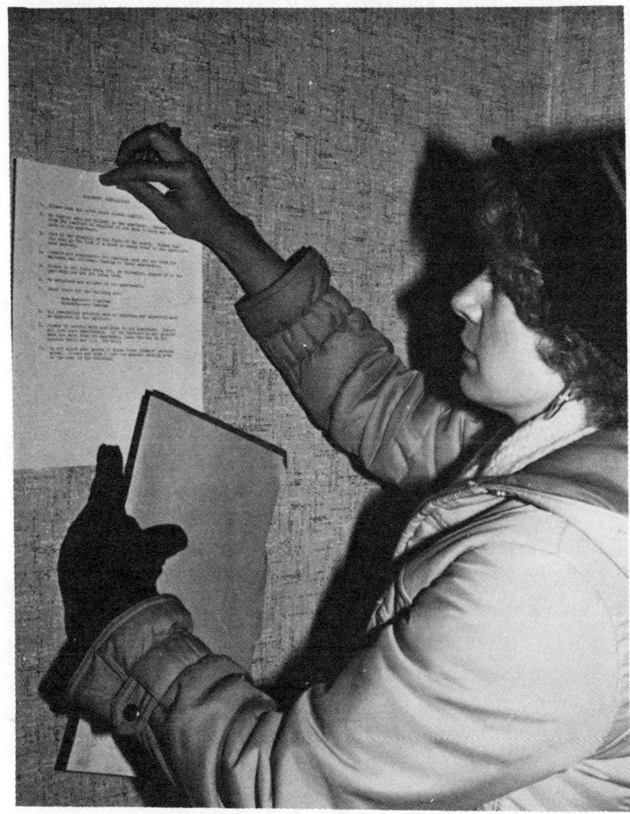

because of unreasonable demands of the other tenants living in the building.

The following policy may help resolve the problem. When the tenants call you with complaints about noise, listen politely. Go to the building immediately and assess the noise level for yourself. If you feel the noise level is not excessive for the time of day, politely explain this to the complaining tenant. Tell the tenant who is concerned to call you back if the noise continues beyond a reasonable time, such as a city curfew. By setting a specific time for the tenant to call you back, you set a pattern of acceptable behavior for the building.

It is tempting to be critical of the complaining tenant if you decide his complaint is unreasonable, because he has probably ruined much of your evening. But this immediate gratification may cost you time and trouble in the long run. Your restraint saves you some money and a lot of negative feelings between you and the tenants.

As you continue in landlording you will probably find a sympathetic ear tuned to a tenant's complaint is sufficient to solve the problem. Some complaints, however, are serious and require your immediate attention. Some ways you can gauge the seriousness of the complaint are:

1. Learn to listen for hysteria or exaggeration in a tenant's complaint. Does the tenant say he was almost asphyxiated when the upstairs tenant developed film in the bathroom? That probably means he did not like the smell of the developer filtering down from upstairs. Of course, you will want to check into the problem, but you will handle the situation calmly.

2. Note the time of the complaint call. We receive many calls on snowy or rainy weekends. Usually this means people are irritated with the weather. They may forget their differences as soon as the sun is shining. Of course, there are some distress calls that must not be ignored just because the weather has turned nasty. If a tenant complains about lack of heat on a cold winter day, you should follow up on such a complaint immediately.

3. Consider how often the tenant calls you with a complaint. Does the tenant call you weekly to complain about another tenant, gossip about other people in the building or mention minor repairs needed in the building? On the other hand, are you hearing from this tenant for the first time in six months? You will probably listen more closely to the tenant who seldom calls you. Do not ignore the frequent caller, however. This tenant is a good indication of the general climate in the building, and sometimes his concerns will warrant your immediate attention.

You should check into every complaint made to you. Remember, you are legally responsible for the physical condition of your building.

You will occasionally find yourself in the position of mediator between your tenants and the other people living in the neighborhood in which your rental is located. This is also a difficult position and you should be tactful in dealing with complaints. Sometimes homeowners do not enjoy living next to a rental unit, and they may be especially critical of the life style of the tenants living in the rental. Other times the neighbor has a legitimate reason for complaining. Although you do not live in the building, it is important for you to maintain good relations with the other people in the neighborhood. Remember, the property is ultimately your responsibility and concerns about the property should be handled by the landlord. If the tenants are responsible for maintaining the lawn and are neglecting their responsibility, for example, the landlord should remind them of their agreement to maintain the yard.

The neighbors' complaints about the tenants' private lives may require intervention from outside sources such as the police. If neighbors do call the police about a disruptive tenant, the landlord should talk to all three parties: the neighbor who complains, the tenant about whom the complaint was made, and the policeman who answered the complaint.

When you are checking into a complaint, be tactful with all parties involved. When approaching the tenant about whom the complaint has been made, say something like this:

> Another tenant in the building thinks you are too noisy. I said I would mention the complaint to you. What do you think is the best thing to do about the situation?

This statement will elicit a better response from the tenant than if you were to say:

> Mrs. Jones says you are too noisy. She is a good tenant. She always pays her rent on time. I do not want to lose her as a tenant. Keep the noise down.

One of the most important aspects of establishing good public relations is to keep the channels of communication open between you, your tenants and the other people who live in the vicinity of your rental. This means listening when you might prefer hanging up on the caller. It means being polite to all parties concerned. When handling complaints about the people who rent from you, you should:

1. Listen politely and carefully to the person making the complaint.
2. Refrain from making a snap judgment either in favor of or against the person who is complaining.
3. Check into the situation as quickly as possible.
4. Talk with all parties concerned and weigh all the information you have.
5. Assure the person making the complaint you are checking into the situation.

As we have mentioned previously, landlording is a business and it requires the skills necessary for operating any business. We have discussed creative financing and advertising in preceding chapters. Landlording also requires skillful handling of public relations. If you consider the suggestions we have made in this section and use your own good judgment, you should be able to manage this aspect of landlording successfully.

GENERAL MAINTENANCE

Other problems in apartment management occur in addition to keeping the books and mediating disputes between tenants and their neighbors. One of these problems is the general maintenance of the building. Building maintenance can be divided into regular and irregular maintenance. Regular maintenance includes: shoveling snow, cutting grass and changing storm windows. Irregular maintenance includes: plugged drains, cracked windows, squeaking hinges and rattling doors.

The landlord can handle general maintenance of the building in a variety of ways:

1. He can do all the regular and irregular maintenance himself.
2. He can hire someone to do the regular and irregular maintenance of the buildings he owns.
3. He can require the tenants to handle the regular maintenance of the building in which they live.

If you decide to handle all the regular and irregular maintenance of the buildings yourself, you will find it a time-consuming job, especially if you own a number of buildings. Keeping and following a written schedule simplifies your tasks. On a sheet of paper list the days of the week and the hours in each day you can devote to apartment maintenance. In each time slot record the maintenance task which must be accomplished and the address of the unit needing the repair. Underneath this description list the tools and the materials you will need. If you have to purchase any materials, record the name of the store where you can find them. In business, this is called a work order. You will probably refer to it simply as "notes" you write to yourself.

Whatever name you use to refer to this list, you will find it saves you a great deal of time and energy. If you use this list conscientiously, you will arrive at the rental with all the tools and materials you need to do the repair. We have found an entire Saturday morning can be spent driving from hardware store to hardware store looking for a special part. Now we make our list and call stores until we find one in our area that carries the materials we need. This saves us time, gas, and wear and tear on our nerves, which is possibly the most important reason for making our list in the first place.

You may also decide to hire someone to do all the general maintenance of your buildings. Sometimes "handymen" advertise in the local papers. Other times you can locate one through a friend. Occasionally one of your renters will enjoy a part-time job maintaining your rentals.

However you locate a handyman, be sure to check his references carefully. You may want to hire him for a few tasks at first and gradually expand his responsibilities as your confidence in his ability increases. If you are lucky enough to locate a good handyman, you will find that even though his salary may seem large to you, he will save you money in service calls. True handymen are a rare breed, so if you have one, treasure him. If you don't, may you be blessed someday by discovering that legendary "Jack-of-all-Trades."

The third alternative is to require tenants to handle the regular maintenance as part of the terms under which they rent the unit. You may also authorize them to take care of the irregular maintenance. Some landlords prefer to authorize a tenant to repair or hire someone to repair anything which goes wrong with his apartment if the repair does not exceed $25. They reason this practice saves them time discussing the repair, doing the work themselves or arranging to have someone else do the work. Although this practice may save some time, we feel it has too many disadvantages to be practical. Some of these disadvantages are:

1. The landlord does not know how much money the tenant will deduct each month from the rent to cover repairs he did during that month.
2. This practice gives tenants the freedom to do work that may not actually need to be done.
3. You need very reliable tenants for this practice to be successful. Many tenants are not able to safely replace a fuse or fix a leaking faucet. You run a risk in authorizing them to attempt the repair.

APARTMENT REPAIR LIST

Date: 3/12/79

Address:	222 Maple Street
Problem:	Replace Bathroom Fluorescent Light
Supplies:	One 12" Fluorescent Bulb (Super Hardware)
Tools:	None
Address:	120½ Elm Street
Problem:	Plugged Drain
Supplies:	None
Tools:	Plumber's Snake / Pipe Wrench
Address:	15 First Ave.
Problem:	Leaking Kitchen Faucet
Supplies:	Assorted Washers (on hand)
Tools:	Crescent wrench / Screwdriver
Address:	
Problem:	
Supplies:	
Tools:	
Address:	
Problem:	
Supplies:	
Tools:	

An apartment repair list helps you keep track of needed repairs.

If you are tempted to try this practice, remember that little bills add up to big accounts. The landlord who does not monitor his business carefully invites trouble.

We have found a combination of these alternatives for general maintenance works best. In duplexes, we require the downstairs tenant to maintain the yard and sidewalks. In a multi-unit, we hire a student to cut the grass and shovel the sidewalks. In duplexes, each of our tenants is responsible for clearing his own driveway. In multi-units, we hire someone with a small snowplow to plow the parking area. We allow the tenants to paint the units when they need painting. We take care of all the irregular maintenance ourselves because we are qualified to do this; however, we have just met the proverbial "Jack-of-all-Trades" and are looking forward to delegating some of our tasks to him.

You should remember general maintenance is part of managing rental units. You cannot ignore the repairs which must be done on your rentals, because tenants move out of poorly managed buildings. Therefore, decide on a plan to provide for the maintenance of your buildings and follow it faithfully.

MANAGING THE UTILITIES

Utilities—heat, electricity and water—are among the highest costs of living today. Ideally, the landlord rents

715 10th Ave.
Cadott, Minnesota
November 20, 1979

Mr. and Mrs. Ralph Anderson
800½ First St.
Cadott, Minnesota

Dear Mr. and Mrs. Anderson:

In the past six months the cost of home heating fuel has risen sharply. The cost of electricity has also risen. We have attempted to reduce our expenditures for heating your apartment. We have installed weather stripping around the doors and windows of your apartment. The fuel bill for your apartment was still 20% higher for this month than it was for the same month last year. We are, therefore, asking that you make a special attempt to conserve energy.

We are recommending the following as ways of conserving energy:

1. Close all doors tightly.
2. Do not leave doors open while you talk to salesmen, paper carriers or your children.
3. Do not allow your children to make frequent and unnecessary trips out of the apartment during the cold weather.
4. Turn off all unnecessary lights.
5. Notify us immediately of dripping faucets.
6. Set your thermostat at the recommended 68 and keep it there.
7. Close the flue when the fire has burned down.

We cannot afford to lose money on your unit because of the high cost of providing you with utilities. We have done all we can to insure maximum efficiency of your apartment. If we find that we are losing money on your apartment, we will raise the rent to cover the additional costs.

We hope that you will cooperate with us in conserving energy.

Sincerely,

Henry Olson

Henry Olson, Landlord

If you pay some or all of the utilities for your rentals, keep the tenants notified of the increasing cost of utilities. Let them know you expect them to conserve.

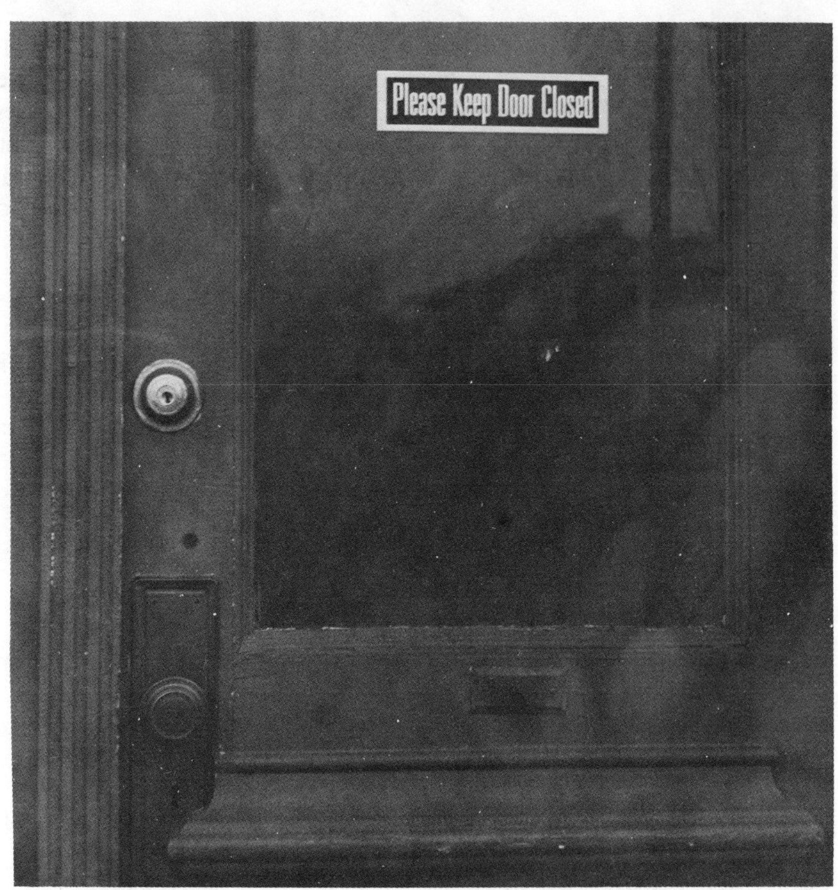

Post signs in your rental which encourage tenants to conserve.

units which have separate utilities because this requires the tenants in each unit to pay for the fuel, water and electricity they use. Many older buildings, however, do not have separate electric and gas meters, nor do they have separate furnaces for each unit. Some landlords who buy older buildings with a single furnace and electric meter have additional furnaces and electrical service run into the building. This is quite expensive, and the landlord usually explores other alternatives.

One alternative is to pay for the utilities and figure the cost into the monthly rent payment. Paying for the utilities has several advantages:

1. When the landlord pays for the utilities and collects the money in the rent payment each month, he knows the building will be adequately heated. When tenants pay for the heat, they may turn the heat down so low when they go away for a weekend that the pipes freeze. We have known tenants to turn the heat off entirely when they were away. Of course there are always the tenants who do not buy fuel or move out without telling the landlord they have left. When the landlord arranges for the heat, he prevents the problems of an unheated building.

2. Many tenants actually prefer renting an apartment with all the utilities provided. This takes the guess work out of their budget. They always know exactly what their housing costs for each month will be. Although the rent seems greater, apartments in which all the utilities are provided actually rent faster in many areas than apartments with separate utilities.

There are also several disadvantages to renting an apartment in which all the utilities are provided.

1. Recently, utility costs have increased rapidly, often and unpredictably. To increase the rent, the landlord must give at least 30 days notice in most states and longer under some conditions. Unless the landlord raises the rent as often as the utility costs increase, the increases come out of his pocket.

2. When tenants do not have to pay directly for the utilities they use, they tend to be wasteful. Although we have enjoyed having tenants in our apartments who were very conservative in their use of electricity, more often we find tenants have little understanding of the price of

715 10th Ave.
Cadott, Minnesota
November 28, 1978

Mr. and Mrs. Ralph Anderson
800½ First St.
Codatt, Minnesota

Dear Mr. and Mrs. Anderson:

Beginning January 1, 1979, your rent for the two bedroom apartment at 800½ First St., Cadott, Minnesota will be raised to $225.00/month. This is an increase of $15.00/month.

The conditions of your rental will remain the same. We will continue to pay the water bill. You are responsible for paying the heat and electricity for your apartment.

The increase in rent reflects increases in the costs of maintaining your rental.

If you have any questions, please contact us. Your first payment of $225.00/month is due on January 1, 1979.

Sincerely,

Henry Olson

Henry Olson, Landlord

Notify your tenants in writing of any raises in rent.

heat and electricity. Another factor to consider when the utilities are figured into the monthly rent is the attitude, "We paid for this, let's use it." If your tenant has this attitude, he may use more energy than he needs.

3. When the landlord pays the utility companies himself, he has more bills to write out each month. This increases his responsibilities as landlord.

A second alternative to the problems of how to handle the utilities in a building is to have the tenants split the costs. Although electricity and water are usually difficult to divide, heat is one utility that can often be successfully divided. Dividing the cost of heating the building is a possibility in a duplex where the units are of equal or near equal size. The cost of heating the building need not be a 50-50 split. It may be a 60-40 split for example, if one apartment is smaller than the other or if one tenant enjoys the sole use of the basement.

The obvious advantage of such an arrangement is the tenants are responsible for the cost of the heat they use.

The disadvantage in requiring the tenants to divide the cost of heating the building is such an arrangement may cause controversy between your tenants. The heat bill is placed in the name of one of the tenants, often the downstairs tenant. Therefore, he must collect the payment from the other tenant. We know landlords who use this technique and are very satisfied with it. You must have very reliable tenants who get along together if this practice is going to work well for you.

If you are responsible for the utilities, watch the costs carefully. When increases in the cost for utilities occur, write to your tenants informing them of the increases. At the beginning of each heating season, send a letter to each tenant urging him to conserve energy in his apartment. If you own a multi-unit, put up signs in strategic places throughout the building which say:

1. Keep this door closed.
2. Turn out the light.
3. Turn faucets off tightly.

We found tenants in a multi-unit feel less responsibility to keep outer doors closed and to turn off entry way lights than they would if they were living in a duplex. We have found signs placed around the building in areas used by all the tenants helps encourage conservation.

Watch the energy bills closely each month. If you notice a sharp increase in a utility bill, call the tenant responsible for the unit in which the increase occurred. If a utility bill rises dramatically, perhaps the tenant has added an air conditioner or basement heater without telling you. Check out any unexplained increases in utility bills. Do not be bashful about reminding tenants to conserve energy. It has been our experience tenants are naive about the actual cost of utilities when they do not actually pay the bills themselves. Use a variety of techniques to continually remind tenants they should conserve energy.

RAISING THE RENTS

Raising rents is an important part of successfully managing rental properties. If you do not raise your rents, you fall behind in net income. But if you raise your rents too frequently, you may price yourself out of the market. Many landlords raise rents haphazardly as they think of it. Other landlords raise rents as a means of getting rid of a troublesome tenant. But the only *good reason* for raising rents is to keep step with inflation and maintenance costs or to reflect improvements you have made to the building.

Factors to consider when raising the rent are:

1. Increases in the cost of utilities if you are responsible for these bills.
2. Current prices of comparable apartments.
3. Increases in maintenance costs, such as lawn care and building repair.

Rents should be raised at regular intervals. If you and your tenant have signed a lease with an escalation clause, the dates on which you can raise the rents and the amount of the increase should be clearly stated. If your agreement with the tenant is oral, you have more leeway in deciding when you will raise the rents. An oral lease does not give you the leeway to raise rents haphazardly, however. Although some landlords will disagree with this, we generally raise the rents every six months. We find January is a good time to raise rents because it is the time when we begin a new bookkeeping schedule for the new year. Although utility increases are unpredictable, January is traditionally a time for increases in various other bills. It may also be a time for a salary increase for your tenant. This may make the burden of increased rent easier for him to tolerate.

We also raise our rents in mid-summer. We do this to protect ourselves against increases in utility prices for the fall heating season. We also raise rents in mid-summer because late-summer is an active renting time for our community. By raising the rents in mid-summer, we assure ourselves of being able to rent any vacant apartments during the late-summer rush. It is wise to determine the peak renting season in your community and raise rents to correspond to that time. If a tenant moves out because he cannot afford the increase in rent, you will have an easier time renting the apartment to someone who can afford to pay the higher rent. We do not raise a tenant's rent until he has lived in the apartment at least six months. We feel the rent agreed upon, even with an oral lease, should hold for at least a six month period.

When you decide to raise a tenant's rent, you should inform him in writing in accordance with your state laws. We find it is best to give the tenant a reason for the rent increase. The reason might be that rising utility costs or your cost of maintaining the building has increased with inflation. It is sometimes difficult for tenants to understand why their housing costs should increase. A brief explanation often makes the rent increase more logical and, therefore, more acceptable.

You may also want to follow your letter with a personal contact. This assures you the tenant has received your notice of the rent increase. If you do not follow up on the written notice, you may find the tenant neglects to pay the increase or does not remember receiving your written notice. Discussing the increase with the tenant also clarifies the amount of the increase and when it is due.

EVICTION

Even though you are an expert at choosing tenants and managing your buildings, you may occasionally have a tenant who does not work out. In that case you have the right to evict the tenant. You also have the responsibility to evict the tenant.

Before you send the tenant an eviction notice, be sure to check your state's laws. Public libraries have copies of the state statutes and a librarian will help you look up what you need. You may also call your city attorney's office and ask for an explanation of the laws governing landlord-tenant relationships. (For more information on the tenant-landlord relationship as it pertains to eviction, see the chapter *Tenants' Rights*.)

In our state, the first step in the eviction process is to send the tenant an eviction notice. The notice must state the reason for the eviction. If appropriate, you may give the tenant an ultimatum for remaining in the apartment, such as to pay his rent or vacate the unit. It must also state the date by which he should be moved from the apartment if he does not comply. Make two copies of the letter. Send one to the tenant and keep one for yourself. You may send the tenant's letter first class or you may decide to send it by registered mail. If you send it by registered mail, request a return receipt. A registered letter is

If a reliable tenant is late with the rent, you may want to send him one warning letter before you send him an eviction notice.

715 10th Ave.
Cadott, Minnesota
January 10, 1979

Mr. and Mrs. Ralph Anderson
800½ First St.
Cadott, Minnesota

Dear Mr. and Mrs. Anderson:

Your rent payment of $225.00 for the month of January is past due. Because of your prompt payment of rent in the past, we assume that there is a good reason for your late payment. We have tried to contact you regarding your late payment, but have been unable to reach you. Please contact us immediately.

We look forward to hearing from you at your earliest convenience.

Sincerely,

Henry Olson

Henry Olson, Landlord

715 10th Ave.
Cadott, Minnesota
January 10, 1979

Mr. and Mrs. Ralph Anderson
800½ First St.
Cadott, Minnesota

Dear Mr. and Mrs. Anderson:

Your rent payment of $225.00 for the month of January is past due. Repeated attempts to contact you by phone and in person have been unsuccessful. Please pay your rent by January 16, 1979 or be moved from 800½ First St.

We look forward to hearing from you before January 16, 1979.

Sincerely,

Henry Olson

Henry Olson, Landlord

A sample eviction notice.

probably worth the additional cost. A return receipt is proof the tenant has received the notice.

Hopefully, the tenant will have moved by the specified date on the eviction notice or will have complied with your requirements for remaining in the apartment. If he does not comply with your requirements and does not leave, you can take additional steps to insure his eviction. You can request your attorney begin eviction proceedings against the tenant.

Direct your attorney to prepare an eviction action and have this paper served by the sheriff. Usually the defendant has 20 days or less to respond to the complaint. If the tenant does not respond to the complaint, the court can grant the landlord a default judgment. This allows the landlord to regain access to the apartment. Sometimes the tenant may not dispute the judgment, but he also may not move from the apartment. The default judgment does not grant the landlord the right to move the tenant. The default judgment only grants the landlord the right to the apartment and the right to delinquent rent and court costs. If the tenant does not dispute the eviction yet does not move from the apartment, the landlord must then ask the court for a writ of restitution. This allows the landlord to have the tenant's belongings moved from the apartment. Usually the landlord must absorb the cost of moving the tenant. This cost is added to the amount the court awards the landlord. If the tenant disputes the complaint, the landlord may have to wait three or four months for the court to decide the case.

Probably the most common reason for evicting a tenant is because of failure to pay rent. We were landlords for almost two years before we encountered a tenant who did not pay the rent. Since then, we have encountered two other tenants who did not pay rent. In these two cases, the tenants moved from the apartments without any problems. The tenant in our first encounter did not move, however. She insisted she would eventually pay the rent. We believed her and continued to grant her extensions when the rent was due. Finally, we doubted she would ever pay the rent and we began steps to evict her. The eviction proceedings went to court.

We were more fortunate than we might have been because she did not contest the decision. If she had refused to move, we would have had to ask the court for a writ of restitution which probably would have cost us additional money in time and moving costs. Or, the tenant could have disputed the complaint and remained in the apartment while the court decided the case. This could have cost us three to four months of lost rent and additional attorney's fees.

We learned some valuable lessons from this incident.

1. Do not be in a hurry to rent to a tenant. (We had not checked this tenant's references.)
2. Be sure you have a security deposit.
3. Do not accept reasons for late rent unless the tenant has a reputation of paying the rent on time and you know the reason for paying late is an unusual occurrence.
4. Do not put off writing an eviction notice to a tenant. Remember your first notice can say the tenant may pay the rent within a specified time period and remain in the apartment. You are not forcing him out in the cold without alternatives.
5. If the notice does not result in payment of rent, start eviction proceedings.

We believe a landlord should do everything he can to avoid having to evict tenants. Even tenants the landlord has screened carefully may be late in rent payments occasionally. The best precaution against having to evict a tenant is to keep reminding him his rent is due. Do not let the tenant's overdue rent payments accumulate.

Although the landlord does have the right and the responsibility to evict tenants, he should use this right wisely. Many things can happen to a reliable tenant which may cause him to miss a rent payment. A death in the family, illness or unexpected expenses may find him short of funds at the end of the month. Although it is tempting to tell a tenant you cannot extend him credit, you should take into account his history of making rent payments. If he is a reliable tenant, you will probably agree to extend him credit for a reasonable length of time. This extension should be formally agreed upon, however, to prevent misunderstandings later. Some tenants may take advantage of the landlord's good nature. You should remember that being a landlord does not require you also be a lender. A later rent payment means the tenant is borrowing money from you free of an interest charge. If you are late with mortgage payments or some maintenance and utility charges, you may have to pay interest on these accounts. The tenant who cannot pay his rent because he spent too much on his vacation or has unexpected car repair bills should be borrowing the money from someone other than the landlord. Landlords provide a housing service and not a banking service. Usually when this is explained to tenants who are delinquent with their rent, the problem is corrected.

CHECKING FOR SAFETY HAZARDS

Another aspect of managing apartments is keeping the buildings safe for tenants. Safety checks are a very important part of the landlord's job.

Begin your safety check with all approaches to the building. See that the sidewalks are reasonably smooth and that stairs and railings are in good condition. In northern states, if you hire someone to shovel the sidewalk in the winter, check periodically to see he actually is shoveling the snow and keeping the sidewalk free from ice. Also check the door frames and thresholds of the buildings to make sure nothing has pulled loose or is protruding. Loose carpet bars or splintered wood may cause tenants to trip.

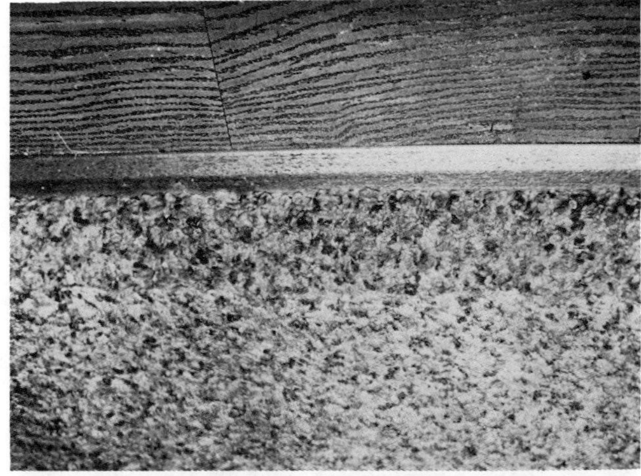

Make sure carpeting is firmly held in place. Tenants may trip on loose capeting.

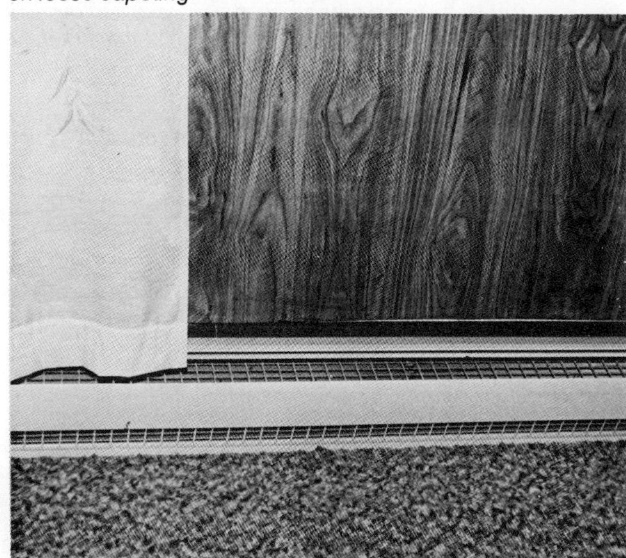

Check the apartments for fire hazards. Here a tenant has curtains hanging too close to an electrical heater.

Keep the outside steps to basement stairs covered. This prevents ice from building up on the stairs. Be concerned about basement safety even if tenants do not regularly use the basement.

Periodically check the fire extinguishers in your rentals.

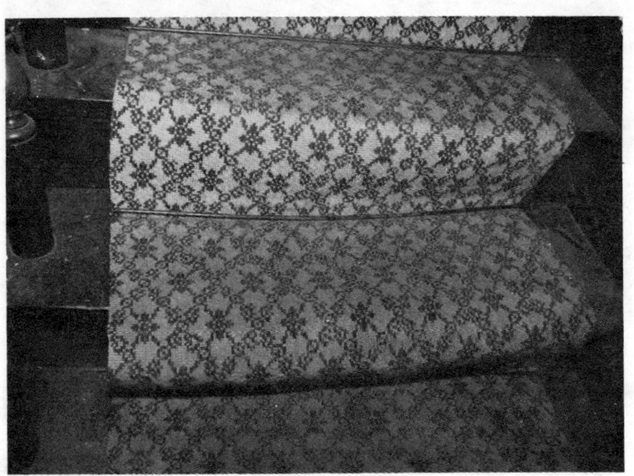

Check for loose carpeting on stairways and repair it immediately.

Loose electrical outlets pose a safety hazard.

Be sure all fire escapes are firmly attached to the building and all doors leading to fire escapes open easily.

After you have checked the sidewalks and entry ways, check the basement. Keep a sharp eye open for any flammable materials near the furnace or the fuse box. The furnace should be checked by a professional heating expert before the heating season begins to insure all jets and nozzles are unclogged. The chimney also should be periodically checked to be sure it has not cracked or become coated with soot. Remember that even in buildings where tenants do not have basement access, servicemen may enter the basement to read meters and make emergency repairs. Regard basement stairs and doorways in the same manner as the stairs and doorways tenants use daily. Also, look for light bulbs that may be near flammable objects or wiring that may have pulled loose or shifted positions. These situations are potential fire hazards.

Inside the building, check the fire extinguishers. Notice the expiration date on the tag. When the expiration date approaches, call an expert to check the fire extinguisher. You will find these experts listed under "Fire Extinguishers" in the yellow pages of the telephone book.

Even though the city code may not require you to install a fire extinguisher, you may decide to do so (especially in a building with three or more units). You may also decide to install a smoke alarm.

Next check the inside stairways. Look for proper lighting on all stairways. If bulbs have burned out, replace them. Be especially alert for loose carpeting on the stairs and repair it immediately.

Inside each apartment, look for raised carpet around carpet bars. Check the floor in every doorway for possible hazards, such as raised tiles or loose door jambs. As you check each room, notice any electrical outlets which may have pulled loose from the wall. Cords to electrical appliances should also be checked. Notice how many appliances the tenant has plugged into one outlet. Request the tenant to correct anything you consider hazardous to the safety of others in the building. At the least, overloaded circuits will cause a fuse to blow.

In the kitchen, check where the stove is located. Tenants may move appliances around to suit their needs. They may not know you have positioned the stove against a non-flammable wall. Curtains hanging close to the stove may be a fire hazard. On gas stoves, check the pilot light and the control knobs for the burners to make sure they shut off all gas flow.

Check all fire escapes from the building. The door to the fire escape should open easily and the fire escape itself should be fastened securely to the outside of the building.

Attics, even when they are not used by the tenants, should be included in the safety check. Look for wiring that may have been chewed by rodents. This is a fire hazard. Also, look for sagging or broken beams and joists

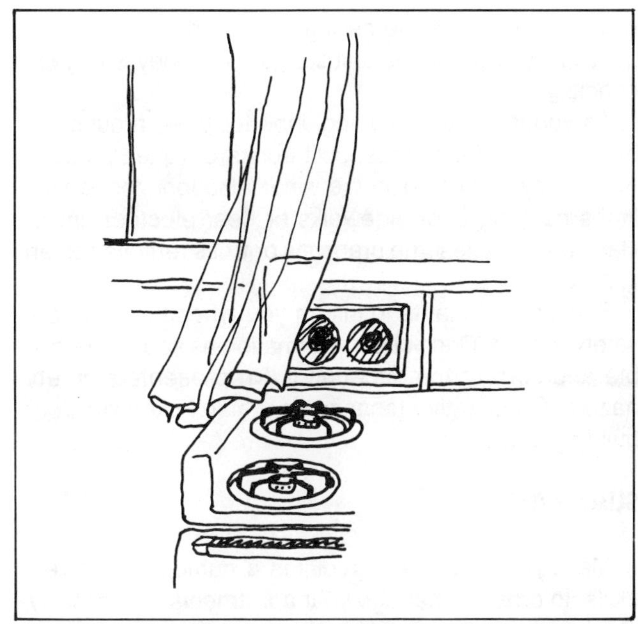

Curtains hanging close to a stove may be a fire hazard.

Bare wires are a fire hazard. This light shorts out when jolted and is a safety hazard to anyone coming into contact with it.

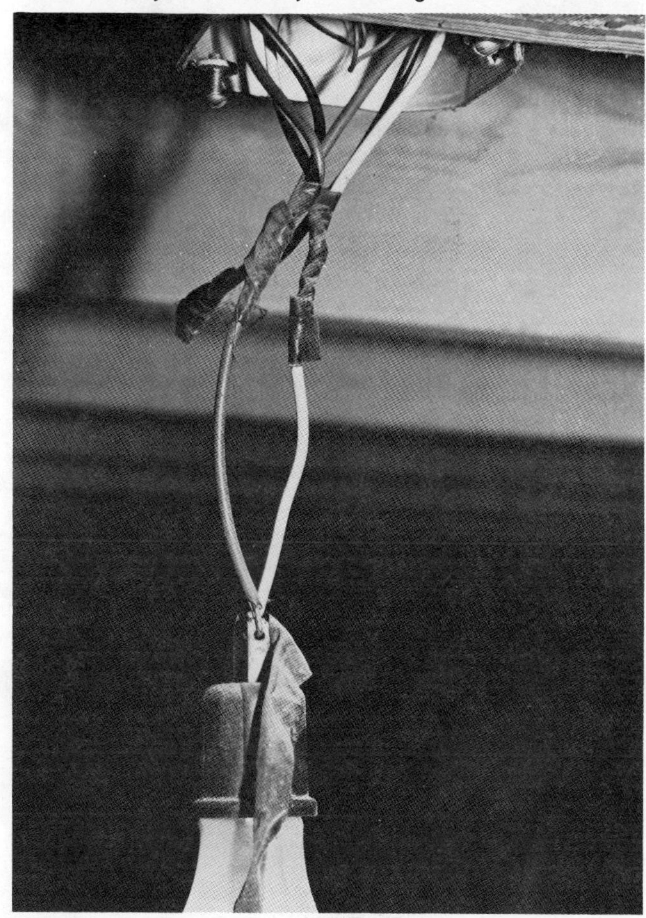

which could cause the ceilings to collapse. An attic inspection is a good time to insure the chimney is in good condition.

As you leave the building, look for trees around the building with dead limbs, split trunks or rotted portions which may blow over in the wind. Also look for healthy limbs hanging over sidewalks or near electrical lines. Have any troublesome branches or trees removed by an expert.

Encourage tenants to inform you when they notice a safety hazard. Check their information as soon as possible and correct the situation if it represents a safety hazard. Cooperative tenants are a help in keeping your building safe.

SUMMARY

Managing apartments requires a number of different skills. In order to manage your apartments successfully, you must know how to keep careful books. Accurate bookkeeping is important so you know how your investments are paying and can make an accounting to the IRS. A landlord also needs to be skilled in public relations to prevent disputes between himself and his tenants and to settle disputes among the tenants in his buildings. Knowing when and how much to raise rents is another important part of the landlording business. The successful landlord is especially aware of increases in utility and maintenance costs as he evaluates his rents periodically. Evicting tenants is often an unpleasant task, but it is a responsibility the landlord must accept. A successful landlord knows his rights and his tenants' rights. When he finds it necessary to evict a tenant, he follows the legal procedure for eviction.

Another aspect of apartment management is safety. The wise landlord checks his buildings periodically to be sure they are safe. He knows the city code and makes sure his buildings conform to the code. He checks his buildings for fire hazards and other factors which might endanger the tenants. He establishes a good rapport with the tenants so they inform him of any problems with the building or with other tenants.

SAFETY CHECK LIST

OUTSIDE OF BUILDING

___Dead or rotting tree limbs
___Branches overhanging sidewalks
___Branches too close to power lines
___Cracked sidewalks
___Snow or ice on sidewalks
___Loose or broken railing
___Projections or loose carpeting in doorways
___Stairs needing repairs

BASEMENT

___Flammable items near furnace
___Furnace jets and nozzles
___Chimney
___Stairs and entryways

INSIDE BUILDING

___Flammable items near stoves
___Loose carpet or tiles
___Outlets pulled loose
___Overloaded circuits
___Proper lighting for stairways
___Inside stairways
___Faulty gas valves on gas ranges
___Cracked windows
___Fire extinguishers
___Fire escapes
___Frayed wiring

5
Maintenance and Repair

EXTERIOR MAINTENANCE

The exterior appearance of a rental property is an important part of any landlord's success. A prospective tenant may arrive early for an appointment to see an apartment. He may decide, just by looking at a poorly maintained building, the unit is not worth further consideration. Any building is a reflection on the owner, so proper maintenance is a good means of making the best impression. Prospective buyers are frequently encouraged to see the inside of a building if the exterior indicates little work will be needed. The following section will cover the techniques for keeping the exterior of any building in good condition.

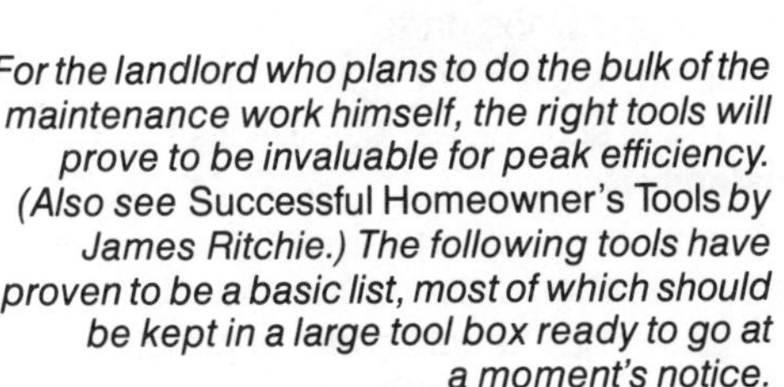

For the landlord who plans to do the bulk of the maintenance work himself, the right tools will prove to be invaluable for peak efficiency. (Also see Successful Homeowner's Tools *by James Ritchie.) The following tools have proven to be a basic list, most of which should be kept in a large tool box ready to go at a moment's notice.*

Tool	Purpose
Square	cutting gypsum board, paneling, etc.
Propane torch	removing old paint and putty, soldering, etc.
Plumber's snake	removing obstructions in pipes
Basin force-cup (plunger)	opening clogged drains
Toilet force-cup (plunger)	freeing clogged toilets
Power circle-saw	cutting paneling and plywood
Flashlight	for dark places
Caulking gun	applies caulk and glue for paneling
Safety goggles	always worn for cement work, paint scraping, etc.

(continued)

Tool	Purpose
Soldering iron	useful in some repairs, electrical and plumbing
Tin snips	cutting sheet metal, linoleum, etc.
Hammer	uses too numerous to mention
Coping Saw	cutting irregular contours or holes
Pressure oiler	oiling furnace motors, blowers, etc.
Block plane	shaping wood, freeing stuck doors, etc.
Hack saw	cutting bolts or any metals
Round surform	finish shaping holes in wood
Flat surform	finish shaping on many wood surfaces
Wrecking bar	use on anything stubborn (not on tenants!)
Trowel	finishing cement work
Paint scraper	removing loose paint
Drywall knife	applying layers of drywall mud, repairing plaster
Level	checking alignments in remodeling
Razor knife	trimming carpet, linoleum, many uses
Vis-grip pliers	holds anything tightly
Scissors	cutting wallpaper, insulation, etc.
Assortments of bolts, nuts, and screws	replacements, if needed
Hand saw	cutting studs and boards in remodeling
Hand drill (with bits)	drilling holes for locks, etc.
Star drill	cuts holes in cement for new bolts
Cold chisel	cuts cement or brick
Wood chisels	one old for scraping, one new for removing wood
Set of allen wrenches	fittings on blowers, motors, locks, etc.
Small steel ruler	gives very accurate measurements on small parts
Old knife	kept sharp for cutting and trimming
Adjustable pliers	many uses
Side-cutter pliers	cutting wire and small bolts
Assorted files	shaping metal and wood parts
Extension cord	power for electric tools or for light
Phillips screwdriver	needed for many screws, especially locks
Regular screwdriver	used constantly
Short-handled screwdriver	for tight places
Center punch	struck with a hammer, makes cone for drill
Nail set	neatly depresses nail heads in trim or paneling
Compass	outlines pattern for irregular fitting
Whetstone	keeps tools and knives sharp
Crescent wrench	for regular nuts and bolts, some plumbing
Large pipe wrench	for drainpipes, water traps, etc.
Small pipe wrench	for smaller plumbing fixtures
Tape measure	measuring windows for new glass, paneling, etc.
Trouble light	examining chimneys, light for dark areas
Wallpaper brush	applying wallpaper paste
Gloves	hand protection for rough work
C-clamps	holding boards or parts when working on them
Circuit tester	fastest way to determine safely if current is on
Brace (with bits)	for drilling very deep or very large holes

Essential items
Stepladder
Extension ladder
Painting equipment (rollers, trays, brushes, etc.)
Cleaning equipment including a vacuum cleaner, mops, pails, etc.
Putty knife
Several additional pieces of equipment that are desirable but not absolutely essential are:
Electric drill
Cutter heads for electric drill
Heavy hammer
Moto-tool for fast inletting for locks
Pick-up truck for heavy hauling
Giant pipe wrench for really stubborn fixtures

In addition to the regular tools listed, the landlord will find a need for "soft" tools, or materials which may be used up when working with them.

Item	Purpose
Large plastic bags	cleaning up garbage left by tenants
Salt	for icy steps and sidewalks
Tapes	(from bottom) ducting tape, pipe insulating tape, masking tape, and vinyl weatherstrip tape
Drywall mud	repairing cracked plaster, filling holes
Caulking compound	sealing windows, cracked wood
Weatherstripping	one of many forms to prevent heat loss
WD-40	stops squeaks and lubricates metals

(continued)

Item	Purpose
Solder	for plumbing and electrical repairs
Flux	helps solder flow
Pliobond glue	flexible fast bond for many things
Elmer's glue	small repairs on loose wallpaper, etc.
Odor killer	the last resort for pet odors
Belt dressing	increases friction on blower belts
Assorted washers	(in 35 mm film cans) replaces faucet washers
Pipe joint compound	seals joints in pipes when reassembling them
Glazier's points	hold window glass in place
Wire	several diameters for various uses
Silicone sealer	seals around sinks and tubs
Fast-drying epoxy	strong rapid repairs
Locking compound	keeps nuts and bolts permanently tight
Graphite lubricant	keeps locks working
Spare fuses	be sure to have spares for every type
Replacement plugs	for small appliance cords

Foundations

Normally, foundations should need little or no attention. Occasionally, however, cracks may appear due to settling of the building. Cracks at least ⅛ inch wide should be repaired. The standard repair material is sandmix cement. This material comes pre-mixed in bags of several sizes. Add as little water as needed to make the mixture barely moist and pound as much as possible into the crack. Watch to see the repair stays tight over the next several months. If cracks open repeatedly, footing problems are indicated. A contractor would be required to correct the problem.

With stone or block foundations, small portions that have fallen out can be repaired by using mortar mix. This material also comes pre-mixed—just add water to make a moist, buttery consistency. Apply a liberal coat of mortar to the broken places and mortar the stones or blocks back into place. Every few years or after extensive repairs, the above-ground portion of the foundation should be painted with a dark-colored oil base or epoxy paint. Patched or flaking foundations are unsightly and may discourage both prospective tenants and buyers. (Also see *Successful Practical and Decorative Concrete* by Robert Wilde.)

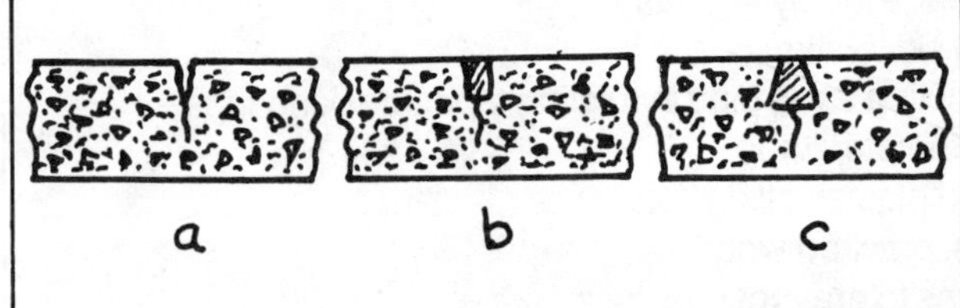

Repairing a wide crack (a), about 1/16 inch or wider. There are two good ways to cut out the crack for patching: (b) a vertical cut for the edges or (c) an undercut.

Sidewalks

Sidewalks and other cement-covered areas often need attention. Kept in good condition, these provide a solid-feeling and "comfortable" appearance. Neglected for too long, they are an all-too-obvious sign the property is not being maintained. Cement work is expensive to have done by a contractor, but most repairs are well within anyone's ability. Probably the worst repairs are on sections of sidewalks that have been buckled or twisted by frost or tree roots. Twisted sections must be removed and the cause of the trouble eliminated before any repairs can be made.

Cement may seem to be very hard, but it does crack easily when it is struck. To remove cement, you will need something to provide heavy blows. You can rent an air hammer or you can purchase or rent a large hammer called a maul or sledge. If you have a good swinging arm, the hammer works fine for normal sidewalks. For large poured concrete slabs though, you may need the air hammer. Cement particles will fly forcefully with either, so wear head-to-toe protection including goggles or, preferably, complete face protection. Cut or break the cement in small portions so you can lift and haul it away.

After the concrete has been removed, you can deal with the trouble. If the problem was tree roots, remove them. If possible, remove the tree so the same thing won't happen again. Do not deal with large trees or limbs unless you are very experienced. Nothing is potentially more dangerous than an improperly felled tree or large limb.

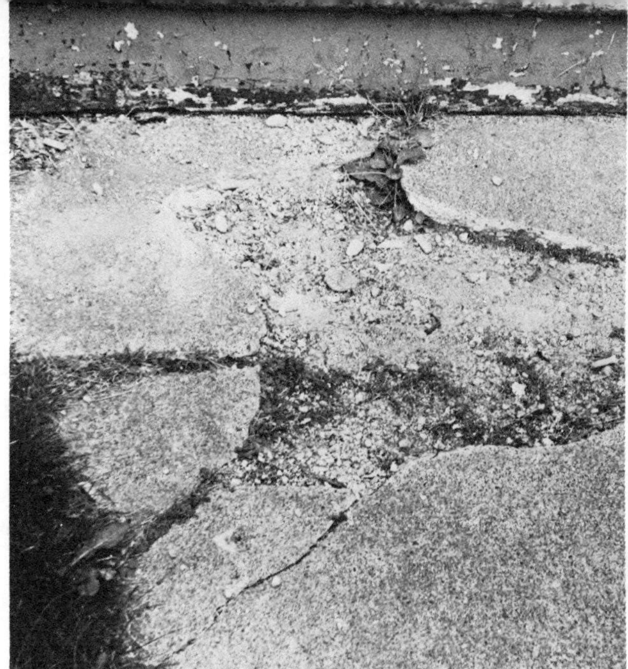

Deteriorated sidewalks are a safety hazard. They also give even a well-kept building a rundown look.

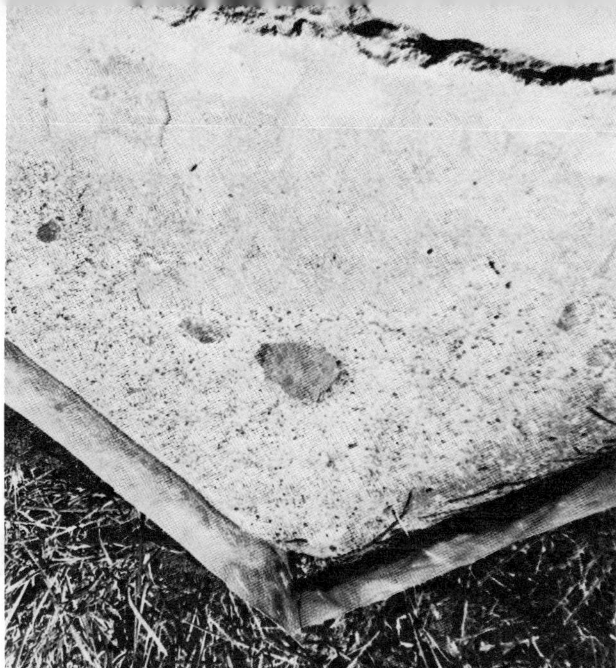

Put wood or metal around the area receiving new cement.

Another common cause of buckled concrete is frost. One way to deal with this problem is to dig below the level of the sidewalk and put a six inch bed of gravel under the new cement work. This will prevent water from rising up through the area and will help provide a solid footing.

After the section has been removed and the problem corrected, the earth should be leveled and tamped to the same depth as the original cement. Make a supporting frame of 1 inch boards along the sides of the area. Hold them in place with wooden stakes driven along the sides. Mix enough gravel cement mix to fill the area and smooth the surface with a trowel. As a final step tamp the surface, spade around the edges and level the surface with a straightedge.

For small areas and cracks, you will find it necessary to enlarge the crack or cut a ledge or shoulder on broken-out portions. Cement only gains strength in thick layers; any thin edges will quickly chip out. Use a cold chisel and hammer to deepen edges or widen cracks so the new cement will have a firmer gripping surface and better thickness on the edges. Remember to wear eye protection and gloves whenever you are cutting cement. Small areas should be filled with sand-mix cement. For even more permanent repairs, you can experiment with epoxy fillers available at any hardware store. These are two-part compounds mixed together to form a very strong bond. The completed work can be lightly sanded and painted if you want a really good appearance. (Also see *Successful Practical and Decorative Concrete*.)

Steps

Porch or other front steps are often a problem. Cement steps can usually be repaired using some of the techniques mentioned under "*Sidewalks*." Wooden steps are seldom as easy to repair if serious rot has occurred. If only the top boards are damaged, cut new boards and nail them into place with sturdy spikes. The understructure is a more serious problem. If the upper surfaces of the step supports are rotted away, a proper repair can be made by nailing 1 inch boards to the sides of the understructure so they form a "sandwich" around the rotted portion. If this proves inadequate, check on pre-cast steps from any concrete company. These are longer-lasting than the wooden types. Contractors will build new wooden steps if you want to replace them. Building them yourself takes a surprising amount of work as well as some experience. Steps are very important to maintain to keep you from possible lawsuits. Regardless of the techniques and choices you apply, be sure to keep all steps in first class condition.

Porches

Whenever prospective buyers look at a building they are normally discouraged from buying if there are sag-

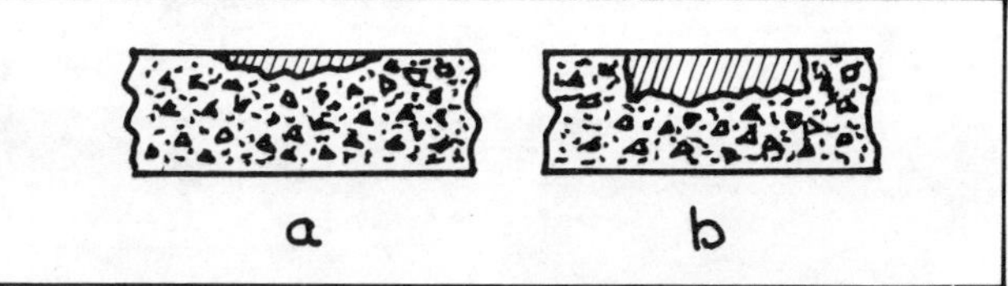

Right and wrong method for patching a small shallow hole in a concrete wall or slab. (a) Wrong—This patch is too shallow. The featheredge will soon chip out, and this patch will not hold. (b) Right—The edges should be vertical. The patch is deep enough for a good body of mortar to be placed; this patch will stay.

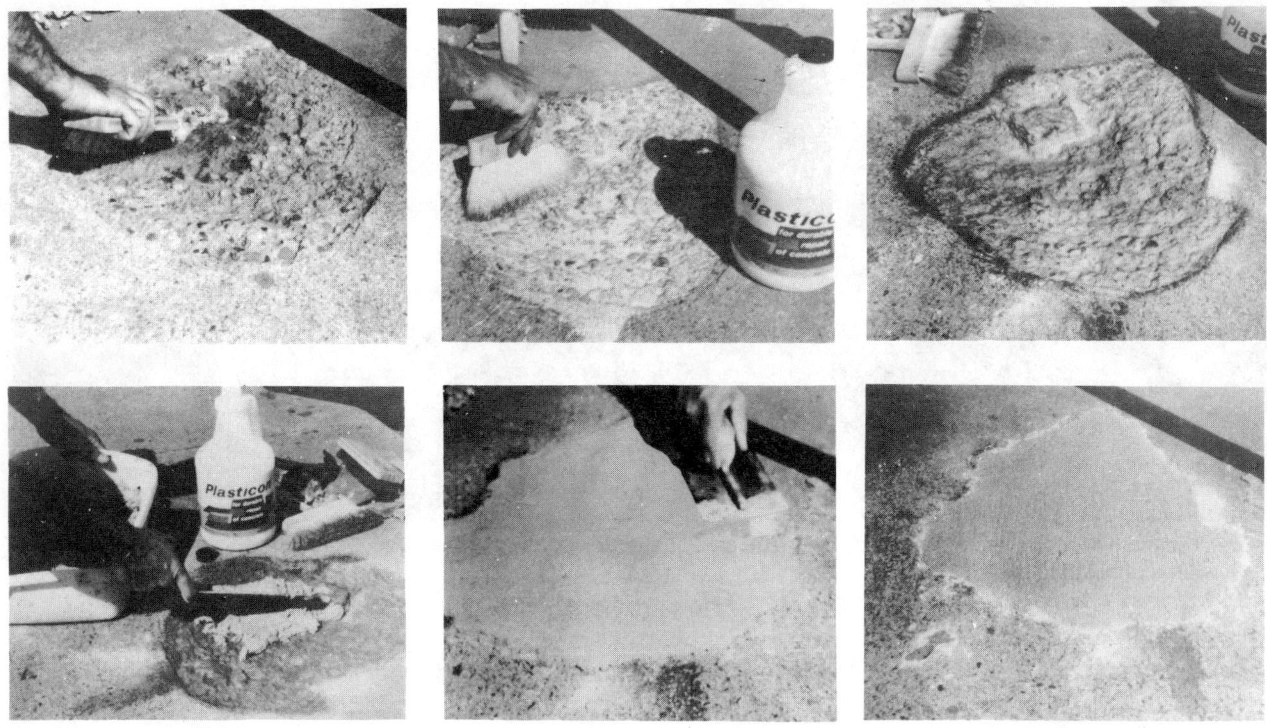

The steps in repairing a damaged concrete slab. Top row (left to right): Preparing the surface by cleaning out all loose debris. Priming the surface. Next, a grout coating is placed. The grout of portland cement and water should have the consistency of thick paint. Bottom row (left to right): Placing and spreading mortar should follow immediately. Finishing the patch with a trowel. Repair completed. (Reproduced from Concrete Repair, Concrete Construction Publications Inc.)

Cement is leveled and smoothed with a trowel.

A sagging or broken porch can often be ➤ restored with very little work.

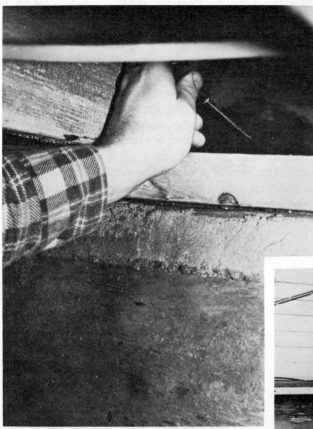

◄ Probe all areas where rot is suspected before buying any building. Darkened areas are a good indication of rot.

▲ A house jack has more than enough power to raise sagging porches.

Replace rotted support members with new ones nailed to sound wood.

ging porches and overhangs. For that reason, an ambitious buyer can often make exceptional purchases on a building with sagging porches and tumbled-down front columns and supports. Porches and overhangs usually turn out to be far easier to repair than you would expect. They also require much less time to correct than less conspicuous defects, such as inadequate electrical wiring or poorly-designed room arrangements.

One reason sagging porches are so easily corrected is because they almost never have any structural support members in common with the rest of the building. They can be jacked up, lowered or re-built without worries about breaking structural supports or cracking interior walls. You must be careful of rotted sections if large portions have separated and been exposed to weather for long periods of time. Check for extensive rot by probing likely areas with a small knife blade or screwdriver.

Repairs on porches require several small to medium sized house jacks. You will probably find them at any rental store, but if you plan to repair a number of sagging porches, you might look for some used ones to purchase. Jack up the lowest part of the porch first, applying the jacks to whatever is most solid underneath. If nothing appears to be solid, use a length of sturdy timber (at least 4 inches by 4 inches) to serve as a support. When you have the lower portion of the structure raised to the correct height, double check it with a level and then re-build the support columns. These are usually brick, block or stone with mortar between. Use mortar mix to re-assemble them, adding just enough water to make the mixture spreadable. You may have to add some support timbers under the porch so it will be properly supported when it is lowered onto the dried columns. Replace any broken or rotted boards on the porch floor. You then have a solid structure and a base for any further work.

If overhangs must be raised, the same jacks can be used with sections of timber to make up the difference in height. Raise the overhang slowly so it will have time to adjust to the new position. The long columns supporting overhangs often appear to be heavy pillars but are normally hollow and very light in weight. Remove these and build up the porch floor under the columns to the correct height. Use short pieces of 1 inch and 2 inch thick board in the required width to match the diameter of the columns.

Cut off rotted porch boards in the middle of a joist.

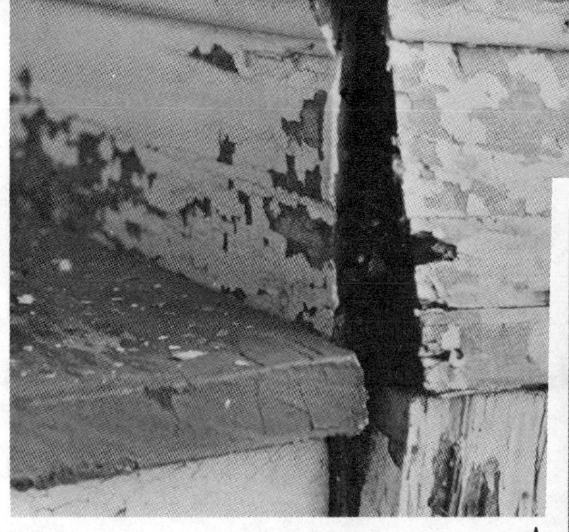

Gaps like this can cause rapid rot.

Where strength is not critical, fit in a piece of board to fill gaps.

Use caulking compound to seal all spaces. When it has dried, sand the outer surface and repaint.

Finish the height by adding thinner boards or pieces of exterior plywood until the columns fit tightly between the overhang and the porch floor. Nail the boards and columns into place with long nails, then lower the overhang onto them by removing the jacks. Fill any splits in the columns with small wood strips or caulk to keep water out, then re-paint the entire porch structure. When you have finished, you will probably find the entire project took less than one day at a cost of about $40. Since you may have saved $3-5,000 on the price of the building less ambitious buyers rejected, consider that your day's pay. You will rarely find such an opportunity in other kinds of investments.

Railings

One source of annoyance is the metal step and sidewalk railings installed on so many older properties. Eventually the bolts embedded in the concrete rust through and break off leaving no easy way to re-fasten the railing. Since many insurance policies require railings on all steps, and the safety of tenants is greatly increased by their presence, you should make every effort to re-install them as soon as possible. It will be necessary to re-embed bolts in the cement. Use a hammer and cold chisel to cut a hole in the concrete base about 6 inches in diameter and about 4-5 inches deep. Embed new bolts in

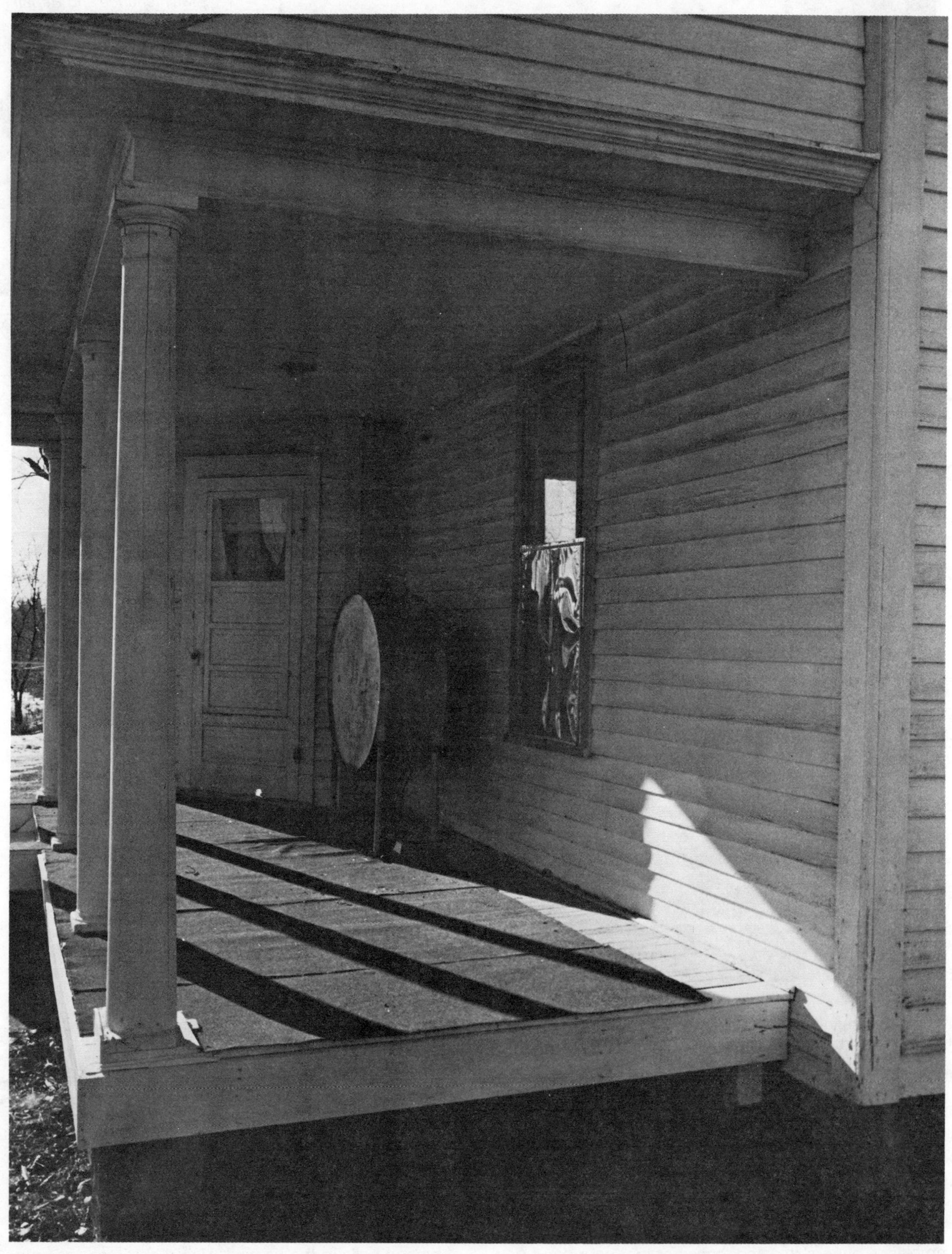

Porch leveled and strongly braced once more.

the holes, using sand mix cement tightly packed in. See that the bolts line up properly with the holes in the bottom of the railing. With the cement fully hardened, tighten nuts down onto the bolts to hold the railing firmly in place. You should then have firm support railings that will last a long time.

Another technique you can try is using the expansion-based bolts available at hardware stores. Use a star drill of the same size as the bolt and cut a hole in the step where the new anchor should be. When the hole is deep enough to seat the expansion-base bolt, insert it and put the railing in position. Then tighten a nut onto the bolt. This is a good technique unless you encounter a piece of rock while drilling. Rocks are almost impossible to cut through, so you will have to try a new location for the hole and patch the old one.

An unsightly porch detracts from the appearance and discourages renters.

Windows

Perhaps the most basic requirement for being a successful landlord is the ability to replace broken windows quickly and easily. Although tenants are supposedly responsible for broken windows, that rarely works out as easily as you might expect. Tenants are reluctant to pay for windows that become broken "accidentally." If you have had the tenant sign a statement all glass was in unbroken condition upon renting, you are more likely to be repaid. Commercial firms charge high prices to replace windows and often take several days or a week to get to a particular window. If the weather is cold and you are paying for heat, this could be a real loss.

Indoor-outdoor carpeting covers worn steps.

Fortunately, windows are very easy to replace. Wearing gloves and eye protection, use a ¾ inch or 1 inch chisel to remove the old putty. If the putty is very old it may be hard and make removal difficult. A propane torch played along the old putty will soften it so it crumbles easily. The old glass is held by tiny metal triangles that are easy to remove with side pressure from a screwdriver. With the old glass removed, clean out the small cut-out, called a rabbet, where the glass rested. Measure the exact distance both vertically and horizontally from the outside edge of the rabbet, and get a new pane cut at a hardware store. Specify the size $^1/_{16}$ inch undersize so you can be sure it will go in. Press it firmly into the rabbet.

With the glass in place, put in new glazier's points, as the tiny metal triangles or spears are called. The spear style is easier to insert, requiring only a slight hand pressure from a screwdriver. The triangular type usually comes with an installation tool that can be tapped lightly

Steps covered—the difference is obvious.

with a hammer to set the point. Two on each side of the pane should be enough except for very large panes. Apply a layer of elastic glazing compound over the points. If the weather is fairly cool, the easiest technique is to take a ball of glazing compound in your hands and roll it out into a string about ¼ inch in diameter and long enough to extend along one side of the glass. Lay the roll in the space over the glazier's points and press it in with a putty knife. Use a firm pressure along the roll to smooth the glaze. Do all four sides uniformly and wait a day or so before you re-paint the glazed areas.

For aluminum windows, you will find some can be replaced and others that will need professional attention. If you do the repair, it is important to put a few beads of glazing into the space where the glass will rest. The glaze acts as a shock absorber to prevent the metal-to-glass fit from breaking the pane. If windows are replaced in any part of a door, follow the same procedure even if the door is wood, since the shock to the glass will be greatly increased in a door.

◄ *Cutting a hole in concrete with a star drill and hammer. Keep all porch railings tight.*

Typical broken window in basement. Have it replaced as soon as you can.

Propane torch softens old putty for easier removal.

Screens

Screens are another concern for the landlord. If the buildings you own have all self-storing screen and storm combination windows, you are indeed fortunate. Few older buildings will have these, however. When storm windows must be removed in the spring, it is far easier to deal with half-screens than the window-sized screens that usually accompany older buildings. Nothing is more aggravating than to reach the top of a 20 foot ladder only to find the screen in your hand is for some other window. If you choose to use full size screens, it is a good idea to paint a number on the frame of each one. This would correspond to a rough sketch showing the windows of each apartment building.

Instead of causing yourself unnecessary problems, remove the storm windows in the spring and give the tenants half-screens to put in whenever they like. These are very inexpensive and most hardware stores carry them. Since they are installed from inside, no ladders are needed. If you are very handy, you can design and build your own from wood strips and a roll of screen for a fraction of the store price. Home-built or purchased, you will find these much easier to use than the older, full-sized screens. Even with self-storing screens, however, you must remember to check at the start of the heating season to be sure the tenants have closed all the windows. Tenants will remain totally unconcerned about such things unless they are paying for the heat, and even then, many will ignore the storm windows. Check them yourself to be sure.

Exterior Siding

Buildings with traditional wood siding require painting periodically, both for protection from weather and for a good appearance. Everything possible should be done to keep the outside appearance pleasing for prospective tenants and buyers, should you choose to sell. You can expect to repaint every six or seven years at best, and more frequently if you use poor quality paints in an attempt to save a few dollars. Money saved on paint is rarely a savings, especially if you are forced to repaint sooner than necessary.

Even the best paints will adhere poorly if the undersurface is improperly prepared. Mildewed areas will cause rapid peeling or discoloration unless the mildew is prop-

Beads of glazing compound at corners and sides prevent shock to glass in doors.

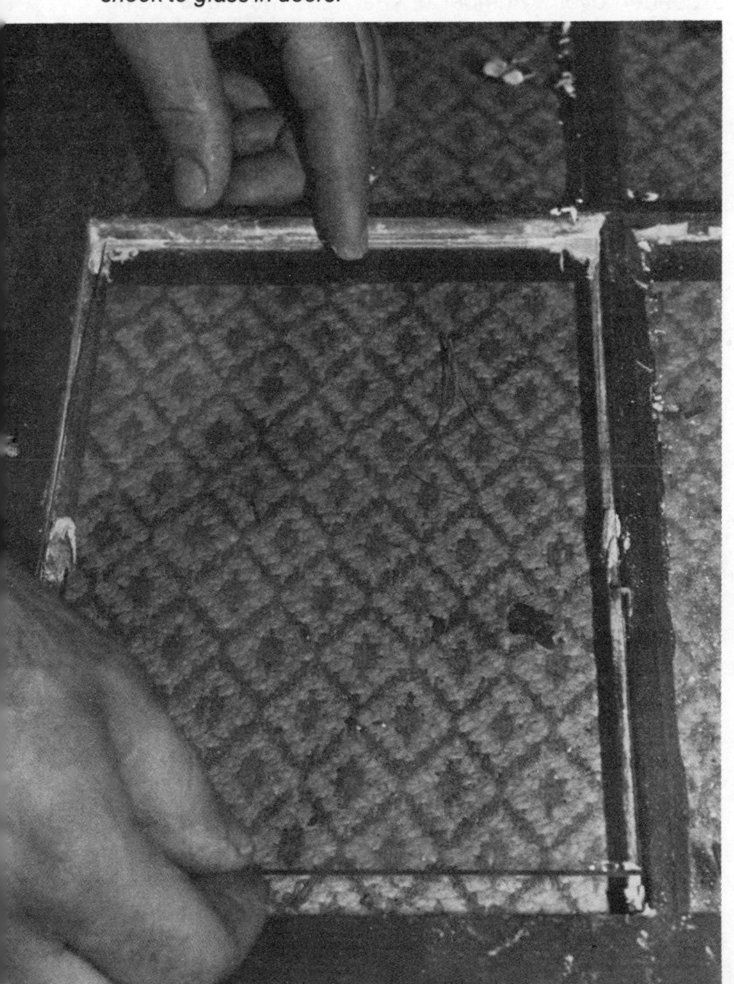

Glazier's points hold glass firmly in place.

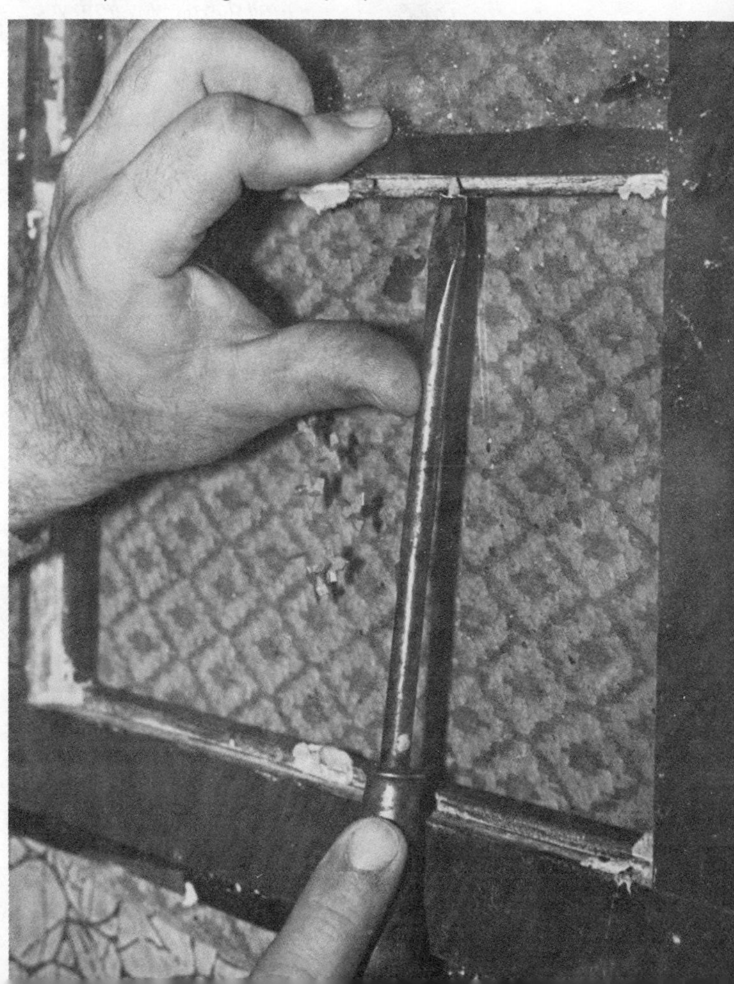

Push the glazing points in straight, with even pressure, and don't push too hard against the glass.

After a bit of practice you'll find the excess putty just seems to roll down away from you.

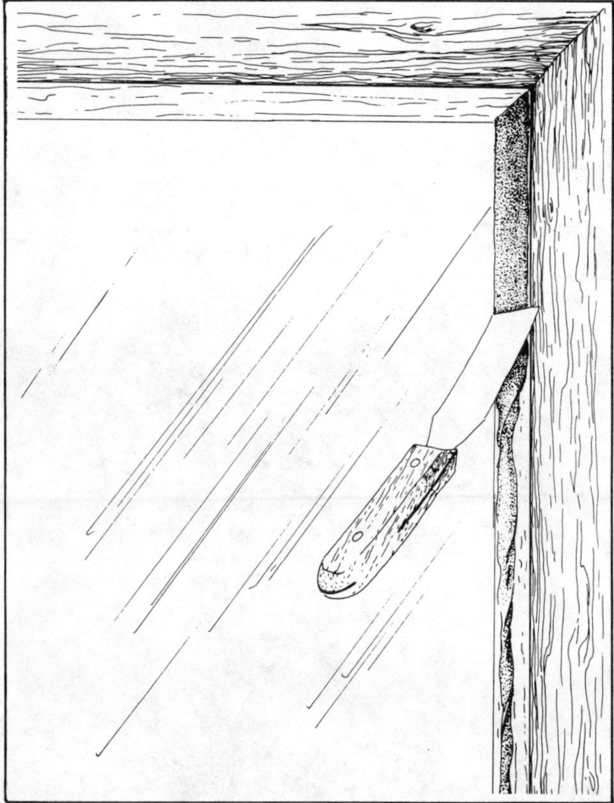

erly treated. Check at a good paint store to find a chemical that will cure the problem. You will also find various formulas for making your own in some of the specialized home repair books. Formulas usually include bleach, trisodium phosphate and water in different proportions.

All peeled or blistered paint must be scraped off and the bare spots given a coat of primer before repainting. Painting over dirt or grease is also a waste of time since the paint will promptly peel. Wash dirty surfaces with one of the special cleaning agents recommended by a paint dealer. It must be a compound that will not interfere with the adhesion of the new paint coat.

In order to reach the upper siding you will have a choice of using a ladder or scaffolding. The scaffolding, available from rental outlets, may be a far safer and wiser choice than the ladder, especially for large buildings. The time spent erecting the scaffolding will end up about equal to the time spent moving the ladder. Whichever you choose, be very sure everything is solid before you head skyward.

When siding reaches a certain stage of disrepair with many warped or rotted boards that obviously need replacing, consider applying metal siding rather than making repairs or repainting. Metal siding is expensive but it is not as difficult to install as you might expect. By doing it yourself you can save at least half the cost of installation and the run-down appearance will be banished for good. Compare the price of metal siding with the paint and time expended over a number of years and the metal siding may begin to look like a good deal. Add on the increased resale value of a building with metal siding and it may look even better. (See *Successful Roofing & Siding* by Robert Reschke for more information.)

Siding and interior walls will be damaged by water. Here, a rotted drip-cap over a window will admit water to the siding.

Roofs

Roofs receive more exposure to weather than any other part of a building. Shingles dry out and crack, metal valleys rust through and flashings around chimneys pull loose. These must all be repaired to prevent costly damage to interior walls and ceilings.

Some people have a fear of heights. If you are in this group, hire someone to inspect and report to you on the condition of the roof. You can keep roofs from leaking much longer than the figures usually quoted as the life of a roof. Where valleys have rusted through, you can often make a waterproof repair with several layers of metal-backed tape available at hardware stores. Sold in several widths, usually up to 3 inches, these tapes have excellent adhesion to any dry metal surface. Make sure all the loose dirt and rust have been removed. Worn or cracked shingles can be repaired with asphalt or plastic roofing tars. Choose a warm day to apply these so the tar makes a good bond with the roof. There is no need to be fancy when applying tar—just spread it on with a flat stick. You should check all repaired areas each year to be sure the repair is still watertight.

When metal chimney flashings have pulled loose or rusted so badly they can no longer be repaired, have a professional replace them. Installing chimney flashings to achieve a watertight fit is a tricky job. The same goes for re-shingling. Unless you are very ambitious or have had some previous roofing experience, you will probably find it wiser to hire a contractor to re-shingle the entire roof. He can then install new valleys and chimney flashings at the same time.

New board fitted to replace rotted drip-cap will keep water out.

Sooner or later all paint will peel. Appearance is important.

Use a scraper to remove all loose paint. Go over bare spots with a coat of primer.

Repainted area has better appearance and is weather resistant.

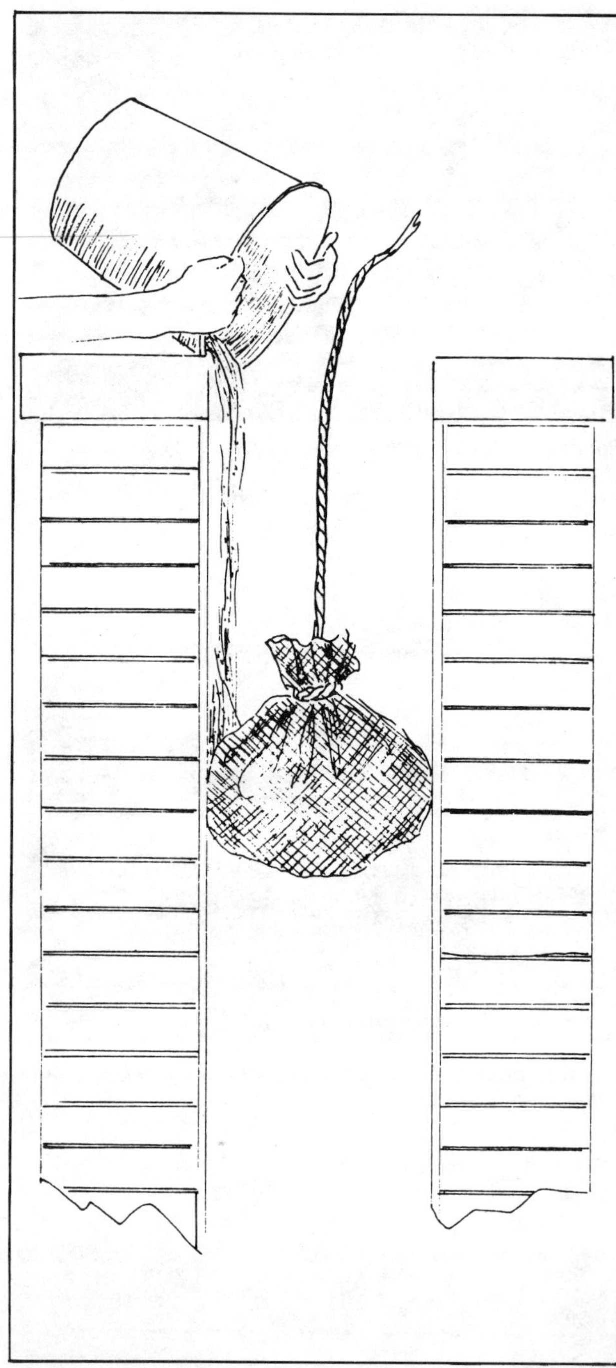

This operation should be carried out with careful eye to conditions in the fireplace below. If too much grout is passing the plug, it may pile up on the smoke shelf, drain into the fireplace and deface it, or, in hardening, may impair the working of the damper. (It is recommended that a professional be consulted before executing this job.)

For garages or small storage sheds in need of a new roof, an alternative well worth considering is a metal or fiberglass roof. Most of the popular catalog companies offer aluminum and fiberglass panels in 8 to 12-foot lengths and 2 to 4-foot widths. If the wood base on the roof is still sound enough to hold nails, these panels are extremely easy to install. They will provide a waterproof roof at a far lower cost than shingles installed by a contractor. The panels come in a choice of colors and textures so the finished roof is reasonably attractive. Follow the manufacturer's directions and avoid windy days when installing it. (See also *Successful Roofing & Siding*.)

Eaves Troughs

Like roofs, eaves troughs should be kept in good condition to allow water to drain off the building without causing damage. If the yard has many tall trees, you may find it worthwhile to install wire screen covers specially made for eaves troughs which prevent leaves from clogging the downspouts. Frequently, older steel troughs will rust through, causing water to gush through at one or more points. Rusted areas can be repaired with the metal repair tapes used for roof flashings. Clean out all dust and dirt, then apply several layers of the tape to the inside of the trough. This procedure will prolong the life of any eaves trough.

Chimneys

The last exterior repair involves the chimney. Chimneys on older buildings should be inspected every year to detect cracks in the flue lining, broken or loose bricks, or soot buildup. From the roof, lower an electric light (an automotive "trouble light" works fine) down the chimney. If cracks appear in the flue you have a fire hazard. Here again, you should get a professional mason to make the internal repairs. If soot or creosote buildup is present, the chimney should be cleaned. A burlap bag filled with rocks or bricks will usually do the job. Lower it into the chimney and scrub it up and down the flue. If you prefer, you can find a professional "sweep" to do the job for you.

As chimneys age the mortar between the bricks disintegrates causing the bricks to pull loose or fall out. Although building a chimney from ground level through a hole in the roof takes some talent, replacing the structure above the roof is a simple matter. Use mortar mix to fit the bricks back together or to fill in where mortar has chipped out between the bricks. You will find re-doing brickwork is not only easy but about as much fun as any repair project can be. It also represents a substantial saving when you do it yourself.

INTERIOR MAINTENANCE

Although well-maintained exteriors are important as a means of encouraging prospective tenants or buyers to see the rest of a building, the inside is the place tenants will be spending their time. The real trick consists of keeping the interior looking pleasant and livable with the least expenditure to consume your profits. Interiors provide unlimited opportunity for anyone with a bit of ambition to save large sums of money by doing the work himself. This portion of the book will offer ideas and techniques to aid the landlord willing to apply himself to maintenance and repair projects.

Walls and Ceilings

Nearly all older buildings have walls made of lath and plaster. The lath is a thin wood stripping nailed horizontally to vertical wall supports called studs. The lath holds a thick layer of plaster. Eventually, every plaster wall cracks or caves in making repairs necessary. These are among the simplest of repairs, requiring no special skill. The market offers a wide array of plaster repair materials. Some come in powdered form to be mixed with water, while some are offered pre-mixed. Probably the easiest repair material is the pre-mixed material called drywall mud. Available at any building center, drywall mud comes in gallon or larger sizes for the most extensive repairs.

To use the mixture, you must first chip out all loose plaster around the edges of the hole or crack so the new plaster has a firm surface for good bonding. Then force the drywall mud into the crack or hole with a drywall knife. Your drywall knife should be at least 6 inches wide for a proper spreading job on large holes. For any hole larger than about 2 inches in width, you will find the material cracks as it dries. Apply a second coat. When it has dried, sand the area smooth and repaint. Take a sample of paint along to the paint store and try to match the old paint as closely as you can. When the area has been repainted, the hole should be difficult to find.

A serious problem is water seepage causing the plaster to pull away from the lath. If this has happened, you can tell right away by the inward bulge on the wall or ceiling. Hand pressure on the area will cause a springy feel, and pieces of plaster may fall out as you push on it. The only means of repairing the area is to use an old chisel or pry-bar to remove all the separated plaster. The resulting mess can be avoided by using a layer of heavy plastic sheeting under the entire area to catch falling plaster.

When you reach the outer edges of the loose plaster, stop pulling the plaster away from the lath. Use the chisel with a hammer to outline the boundaries so you end with a rectangular or square opening. Cut a piece of gypsum board to fit the opening and nail it to the studs and lath behind. Fill the space between the gypsum board and the old plaster with drywall mud, then apply a thin layer over the gypsum board. Probably several applications will be needed to level the area, followed by sanding and repainting to match the original surface. With patience, whole walls can be repaired by this technique.

For newer walls built from gypsum board and drywall

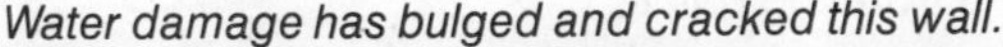

Water damage has bulged and cracked this wall.

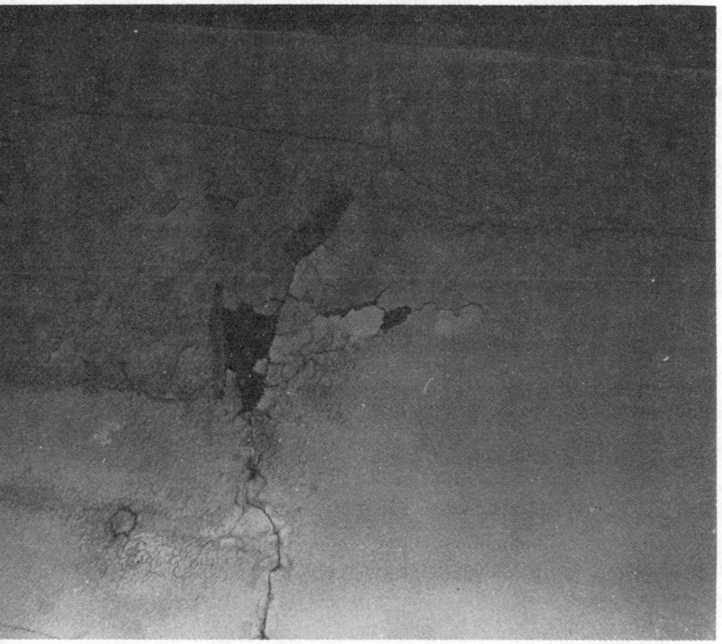

Bulged plaster cut out to expose firm lath beneath.

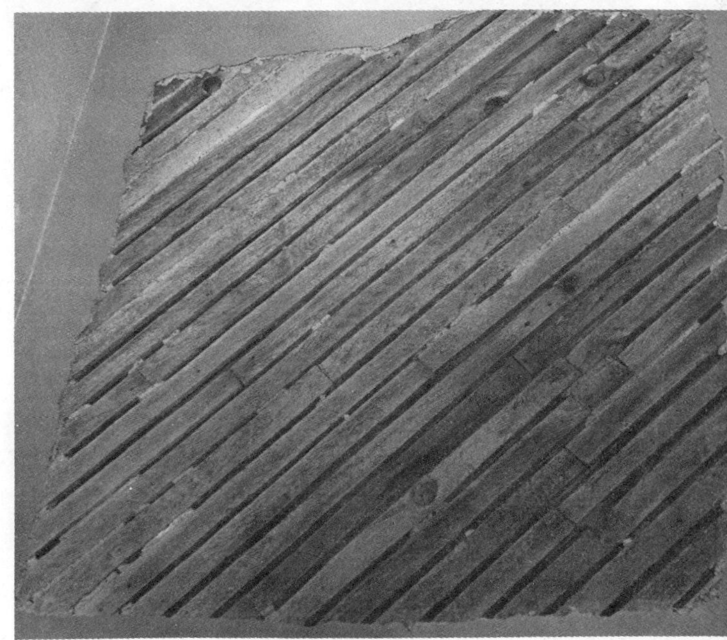

Sections of gypsum board fitted into place.

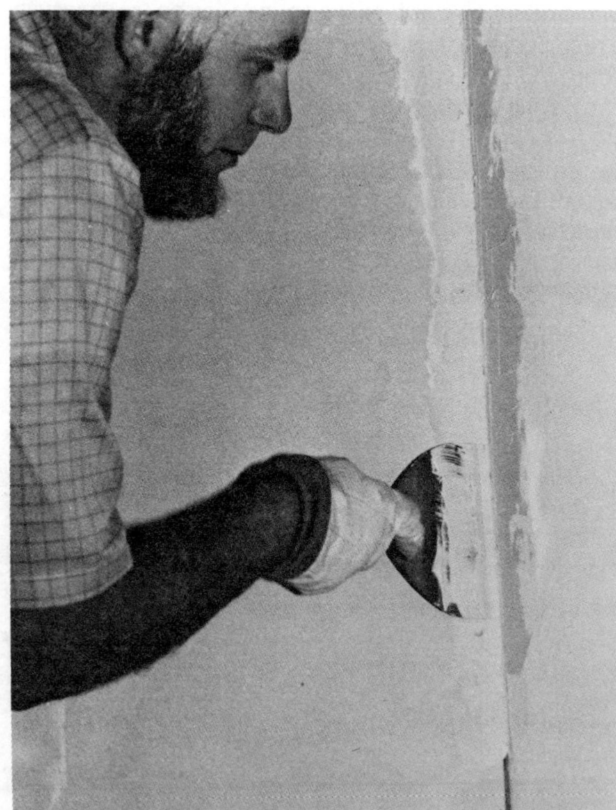

Drywall mud fills in all cracks around the gypsum board. Several coats will be required.

mud, the very same technique can be used to make repairs. Cut out the old gypsum board, fit in a new piece and replaster with drywall mud. The only difference lies in matching the final texture to the original area. If the texture is a bumpy finish, add a finish coat of sand-texture drywall or use a paint containing sand that will match the original finish. To match other textures (and there are many currently being used) try to determine how the original was done. Circular sweeps with a trowel are common; so are brush strokes, coarse roller marks and designs from specially built tools. The only method to use is trial and error until you find what works. If your experiments produce no acceptable results, you may have to call in a professional to do the finish coat.

If the walls or ceilings are discolored or peeled you may want to repaint them. Scrape off any peeled paint and wash off any dirt or grease. If the discoloration was caused by water damage, you may be surprised to find even the best paint will still allow the discoloration to show through. This is often the case with dark stains and light paint applied over the stains. Experiment first to be sure the paint will cover. If it doesn't, refinish the plaster in the stained sections before repainting.

Latex paints are by far the easiest to apply, but disregard any claims of one-coat coverage. Rarely will even the best paints cover well in one coat. Use a 2 inch brush to paint around the windows, doors, and irregularities. Use a 9 inch roller to paint the rest. Rollers with extension handles will save time moving ladders when you are doing upper walls and ceilings. Also, look for plastic roller pan liners to save washing time and water. Wash all roller pads thoroughly after you are finished with them and remove the pad from the roller.

To suit the greatest variety of tenants, avoid any unusual colors, even if the paint is on sale. Instead, select whites, creams, or pale beiges to match the greatest number of colors. (This will also make the apartment appear brighter and larger.) Always use one brand of paint for all the painting you do. You will then know what to expect for coverage and, most important, you will be able to match the color more easily if areas need to be repainted. Keep a log of the names of the paints you have used to save time when matching paints. If you have a heated storage area, save any remaining paint for later touch-ups. Freezing destroys many latex paints, so be prepared for damage to paints if stored unprotected. (See also *Book of Successful Painting* by Abel Banov and Marie-Jeanne Lytle.)

Wallpaper presents a much bigger problem than painted surfaces. Where it is torn or discolored from water damage, it must be replaced. Check the attic and basement for any remnants that might be left. If you find none, take a sample to a wallpaper store and try to match it. If you are lucky enough to find some that matches, tear out the damaged part and fit in a new piece, aligning the pattern carefully. The glue used for wallpaper is a wheatpaste that must be mixed with water and allowed to stand until it thickens. Apply it with a wallpaper brush to the back of the wallpaper and press it into place with your hands. Where the wallpaper has separated from the wall but remains intact, the repair is simpler. Glue down any seams with the wheatpaste. If the separation is not near a seam, make several small cuts across the face of the bulge with a razor blade. Then use a piece of fine wire to work some wheatpaste back under the cuts until the paper adheres.

For seriously damaged or unmatchable wallpaper, the only solution is to repaper the whole wall. The difficult part is often in removing the old wallpaper. Hot water soaking is the usual procedure for removing any parts that refuse to peel off. Using the largest sponge you can find, sponge hot water over the stuck wallpaper until the paste softens behind. If this fails, you may have to rent a commercial steamer. When the wall is bare, fill in any holes or gaps with drywall mud and apply the new wallpaper with the wheatpaste. Wallpapering is not particularly difficult, but can be very trying to the patience—so try to stay relaxed. Some wallpapers come with wheatpaste already on the back, ready to moisten and apply. The glue is seldom adequate on these and you may be in for a great disappointment when it bubbles. Treat these wallpapers the same as those with no adhesive on them by adding wheatpaste to the back. Make all cuts with a razor knife or scissors. Smooth out wrinkles and bubbles with your hands by moving them toward the edges of the paper to squeeze out excess wheatpaste. Wallpaper shrinks slightly on drying which helps remove small bubbles or wrinkles that could not be worked out. For unusual contours, you should consult one of the specialized books on wallpapering techniques. This is also a good idea if you plan to wallpaper a ceiling. Ceilings should be wallpapered only after you have first gained some experience on flat wall surfaces. (See also *Wallcoverings and Decorations* by Banov, Lytle and Rossig.)

Another wall covering that may need occasional attention is ceramic tile usually found in bathrooms. The grout holding the tile in place may chip out or crack. Even though the tile may be held firmly in place, the grout should be repaired to prevent water from seeping behind the tiles, causing rot inside the wall. Silicone rubber sealers work well for sealing the spaces between tiles. If tiles have fallen out, the easiest technique is to re-set them using two-part epoxy to hold them in place and then seal the space around the tiles with the silicone sealer. This will provide a repair needing no attention for many years.

◄ *Water damage on gypsum board textured walls usually involves lifted paper. Cut away any loose paper before repairing the area.*

Small rollers often duplicate rough textures on drywall. ►

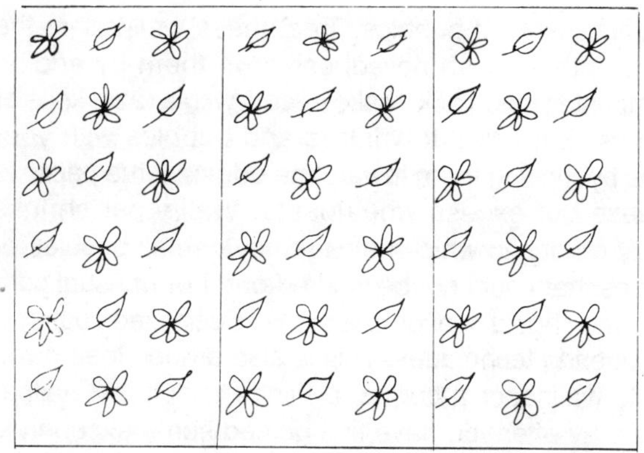

In a drop-match pattern, once you line up the marks, you will find that the first strip has the full pattern at the top. The number two strip will have a half-pattern at the top; the number three strip will also have the full pattern at the top. These three strips illustrate a drop match pattern. Note that every other strip is the same at the top.

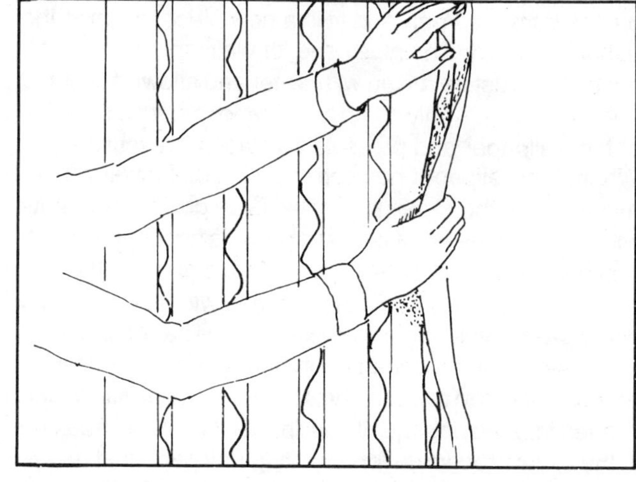

Unfold top part of strip only. Position near ceiling, leaving 3 inches to trim off later. Line up the right edge of the strip with the plumb line.

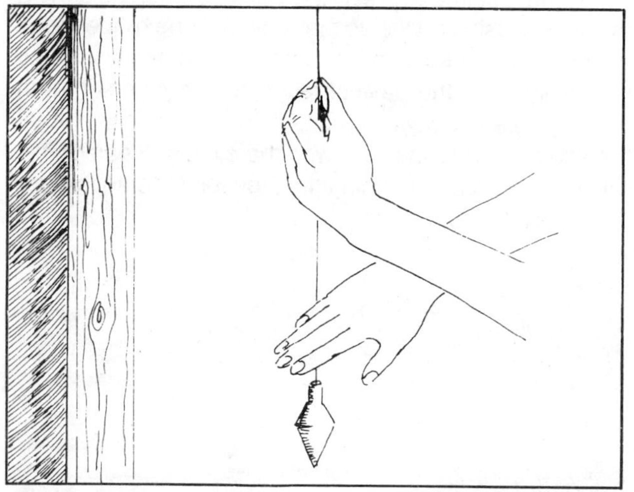

One strip (less ½ inch) to the right of the door, fasten plumb line from ceiling. Chalk the string and, holding it near the bottom, snap a line onto the wall. Measure ceiling height. Allow 3 inches extra top, 3 inches at bottom.

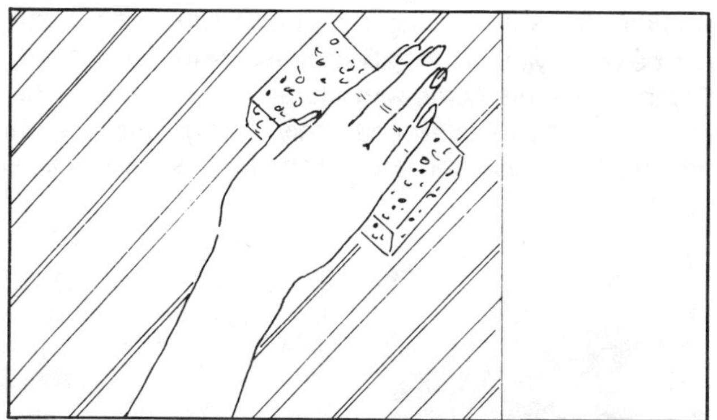

Smooth strip, working from center to edges. Unfold bottom, align with plumb line, smooth out entrapped bubbles with sponge. Small bubbbles disappear with drying.

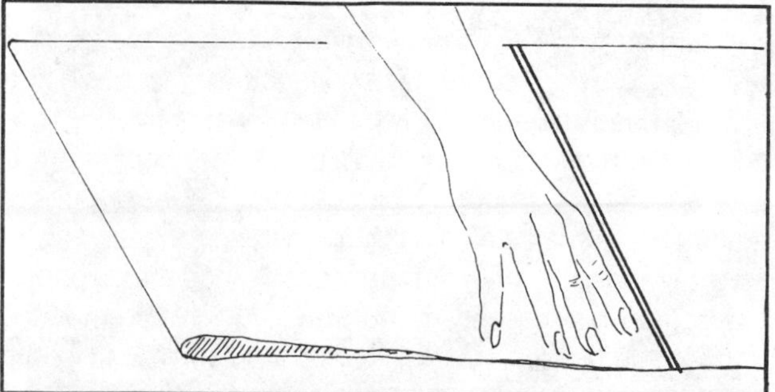

After pasting smoothly, fold paste to paste so edge ends up just short of center of strip, pattern up. Fold other edge to just beyond the edge of other fold, which should have a few inches without adhesive. Do not crease folds.

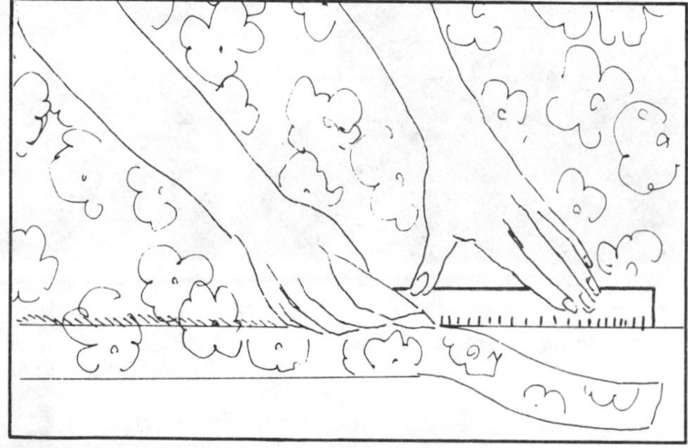

Use ruler with knife or razor blade to trim top, bottom and around door frame. Wipe off paste with wet sponge. Smooth entire strip. Roll down edges with a seam roller. Don't use roller on flock wall coverings. Tap seams with sponge to avoid matting flock pile.

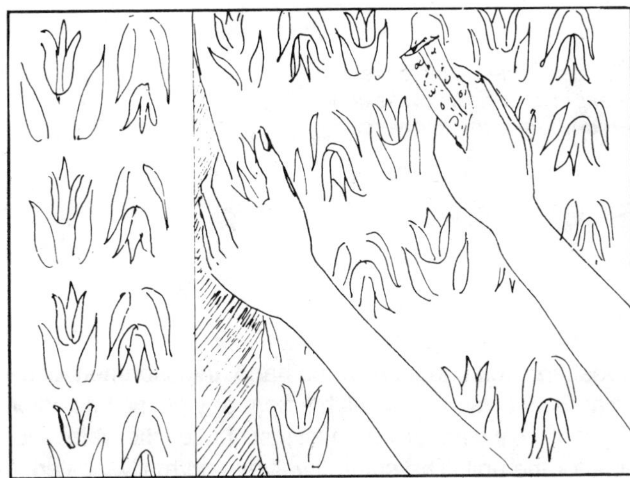

Hang succeeding strips. Carefully match pattern at left edge of new strip with previous strip. Butt edges, sponge, and roll edges.

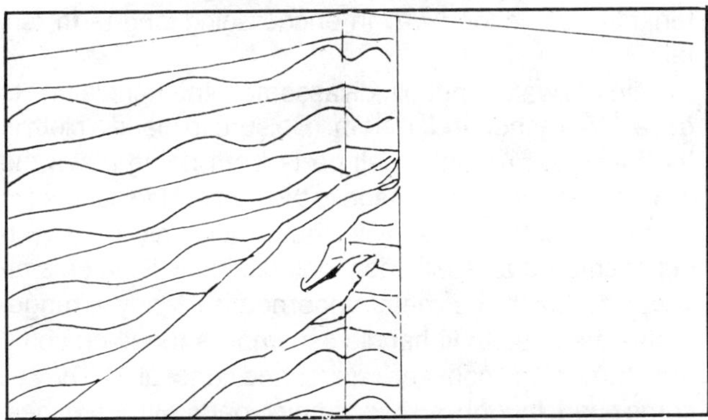

At corner: Measure edge-to-corner at top, middle and baseboard. Take widest measure; add ½ inch. Cut vertical strip this width. Apply, overlap corner ½ inch. Measure next strip. Add ½ inch. Drop plumb this distance from corner. Follow plumb; apply, match pattern and lap at corner.

Windows: Measure ceiling to frame. Add 1 inch. Cut vertical strip, apply so it extends over top of frame 1 inch. Trim around frame. Match pattern; use short lengths above, below frame.

Plumbing

Plumbing requires frequent maintenance, especially in older buildings. With the exception of very unusual occurrences, all plumbing maintenance is relatively simple, requiring only a basic knowledge of plumbing construction. Plumbers are expensive and any landlord who must call a plumber for every problem will find his profits shrinking quickly. This section of the book covers the basics that anyone can do. Once you become proficient at these, your confidence will increase until you will find yourself able to tackle much larger projects, such as complete remodeling of existing plumbing to fit new room arrangements. If and when you want to experiment you will find techniques outlined in other reference books. Since the water must be shut off for nearly all repairs, do your experimenting a a time when supply stores are open. You may be in need of extra parts you had not planned on or some advice easily supplied by a clerk. Keeping a tenant's water shut off longer than absolutely necessary is a poor policy, so plan ahead.

The appearance of washbasins and lavatories is a major factor in a prospective tenant's decision to rent the apartment. Every attempt should be made to keep all these fixtures in top condition. Porcelain washbasins sometimes become chipped. Rather than replace the unit, try one of the epoxy patching enamels. Clean the area thoroughly with a solvent such as benzene and dry the area. Then apply the epoxy following the manufacturer's directions.

Even more noticeable than chips are the stains resulting from dissolved minerals in the water. Copper and iron seem to be about the worst offenders. While these stains have no functional effect on the unit, their appearance is a real detriment. Try a mild cleanser to remove the worst part, then leave a coating of cleanser on the area overnight. If the stain still shows, try bleach or use a commercial rust remover or a mild acid like vinegar. If stains persistently show up you may want to consider a water softener for the building.

Basin stoppers often work poorly because of clogging or by becoming disconnected. Check first to see if the stopper needs cleaning by removing it with a twisting motion. If cleaning fails to cure the problem, check the rod connections underneath. The tightness of the stopper is adjustable with a small nut that joins the connecting rods. Sadly, some of the new stoppers and fittings are so poorly made they disintegrate in no time. If the system is inoperative either replace the stopper and linkage or install a rubber stopper on a chain. The latter is old-fashioned but amazingly serviceable. We have never had a tenant upset over one of these.

Faucets, too, need occasional attention. The most frequent problem is dripping caused by worn rubber

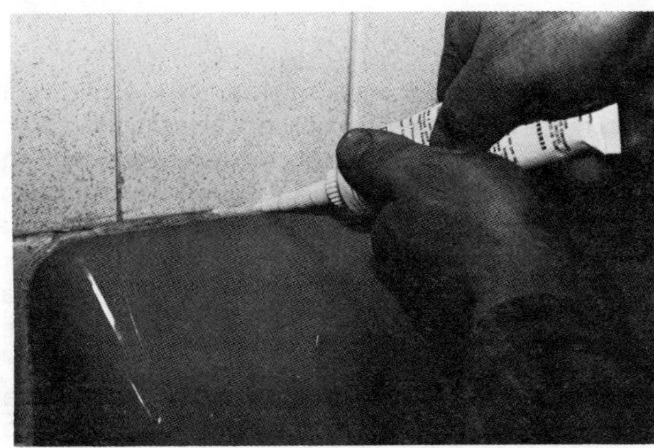

Use a silicone sealer to prevent leaks in ceramic tile walls and around sinks and showers.

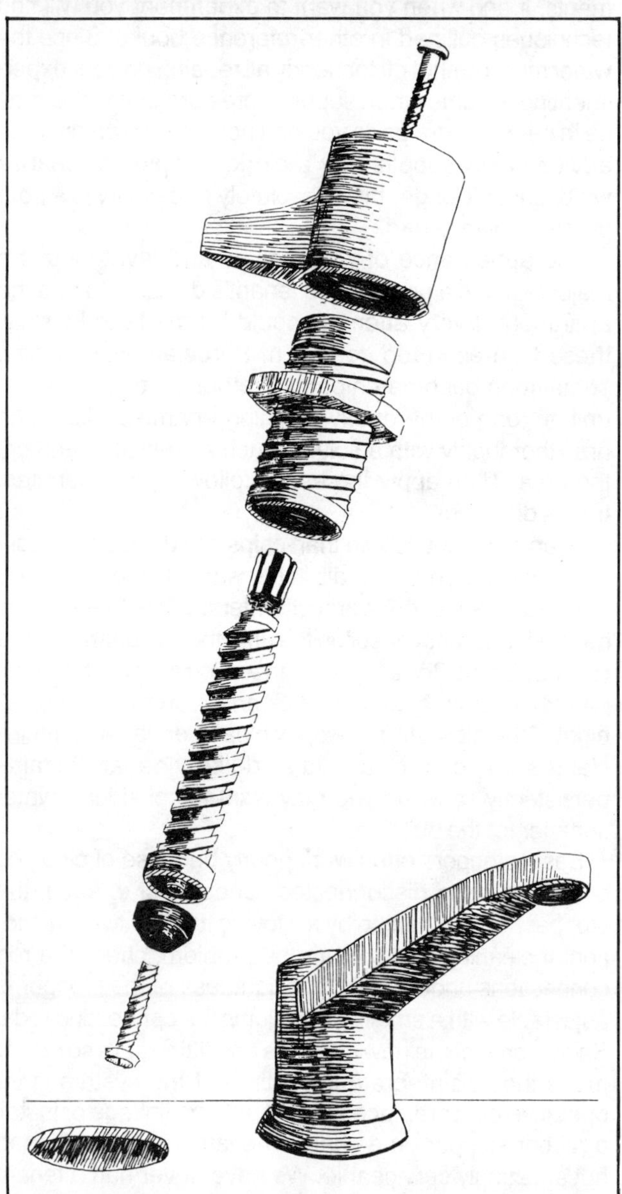

The washer is at the very bottom of everything. One nice feature is that faucets usually come apart easily because they are used so much.

washers. You should have on hand an assortment of replacement washers available from any plumbing center. To replace a washer you must first shut off the water supply for the unit. The shut-off valve is normally located in the basement. Even for short repairs like replacing a washer you should let tenants in the building know if the water is to be shut off. Someone might be taking a shower, washing his hair or be involved in some other project like developing photographic film. Thoughtfulness toward tenants goes a long way in encouraging long-term rentals.

With the water shut off, disassemble the handle unit to get at the washer underneath. (Be sure to place a cloth in the basin to prevent small parts from going down the drain and to prevent damage to the basin. Use care not to scratch faucets and handles. These have only a thin coating of chrome and will soon look unsightly if water is allowed to reach the metal underneath.) Many arrangements are used to fit handle assemblies together; some are obvious and some are clever and concealed. They all come apart, though, so keep turning parts with wrenches, screwdrivers or other tools until the assembly comes apart. You will find a central shaft in most units that will lift out after being unscrewed. At the bottom is a rubber washer usually held in place by a single screw. Remove the screw and pry out the old washer with a small screwdriver or a knife blade. Then replace the washer with a new one that will fit snugly into the opening in the bottom of the shaft. Re-assemble everything and turn on the water supply to the unit. You should find the dripping has stopped.

Another problem sometimes develops with faucet handles. As they age, the threads that hold them to the shaft may become so worn the shaft no longer rotates with the handle. Most parts for older faucets are difficult or impossible to find. Fortunately the market offers a universal replacement handle you can find at most plumbing stores. These may not match the original fixture in appearance but they do provide an alternative to replacing the entire sink unit, which is far more costly.

The only other problem that may need occasional attention on washbasins is the aerator sometimes found on the end of a faucet. These may become clogged by particles and mineral scale in the water. Unscrew the unit and disassemble the parts, being sure to keep them in their correct order. Clean screens or clogged holes in plastic plates with a small wire or pin before reassembling the unit. These procedures should keep all faucets and basins in good operation.

Another problem area, and certainly one of the more frequent problems encountered by a landlord, is clogged drains. Drains may be clogged by grease, hair, food particles or solid objects like hairpins. Most often the blockage is in the trap, a U-shaped piece of pipe under the basin. A trap is very easy to clean by disassembling the U-shaped piece of pipe from the upper and lower pipes that connect it. Put a pail under the trap to catch any spillage; then use a large wrench to unscrew the couplings that fasten it. Clean the trap with a piece of wire and check the upper and lower pipes to be sure the blockage has been removed.

If the trap and upper drain were free of obstruction, or if cleaning out those sections failed to restore proper drainage, the blockage is in the lower section of pipe. To clear pipes (other than a trap) use a plumber's snake. Push the end of the snake into the pipe as far as it will go. When it seems to stop, tighten the handle unit down close to the pipe and turn the crank or rotate the unit to make the cable go in farther. Keep feeding the cable into the pipe until you can go no farther. By using this method you can clean out obstructions the length of the cable—about 15 or 20 feet. For really stubborn obstructions, or for those farther back, you may need to rent one of the larger motor-driven snakes or disconnect the pipes to start closer to the obstruction. This is usually a rare situation.

When the drain has been cleaned and reassembled, run the water for several minutes to be sure the blockage has really been removed. Then do what you can to prevent future problems. Some renters are very reasonable and a simple explanation, such as telling them not to pour grease down the drain or to be careful with hairpins, will eliminate the problem. Plastic screens are available to put over sink drains to catch loose hair or other debris. If necessary buy one and insist it be used.

Toilets also require occasional maintenance. For some reason, seats and covers frequently become cracked in rental units. Fortunately, these are separate from the tank or bowl and take only a couple of minutes to replace. You can purchase a new cover and seat unit at any plumbing center. The units unbolt from underneath, immediately behind the bowl. Use a wrench to remove the nuts, then lift the unit off and bolt in the new unit.

Sometimes, the problem of water running continuously in the upper tank develops. There are several possible causes. If the tank is not filling up, check the rubber ball or flap that seals the outflow at the very bottom of the tank. It may have become clogged with mineral deposits or

Shut off the water main in the basement before working on water lines.

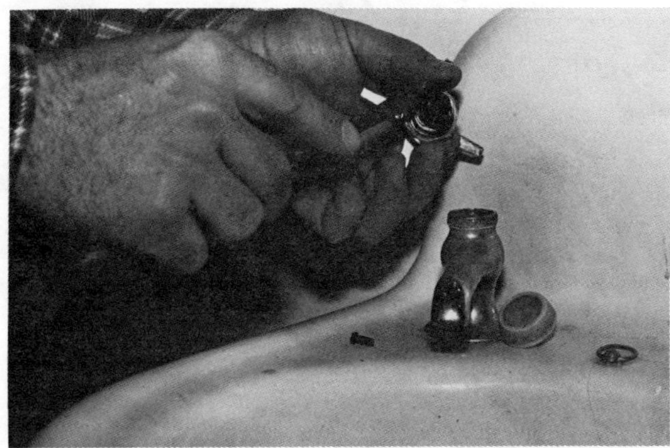

With faucet disassembled, pry out the old rubber washer.

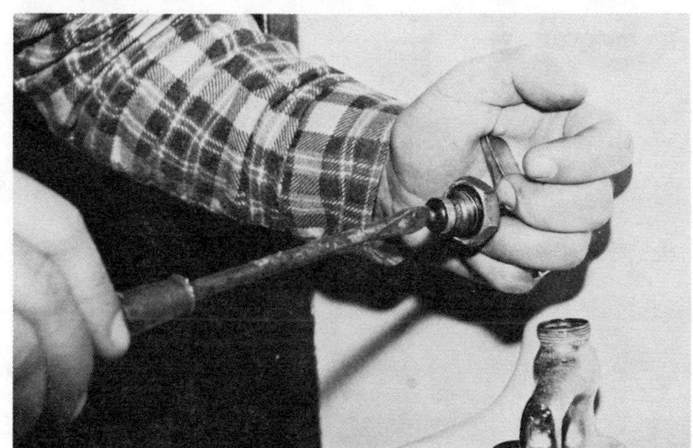

Fit in a new washer and tighten the screw. This should stop leaks.

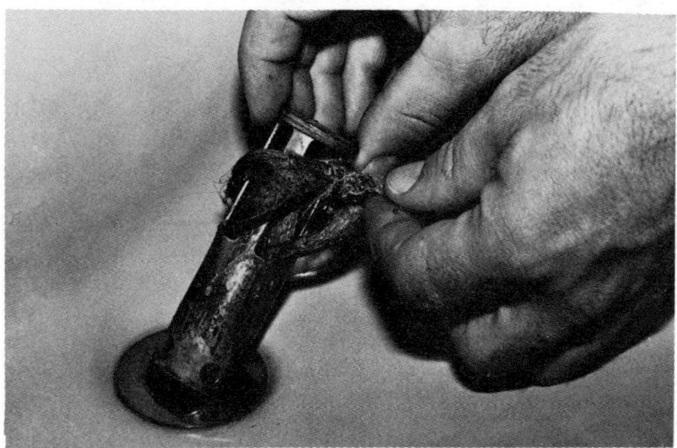

Hair and other obstructions will block drains. Start from the top drain stopper and work down until the problem is solved.

Disconnect water traps with a pipe wrench.

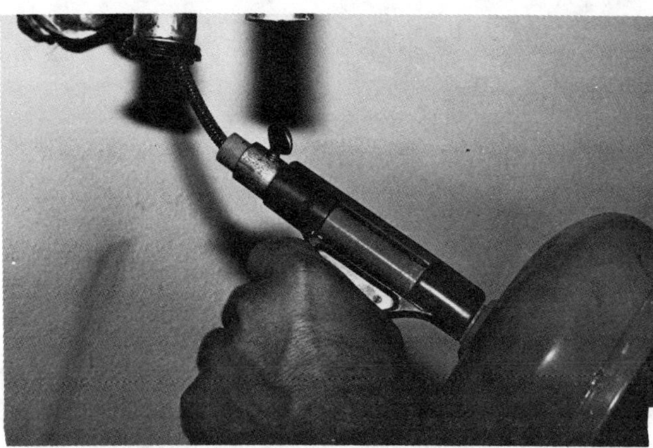

Use a plumber's snake to remove obstructions inside pipes.

cracked with age. Mineral deposits can easily be cleaned off but a cracked or broken seal should be replaced. With the ball sealing properly the tank should then fill up.

If the tank fills but the water continues running, one of two problems will be the cause. You will find a ball-shaped float connected by a 12 to 14 inch rod to a shut-off valve. Lift up on the rod. If the water shuts off, the ball is the problem. It may have become corroded, allowing water to get inside. If that has happened, unscrew it and put on a new ball. If the ball is not waterlogged, bend the metal rod down so the ball makes contact sooner with the water in the tank. This will shut off the water flow sooner.

If the water did not shut off when the metal rod was raised, the problem is in the shut-off valve. To repair the shut-off valve you must first turn off the water supply to the toilet tank. Usually you will find a valve between the tank and the wall right in the bathroom. If you do not, shut off the main in the basement. Then remove the whole ball assembly and lift out the shut-off valve unit. If it seems to be badly corroded, it takes only a few minutes to replace the entire ball and valve assembly with a new unit available at any plumbing center. If the metal part seems to be in good condition you should replace worn washers or gaskets with identical ones and reassemble the mechanism. This should cause the water to shut off properly.

If a toilet bowl becomes plugged use a toilet force-cup (plunger) to clear the obstruction. These have an elongated central core that gives much better results on toilets than you will have with an ordinary sink force-cup. If this method fails to clear the obstruction you have a situation that will require a toilet auger. Either purchase one and ream out the pipes or call a professional to do the job.

Eventually a toilet bowl will need replacement due to cracking or severe discoloration. This is surprisingly easy and requires only a wrench. It is also not the messy or smelly job you would expect. To replace the unit shut off the water supply to the tank. Get rid of as much water as you can by flushing several times followed by bailing the tank. Put down newspapers to catch any spillage.

Disconnect the piping to the tank, since you will be removing both tank and bowl. Then remove the nuts from the bolts holding the tank to the wall. Remove these with care, remembering they are very heavy fixtures. Take both tank and bowl outside for disposal. Invert the new bowl on a pad or rug to install the wax ring used to seal the joint between the bottom of the bowl and the floor pipe. Slide it onto the flange on the underside of the bowl. Run a bead of setting compound around the very bottom of the unit where it will rest on the floor. Set the unit upright in position on the floor pipe and tighten the nuts to hold it in place.

Now attach the tank to the bowl according to the manufacturer's directions and bolt the unit to the wall if it is a wall-hung unit. Connect the water line and assemble the flush mechanism in the tank. (Read directions on the package.) Turn on the water and make any necessary adjustments to the ball and shut-off so the fill level will be correct. Flush the unit and be sure everything works. At this point you have saved enough on plumbing bills to take someone out to dinner several times. Enjoy yourself. (See also *Successful Plumbing* by Robert Scharff.)

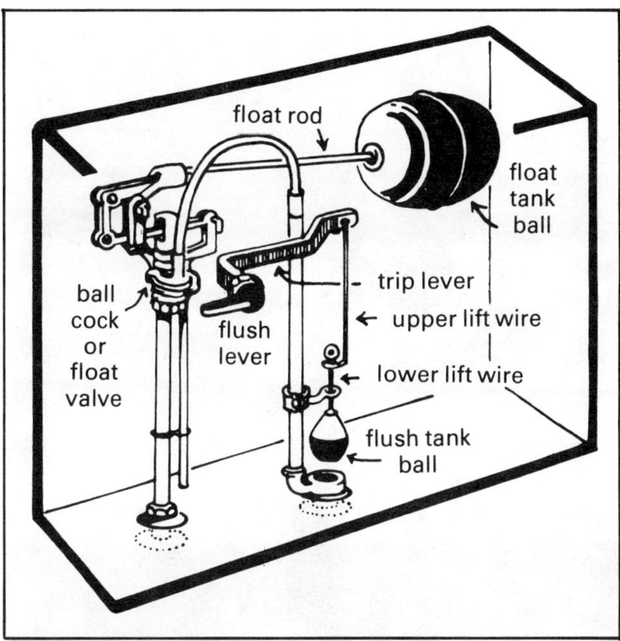

Diagram of toilet tank.

Electrical

While there are numerous books for the do-it-yourself electrician, this book takes a very conservative stand on the matter of learn-as-you-go electrical work. People are unlikely to be injured from a poor paint job or even a badly installed toilet. Electricity is quite another matter, however, so it is best to save your experimenting for other areas.

Three types of problems can be handled by anyone, however. The first is a problem involving fuses or circuit breakers. Older buildings will normally have screw-in

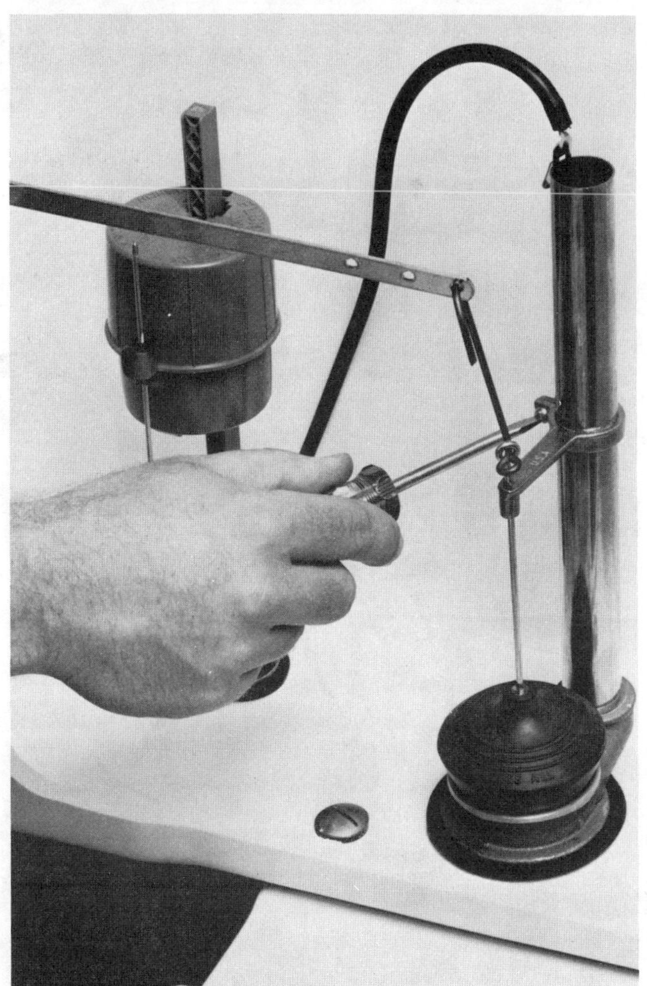

how to repair a toilet

Leaky flush valves attributable to conventional toilet tank mechanism can be eliminated with a Flusher Fixer Kit available from hardware and lumber dealers. The kit replaces the worn-out tank ball or flapper and does away with lift wires and brackets that often become bent. Unlike conventional flush valve assemblies, the Flusher Fixer Kit is installed without tools and without removing the tank from the bowl. The kit's seat is simply bonded directly onto the existing seat with a patented watertight sealant.

As detailed in the accompanying photographs on page 84, the old tank stopper ball is first removed from the toilet along with the left wires and bracket guide. (1) Steel wool is then used to clean off the old brass flush valve seat and water used to rinse the seat clean. (2) Waterproof sealant is applied to the underside of the new stainless steel ring using the entire contents of the tube supplied with the kit.

After placement of the new seat on the old brass seat, a 9-ounce can is placed atop the unit (3) to apply necessary bonding weight. The seat is allowed to set in this position for two hours with water level just enough to cover the top rim of the seat. A chain is then secured to the flush valve (4) and attached to the lift arm. Excess chain may be cut off or fastened to the clip and the toilet is ready to use.

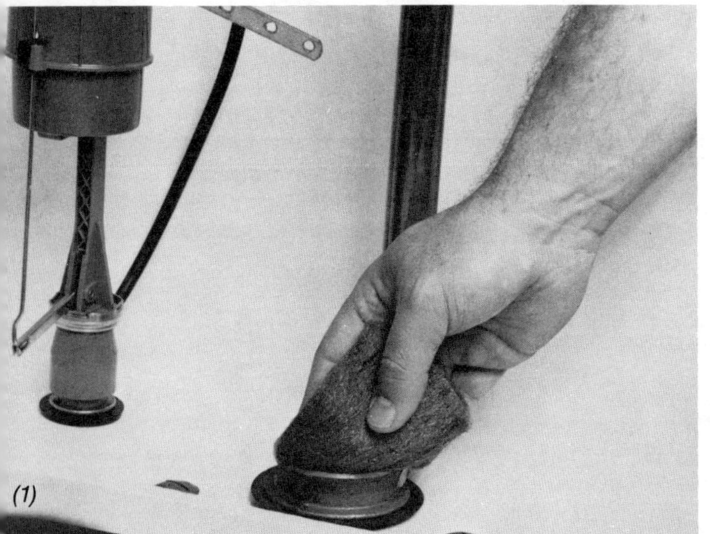
(1)

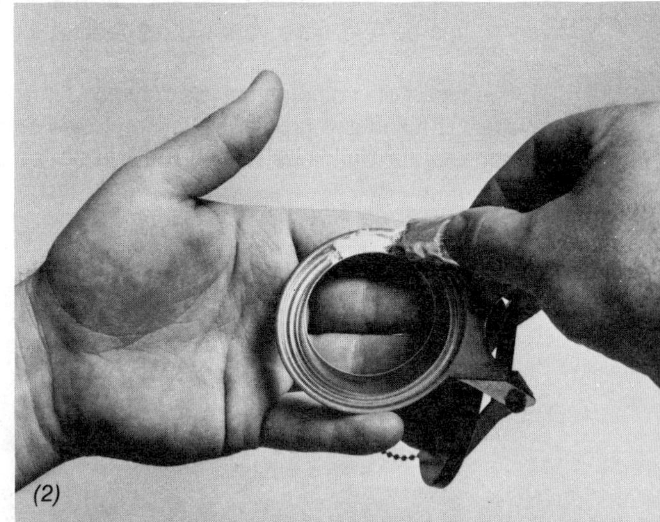
(2)

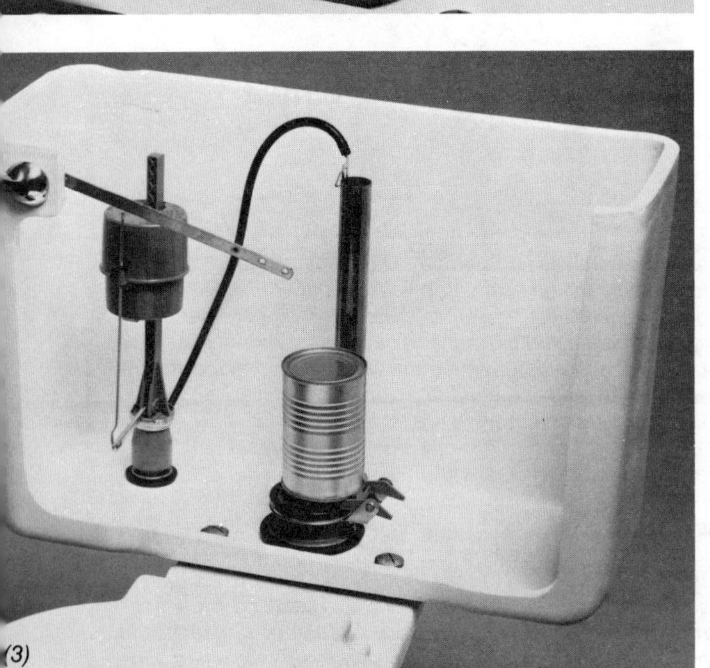
(3)

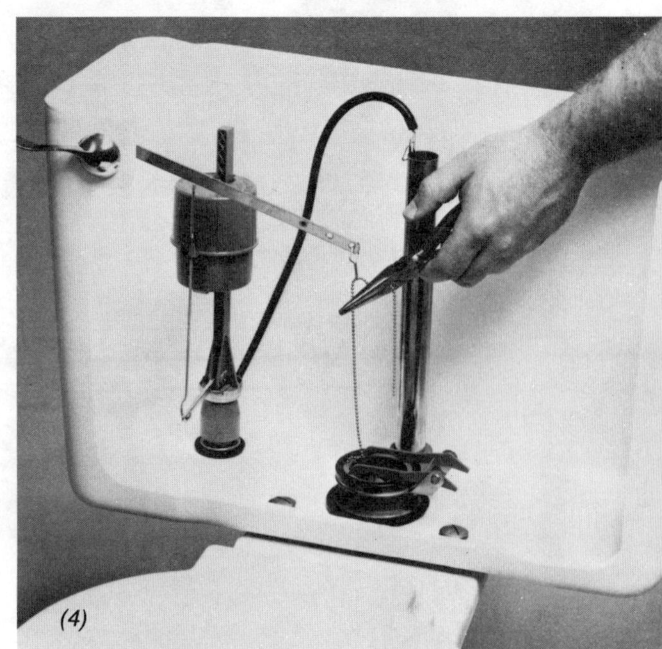
(4)

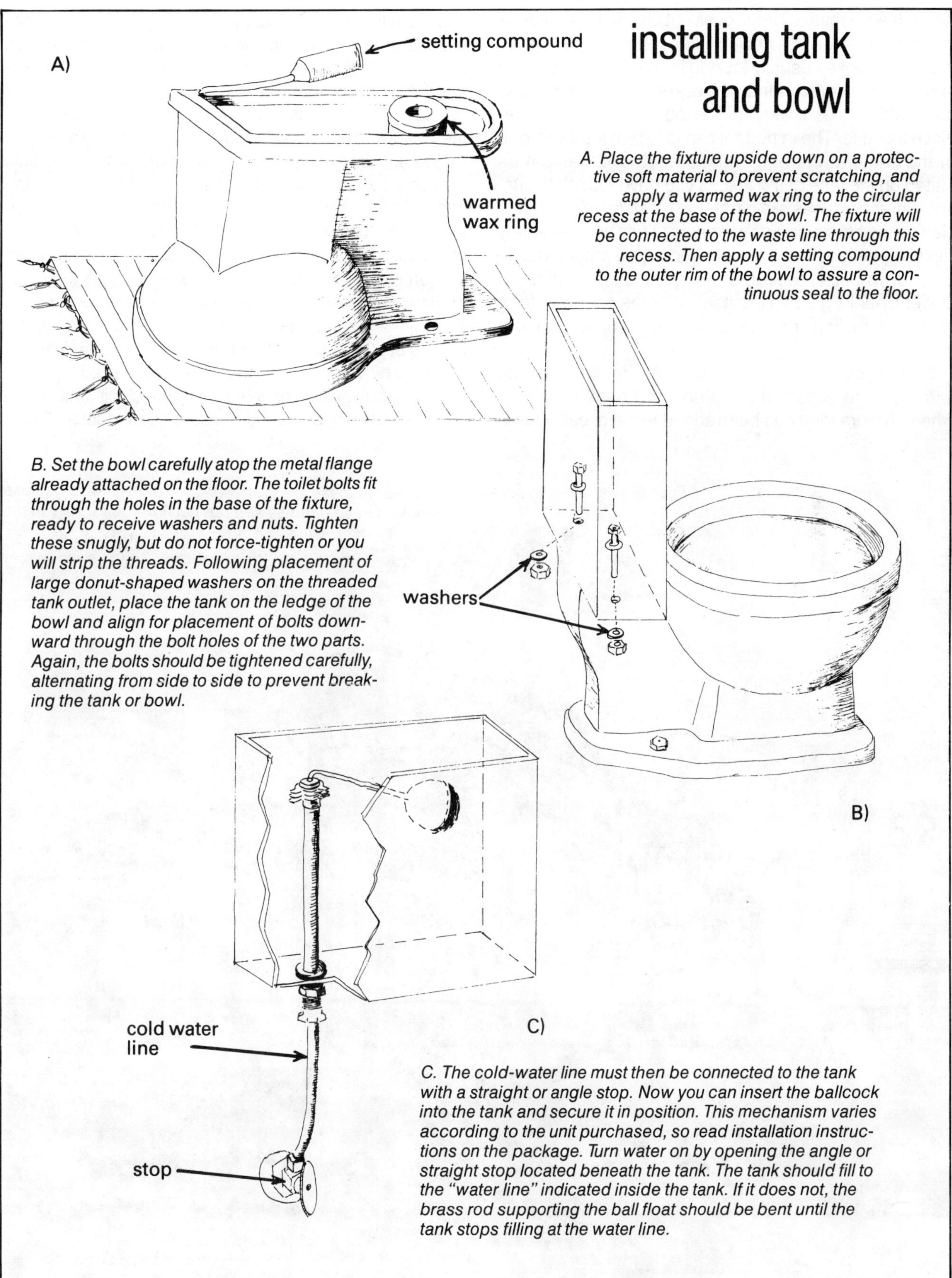

installing tank and bowl

A. Place the fixture upside down on a protective soft material to prevent scratching, and apply a warmed wax ring to the circular recess at the base of the bowl. The fixture will be connected to the waste line through this recess. Then apply a setting compound to the outer rim of the bowl to assure a continuous seal to the floor.

B. Set the bowl carefully atop the metal flange already attached on the floor. The toilet bolts fit through the holes in the base of the fixture, ready to receive washers and nuts. Tighten these snugly, but do not force-tighten or you will strip the threads. Following placement of large donut-shaped washers on the threaded tank outlet, place the tank on the ledge of the bowl and align for placement of bolts downward through the bolt holes of the two parts. Again, the bolts should be tightened carefully, alternating from side to side to prevent breaking the tank or bowl.

C. The cold-water line must then be connected to the tank with a straight or angle stop. Now you can insert the ballcock into the tank and secure it in position. This mechanism varies according to the unit purchased, so read installation instructions on the package. Turn water on by opening the angle or straight stop located beneath the tank. The tank should fill to the "water line" indicated inside the tank. If it does not, the brass rod supporting the ball float should be bent until the tank stops filling at the water line.

fuses. If an electrical circuit goes out check the small windows in the faces of screw-in fuses. They will be in large metal fuse boxes usually located in the basement. If you find a fuse with the window blackened or one with the metal strip inside broken or melted you will have to replace the fuse. The important part is to replace it with one of the same amperage rating (10, 15 or 20 amps) as stated on the face of the fuse. If you have reason to suspect improper fuses are already in place have an electrician go over the fuse box to be sure. Then you can safely replace any fuse with one of the identical amperage. To be sure you don't receive any shocks, either shut off all power by pulling down the handle for the power main or touch only the top rim of the fuse when you insert the new one.

Before you put in the new fuse, however, you must eliminate the cause of the problem. Fuses only blow when an extra load has been added to the circuit. This is usually in the form of an extra appliance, such as a portable heater, a curling iron, stereo or anything added since the fuse was installed the last time. Most difficult to detect are the combinations that can blow fuses. Some electrical devices are controlled by thermostats or timers so they do not operate continuously. Electric frying pans and forced air furnaces are good examples. If these should kick on at the same time other electrical appliances on the same circuit are in use, a surge of current can blow a fuse that would otherwise operate perfectly. Remember that a blown fuse is not a problem in itself, but rather a symptom that an overloading problem exists. First solve the overload problem, then replace the fuse. Also before replacing any fuses, see that the appliance which caused the fuse to blow has been disconnected or the new fuse will promptly blow as soon as the power is restored.

One handy means of determining which circuits or outlets are still in operation is to use a circuit-tester. These

Fuse boxes, showing screw-in fuses. Above these are the handles to remove the larger fuse blocks. Grasp handles and pull out firmly to remove them.

consist of two prong-capped wires with a tiny bulb connected to them and cost under $2. You can safely push the prongs into opposite sides of any outlet or check wiring anywhere to see if the circuit is operating. Whenever the bulb lights up you can be sure current is flowing. A circuit-tester should be in your tool box at all times.

Occasionally, fuses in the main blocks will blow. If power to some parts of the building remains out after you have checked all the screw-in fuses, this is probably the cause. Pull out the fuse blocks by using the small metal handles that slide in and out in the center of the fuse box. Behind these you will find fuses of a different type, long and cylindrical, held into place by spring clips. Pull firmly on each cylinder to snap it free. The only way to determine if one of these fuses has blown is to replace each one alternately with a new one of the same amperage. Keep trying until you find the right one. Before checking to see if one of these fuses was the cause of the trouble, be sure you turn the main power handle back on if you turned if off earlier. If fuses do not solve the problem call an electrician.

For modern buildings or those recently rewired, you will find the fuses have been replaced with circuit breakers. Instead of blowing out and being replaced, circuit breakers kick out when they overload, needing only to be reset to be put back into operation. Usually a tiny red flap or spot appears in a small clear window when the circuit has blown out. With the appliance that caused the overload disconnected, snap the breaker switch to the off position momentarily and then turn it back on. The red spot should disappear and the circuit be operational. Sometimes the red spot will show up poorly. If you suspect a breaker is out, snap each breaker off and on to be sure they are all reset. If this procedure fails to restore power, you should call an electrician.

You will probably find fuses blow or breakers go out when appliances such as ovens, hair driers or other high wattage appliances are used along with frequent furnace starts. Translated, that means between 5 p.m. and 8 a.m. on the coldest night of the year. A good idea is to plan ahead for that situation. Buy spare fuses for every one that might need replacing and put them near the fuse boxes where they will be handy. See that some reliable tenants know where the fuses are and show them how to replace a fuse. Attention to this detail may save you an evening's drive through a blizzard to keep tenants from freezing. Electricians and furnace repair men are often difficult to locate at critical times, even if you are willing to pay the price of an emergency call.

The last electrical problem is broken cords on lamps or small appliances where such items are furnished by you. No electrical knowledge is required with the replacement plugs now available. It is difficult to believe anything so simple can really work, but after many years of testing

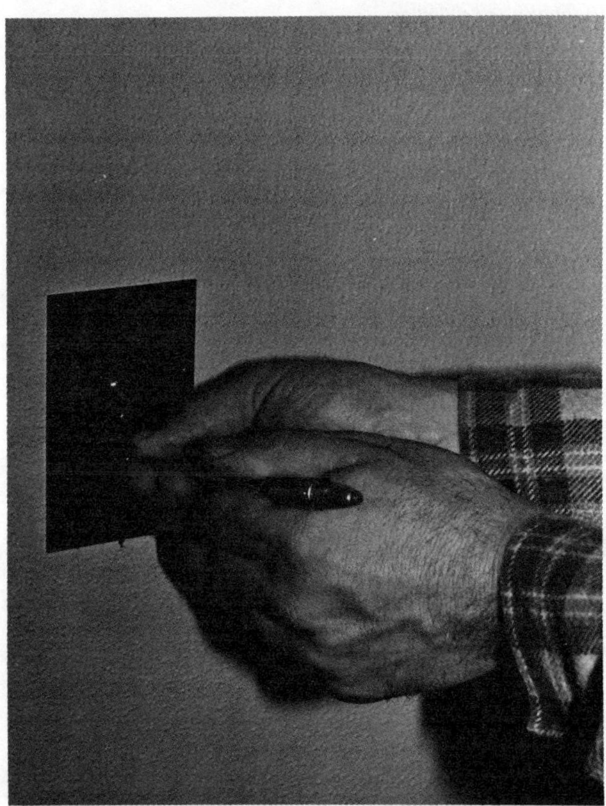

Circuit-tester lights up when current is flowing.

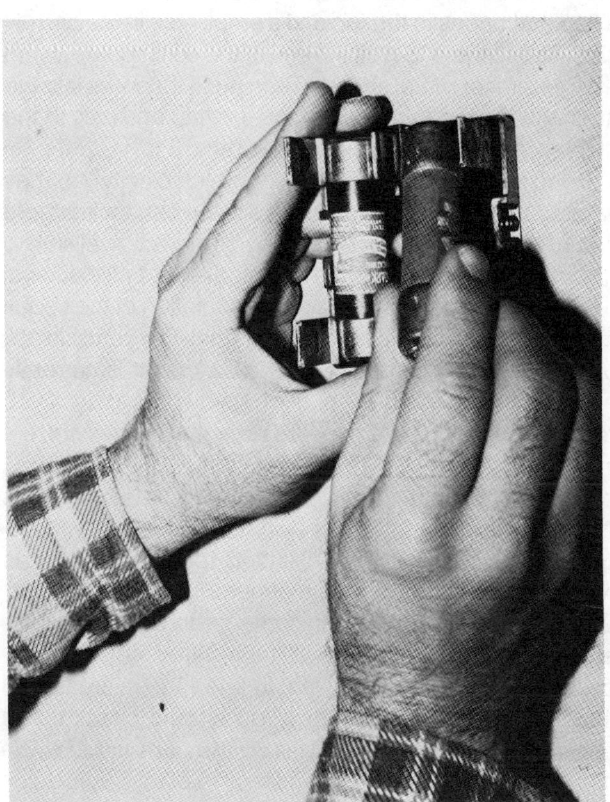

Removing a cartridge-type fuse. Keep replacing these until you locate the one that has blown.

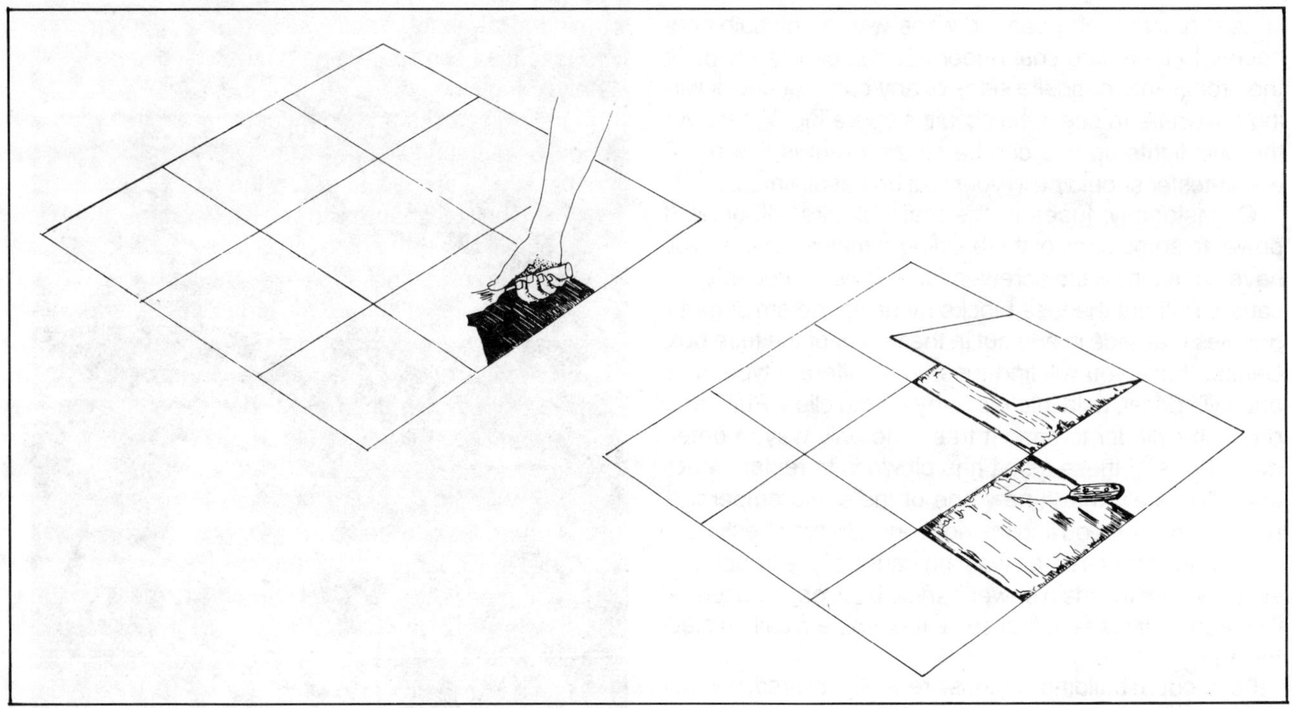

Broken tiles will come out easily with leverage from a screwdriver. Lay a new bed of adhesive with a putty knife or other edge, and after waiting 10 or 15 minutes lay in the new tile.

they have been proven reliable. You can identify them by a flap that opens in the top and a small hole in the narrow side. To use them, cut off the end of the cord squarely with a wire cutter or metal shears. Then push the wires into the hole with the top flap open, close the flap and plug in the appliance. It should be as good as new.

If you feel comfortable working with electricity you may want to expand your knowledge so you can tackle more complex repairs or re-wiring. Many books are available to give detailed information on techniques, but all electrical work is strictly governed by codes. Violation of the codes may leave you open for legal problems. The sensible approach is to find someone who knows what is currently acceptable and ask him about what you plan to do. If you rely on books, be sure they are recent and have current information.

A final thought on the subject of electricity is light bulbs. Anyone can change a light bulb, of course. As you acquire more buildings, you will find there will be areas which are designated for the general use of all tenants. Common entryways and basement storage or laundry areas are examples where all the tenants may have access. You will, of course, want to keep these areas well lighted to prevent accidents. You should check these areas occasionally to make sure they are lighted. We have found tenants have a tendency to borrow light bulbs from general-use areas for their own apartments. Also, when choosing light bulbs for general use areas, fit the wattage of the bulb to the space to be lighted. Some areas do not need to be brilliantly lighted while others should have very bright lights. If you match the wattage of the light to the purpose of the area, you will have happy tenants and save on utility costs. (See also *Successful Home Electrical Wiring* by Larry Mueller.)

Floors

Eventually, all flooring materials suffer wear or damage extensive enough to require replacement. To prolong the life of a floor, you may find the following techniques helpful. This portion deals only with repair of flooring materials. For stains or other problems, see the section on "Cleaning an Apartment." To install new materials and decide which floorings to choose, see the section on "Remodeling."

Tile floors have several problems that may develop. Edges of the tiles may become lifted or curled, often from water damage. A helpful tool to use for tiles is a propane torch with a spreader head to distribute the flame. By warming the edges of the tiles, you will find they become flexible enough to re-glue by forcing flooring adhesive underneath the edges. Allow it to dry about 10 minutes, then hammer the edges back down with a wood block under the hammer. This is time consuming, though, so use that technique only for small areas.

For badly damaged tiles, try to find replacements. Use

an old chisel to pry out the damaged tiles, applying the propane torch wherever they are tightly stuck. Scrape out all the old adhesive and apply a new layer of tile adhesive. Set the tiles into place after the adhesive has set for the required 10 minutes.

For linoleum, the usual problems are bubbles, cuts or worn areas. For bubbles, the raised part should be slit in several places with a sharp knife or razor blade. Force adhesive back under the bubble with a piece of wire, then place a heavy weight on the area until it stays down. For cuts in linoleum, use the same procedure, forcing glue underneath and then weighting the area.

Worn patches can be cut out and replaced if you can find matching material. Cut out a rectangular area around the worn spot and glue in a new piece cut to fit. Apply weight to all edges until the adhesive has set firmly and the corners remain tight.

Carpeting is one of the most common floorings and you should be thoroughly familiar with its problems and solutions. Where the carpet is burned or badly damaged, cut the area around the damage in a rectangle. Replace the section with a matching piece of carpet, bonding the new piece with heat-tape strips available at any carpet store. Put the tape in place around the edges of the replacement piece. Seal by placing a hot iron (with a cloth pad underneath) on top of the carpet to set the tape. Cuts or tears can be eliminated by using heat tape underneath the cut. For wall-to-wall carpet that develops cuts or tears, a professional will be needed to make the necessary repairs.

Locks

Every apartment will need a lock on every door. Most locks are relatively trouble-free, but many tenants will refuse to rent an apartment unless all the locks have been changed since the last renter. Since keys may have become misplaced by previous tenants and you can never be sure how many spare keys anyone may have made, changing locks is a good policy. The important consideration is to find one particular kind and brand of lock and use that lock every time you change. This will offer two advantages. The holes will line up every time you install a new lock and you will not need to drill new holes in doors. Second, the locks you take off can be re-used at a later date on another apartment door. This system saves many wasted locks and ruined doors. Keep all keys and locks labeled so you know what keys will open which units.

Many tenants also request chain locks in addition to the door lock. These cost under $3 and take only five minutes to install. Attach them to the strongest surface near the door. Only in rare circumstances can they be attached strongly enough to resist a determined entrant, but they are a definite hindrance to illegal entry and provide peace of mind for tenants. Their use is highly recommended. You may also consider using deadbolt locks as another safety precaution.

For sticking locks and door knobs, your first approach should be a graphite lubricant sprayed liberally inside the mechanism to see if that eases the lock. If not, remove the entire lock mechanism to see if it operates apart from the door. If it does, the problem is likely caused by faulty alignment from shifting. To re-align the lock you will need to fill all the original holes. Use small wooden dowels or wooden match shafts dipped in fast-setting epoxy. Drive the dowels into all the holes, then cut them off and file the surface smooth. Re-drill the holes and replace the lock mechanism. You will find an electric drill works best when re-drilling since it has less tendency to cause splitting. You may also have to enlarge the hole for the key cylinder. Use a round file or round surform tool to enlarge holes. If you must drill a large hole in a door where none existed before, the easiest way is with an electric drill combined with a hole saw of the correct diameter. (You can find hole saws at any hardware store.) If you lack an electric drill, you can do the same job with a brace and a large bit, or with any size drill and a coping saw or a keyhole saw, finishing out the curvatures with a round file. It just depends on the amount of work you want to do to accomplish the same job.

Chain locks provide good protection against illegal entry.

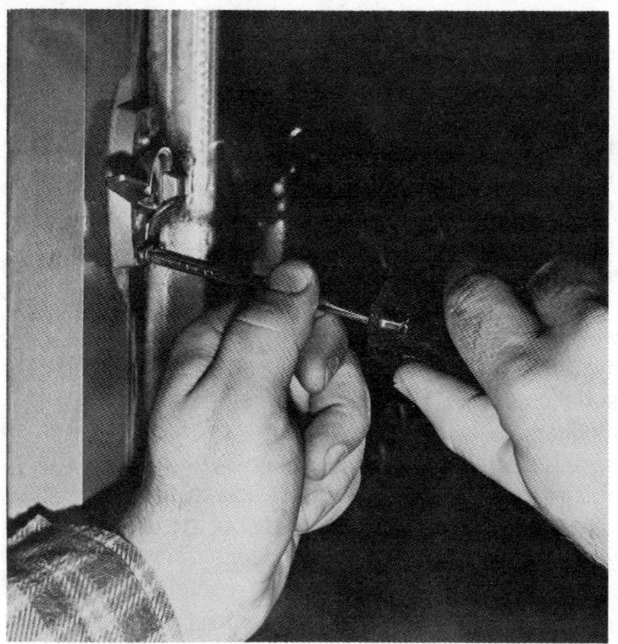

Remember to install locks on every window.

Door handles may have to be realigned or lubricated occasionally.

Bannisters and Railings

Railings and bannisters often become loosened from extensive use. This is especially true of handrails mounted by metal brackets. The brackets break or pull loose inside the wall, causing the plaster to break around the area. This must be repaired by opening the wall to provide a new anchor point inside. If the stud inside is split where the fastener pulled out, you will have to nail on a support 2 by 4 to add strength. Re-fasten the railing to the new wood surface and replaster the wall as described in "Walls and Ceilings."

For heavy bannisters in older buildings, check to see they are tight at all points. Where they are loose use epoxy and long screws to tighten. Decorative wood balls or other turned shapes often top these bannisters. They may become loose and turn or lift up. This presents a hazard and they should be re-set using epoxy or removed entirely along with any bolts or fittings underneath. Safety is the prime consideration. Good appearance is beneficial but of far less importance.

Cleaning an Apartment

Sometimes tenants will move out unexpectedly leaving behind a frightful mess. You can help minimize this by checking periodically to see tenants are being reasonably neat. Good references are often a help in finding out about tenants' past habits, but we have found even some tenants with the very best references vanish with the law in hot pursuit. Consequently, you may have a surprising amount of personal goods and trash to clean out before the apartment can be re-occupied.

If you find yourself with such a problem, the first thing to do is check both state and city codes to see what is legal in regard to personal goods. Some states require personal goods be stored for varying lengths of time before they can be sold. You will probably be required to write letters to the person's last place of employment and last known address. Some states place personal goods in categories, depending on value, with specific directives for each category. Be sure you understand all the laws that apply in your area and follow as many as you can to protect yourself.

Garbage, beer cans, etc., can be picked up in large plastic bags. Unless you have city garbage pickup that, by chance, is coming immediately, it is not a good idea to leave these bags out on the boulevard. Neighborhood dogs or cats will probably have everything strewn all over after one night. The only alternative is to have a place to store garbage until it can be picked up or, better still, have your own pickup truck and transport everything to the dump yourself.

installing a new lock

a. Remove worn out, broken, or low-security lock.
b. Remove latch of old lock.
c. Use template packed with new lock to mark area to be enlarged.
d. If a jig is available (as shown), use hole saw to enlarge area to accept new lock mechanism.
e. If hole requires only minor enlargement use a wood rasp or similar tool.
f. Cut away excess wood in edge of door, if necessary, to accommodate new latch plate.
g. Install latch.
h. Insert lock mechanism from outside of door.
i. Attach mounting plate on outside of door and snap on trim and knob.

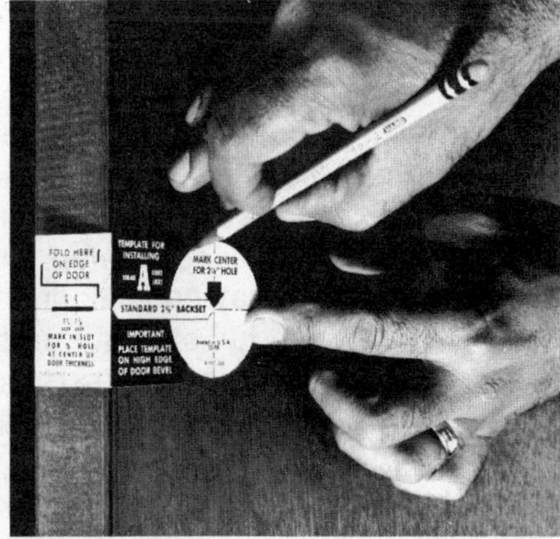

With all the trash and personal goods removed, thoroughly clean all sinks and lavatories using a combination of cleansers and strong detergents. Scrub linoleum or tile floors with a sponge mop, using hot water and a strong floor cleaner.

Refrigerators are often left unplugged and closed, causing bad odor problems. The market offers various deodorizing cleaners for such purposes. Remove all food items and scrub the inside thoroughly and leave the door open to air out. You may want to place a small deodorizing unit inside before putting it back into service.

Carpets, too, are often stained, with pet odors being especially troublesome. Even if you had specified "no pets," you may be surprised to find the tenants had one anyway. The carpets should be completely steam cleaned. The place where you rent the steam cleaner will supply you with several cleaning solutions. You should find one especially concentrated for pet odors. The suggested dosage may not work and you may have to apply the solution full strength on both carpet and baseboards if the odor is really bad. Allow the apartment to air out thoroughly for awhile. More than one application may be needed but eventually the odor will vanish unless the carpet was thoroughly saturated by un-housebroken dogs. You may have to replace the carpet if that has happened.

For carpet that is dirty and stained, deal with the stains first. If stains are exceptionally bad, you will rarely get rid of them entirely. Try the solutions recommended by a store that specializes in cleaning products, then decide whether new tenants of the level you hope to attract will accept the results. If not, you have three choices, depending on the location of the stain and the overall quality of the apartment. You can cut out and replace the stained section; you may be able to cover the area with a small decorative rug; or you can re-carpet the entire room (see "Remodeling").

After you have dealt with the stains, the remaining dirt will usually come out with a steam-cleaner. These are available at rental stores, carpet stores and hardware stores. Carpet or hardware stores often run specials, including free or greatly reduced rental fees for buying the cleaning compounds. Usually the rentals are for either one-half day or for a full day. It takes only a few minutes to clean a room, so you may be able to combine the cleaning of several units while you have the cleaner rented. The cleaning agents usually come in a series, including one for use directly in the machine and another for pre-treating especially dirty or greasy areas. These pre-treating compounds are effective, so try them for the worst areas. The steam-cleaning is really easy. The hardest parts are getting the machine into apartments, especially those with long stairways, and moving the furniture. Be sure not to put the furniture back until the carpet has completely dried. The metal bottoms on most furniture legs will cause rust spots on the carpet.

Another problem is the walls when cleaning apartments. Where tenants have fried foods extensively you may find grease spots. Ordinary detergents will usually remove the grease from tiled or enameled surfaces. On wallpaper, however, harsh detergents may damage it even more than the grease. Try a paste made from cornstarch and water. Allow it to dry completely, then brush it off. This usually works and is harmless to the wallpaper. If that fails, you will have to try light detergents. If grease continues to be a problem around stoves, consider applying a more easily washed wall covering near these areas. By following these techniques, you will keep the job of cleaning apartments to a minimum. (See also *The Building Primer* by Robert Taylor.)

SUMMARY

Exterior and interior maintenance on rental properties is a matter of constant concern. Since it is so expensive to have most of the work done by contractors and specialists, the landlord can save greatly and add to the value of his buildings by doing much of the work himself. With the exception of electrical connections, the field for experimenting and learn-as-you-go work is wide open for anyone ambitious enough to try. The prime factor to keep in mind is to be prepared for potential problems and have the tools and replacement materials handy when the need arises. If you are handy and prepared, you will have a big head start toward keeping any building attractive, comfortable to live in and, most of all, safe for your tenants.

6 Winterizing

With today's soaring energy prices, winterizing any building should receive the most careful attention. Those who live in the northern states should especially take note. It matters little whether the landlord or the tenants are paying for the heat. Tenants unhappy with their fuel bills may move out, causing as much trouble as the same high fuel bills may cause for the landlord. Some parts of winterizing are very inexpensive and provide an excellent way to build a better working relationship with tenants.

FURNACES

Winterizing should begin in late summer or early autumn with the heating system itself. With a forced-air system, measure the size of the furnace filters and purchase at least three spares for each furnace, putting them near the furnace where they will be handy. Whenever they become dark and clogged replace them. You will probably have to replace them about two or three times each season to prevent wasting heat from poor circulation.

In the furnace itself, oil the bearings of the blower and blower motor. This is a simple procedure that will provide a quiet furnace operation and prevent costly replacement of motors and bearings. Do not, however, use the aerosol cans of super-fine oil that have become so popular for squeaky doors and automobile parts. They lack the "body" to stay in the oil fittings found on bearings and motors. Instead, go to a good hardware store and invest several dollars in a pressure oiler with a trigger. Fill the oiler with number 20 motor oil and you will have a combination that can save you a small fortune in repair bills. All you have to do is use it two or three times each season. Look carefully on every motor, blower, or circulating pump (on hot water systems) for the cup-shaped fittings. These usually have a small spring-operated cap that must be held to fill the cup below with oil. Use a flashlight and look carefully to avoid missing any.

While the furnace door is open during oiling, check to be sure the blower belt is properly tightened. It should not be drum tight, yet there should be no noticeable slack. If the tension is incorrect, loosen the bolts (usually on the motor mount) and change the tension, then tighten the bolts. If the belt shows any amount of wear or has visible cracks, replace it now. With the belt properly tightened, apply a thin coat of belt dressing to the inner surface. Belt dressings come in either stick or squeeze-can. (The can is easier to use on a non-moving belt, which is usually when the dressing is used.) The belt dressing adds friction to the belt-pulley joint to prevent slippage and prolongs the life of the belt.

With oil-fired furnaces, the nozzles that inject the oil may become clogged occasionally. If the furnace has been operating erratically or going out, have a specialist replace the faulty nozzle. Clogged nozzles can be dangerous, so it is better to have a specialist deal with the problem.

Hot water systems have no filters to replace, but they do require a process called "bleeding the system." This should be done every month or so during the heating season to keep the water circulating properly. On the outside of the furnace you will find a faucet-like structure with a control knob. Put a catch-bucket under the faucet, then open the control knob until water flows out smoothly. This shows all the trapped air has been allowed to escape. There is no need to replace the water, since the heating system is connected to the building's water system and will refill automatically.

Each radiator also has an air vent somewhere near the top, usually with turn-screw to bleed out air. The radiators should be bled at the start of the heating system. Begin with the highest radiator in the building and work down, opening each valve until water starts to flow and then closing it tightly. Also, vacuum the grillwork on radiators to prevent layers of dust from acting as insulators.

In steam systems watch for a radiator that fails to heat. This is usually caused by a clogged pressure vent. Vents can often be cleaned by boiling them in a pan. If this fails, replace the vent.

Many people are unfamiliar with the operation of heating systems other than forced air systems. With thermo-

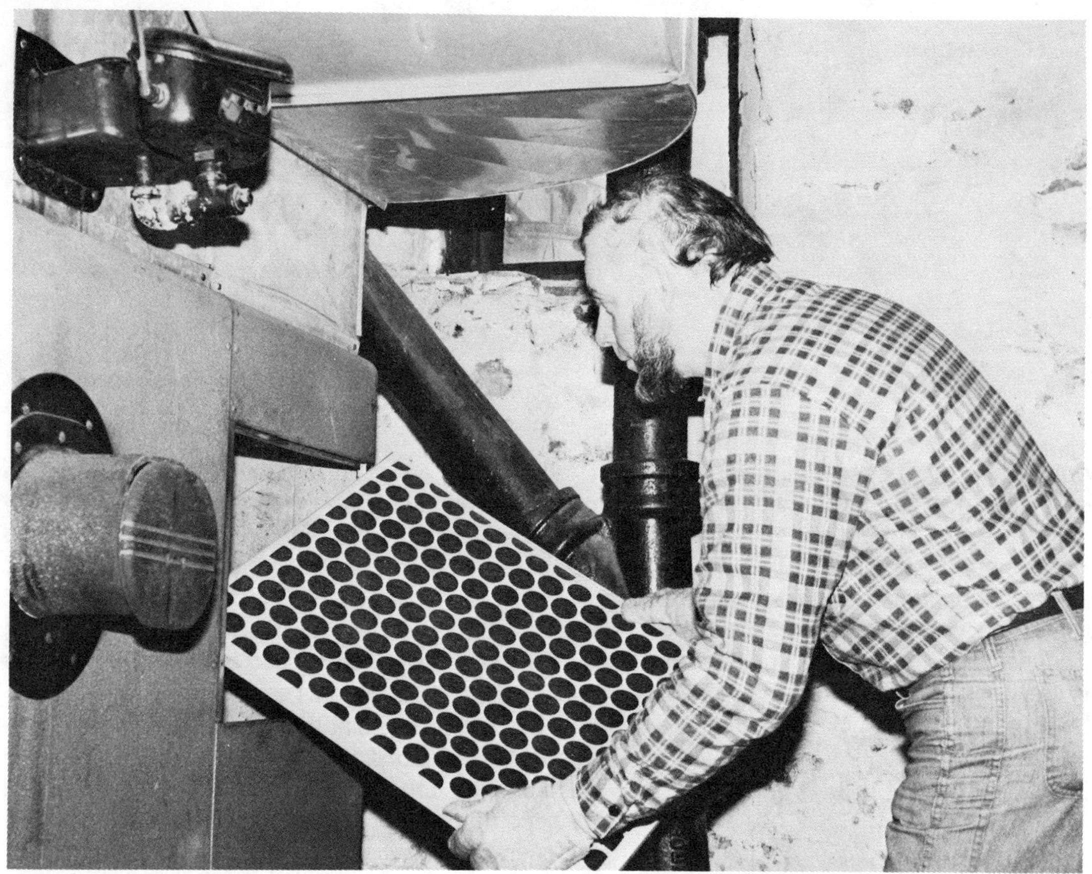

Replace furnace filters each season to prevent wasted heat.

Oil furnace motors and blowers periodically to prevent wear.

stats being lowered across the country, you may find upper units suddenly left without heat. The reason is with only one thermostat in a lower unit, (very common in older buildings). The lower unit heats to the temperature so rapidly no heat ever reaches the upper radiators. The problem can easily be solved by closing the valves on the lower radiators almost entirely. This allows more time for the heat to reach the upper radiators and equalizes the temperature. The system should then work very well.

Thermostats

Another consideration is the location and adjustment of thermostats. Surprisingly, thermostats often end up being poorly located. Be sure each thermostat is located on an inside wall with no heat source or drafty spaces to interfere with its operation. Windows close to a thermostat may cause it to start the furnace too frequently. Lamps or other heat sources nearby may prevent if from turning the furnace on. We learned several years ago to check for such problems when we received a call from tenants who were cold in one of our buildings. They thought the furnace had gone out. The building had three units regulated by one thermostat in a lower apartment. When we entered the lower apartment, the tenant was wearing a coat and our breath made a cloud. Glancing at the thermostat area, we discovered the tenant had turned on all four burners and the oven on the gas range in an attempt to raise the room temperature above the locked setting. A small area that included the thermostat had actually reached 92 degrees! This situation had kept the furnace from coming on and the rest of the building was down to 45 degrees. Needless to say, the relationship between the thermostat and the stove was promptly changed. Although it is not a large project to re-locate a thermostat, this should be done only by an experienced electrician or heating specialist. You may easily save the price of the service call in lower heat bills by re-locating a thermostat.

TEMPERATURE ADJUSTMENT

The entire heating system must be adjusted for maximum efficiency. Where the landlord is paying for the heat, it is unwise to allow tenants to adjust their own thermostats. Tenants seem able to remain totally unconcerned about energy costs and cheerfully set their thermostats at much higher temperatures than an energy-conscious person would select. The only answer is to replace older thermostats with locking models. You may have to search several heating supply stores before you locate them, but they will be worth your time and the installation cost (again, by a competent electrician or heating specialist) in just one season. Once installed, they are very simple to set. Several styles are available. One style has a locking plastic cover that completely encloses the thermostat. This style is the most tamper-proof. However, it prevents the tenant from turning the thermostat below the set level, perhaps wasting some heat on a few days in spring or fall. The other style locks only the control knob, allowing the landlord to set a maximum temperature and permitting the tenant to select any temperature below that maximum.

Either style can be of great use in saving heat and the serious landlord should give them careful consideration. When setting temperatures, you can use any current governmental guidelines, but remember to take into consideration the room layout and the height of the ceilings. A temperature that might be comfortable in a modern apartment with low ceilings may cause great discomfort in an older apartment with a combination of high ceilings and large windows.

INSULATION

Another major factor in winterizing is insulation. Many older buildings have no insulation at all. No one should pay to heat a building today unless it is properly insulated. Whatever your insulating costs, you will be repaid in a few years by the heat saved. Proper insulation also makes the building much more attractive to prospective buyers and, if tenants are paying for their own heat, much more likely to attract good tenants. Fortunately, many parts of insulating are very simple and require no experience.

Begin in the attic to see what insulation has already been installed. If the insulation is less than 6 inches, you should seriously consider adding more. You can select from loose filling, rigid panels or rolled blankets of fiberglass. The loose fill is usually the cheapest and easiest to install, but it settles and mats together over a period of time, reducing its efficiency. Rigid panels, such as the plastic foams, are excellent insulation but nearly impossible to get into an attic unless the opening is unusually large. That leaves the rolled fiberglass blankets as the best choice for placement between ceiling joists.

The rolled blankets are available in 56 to 70-foot rolls in widths to match the space between ceiling joists. With the new coding system, an R factor is used to designate insulating efficiency so you can easily make comparisons. An R factor of 11 is most common on fiberglass blankets that expand to a thickness of about 3½ inches. This is very good insulation. The rolls can easily be cut to length with an ordinary scissors, but for convenience, measure the length you will need to reach from one side of the attic to the other and cut as many as you will need at one time. To make the job easier, do your cutting in a room with a long flat floor. Cutting insulation this way will prevent you from doing a balancing act on the joists and chasing escaping rolls. The less balancing you have to do, the less your chances of unexpectedly ending up in a lower apartment. The fiberglass can be a great irritant to skin and lungs, so wear protective gloves and nose protection, such as a painter's face mask. The material should be pressed firmly between the joists, but needs no fastening.

Often old attics will have small sections boarded over. For any section four feet or less the insulation can be pushed underneath with a broom handle. For larger sections you will need to remove some boards to get at the space underneath. Where other irregularities occur, such as at electrical connections, or around chimneys and pipes, it may be necessary to fill in with some of the loose fill insulation that comes in bags. You might even find an attic that is completely floored over. If the attic is to remain unused, you can insulate by laying the roll insulation directly on the flooring.

If the attic is to be occupied, it will be necessary to insulate the upper portion between the rafters. Here, the blanket insulation must be stapled into place. If the walls and ceilings are already finished, insulation is available with a decorative side so it can be added right over any finished surface.

Staple or tack polyethylene vapor barrier between joists. Seal seams and holes with tape (Dept. of Housing & Urban Development).

If both your existing insulation and the added insulation have vapor barriers, cut holes in the new insulation's vapor barrier (National Mineral Wool Insulation Assn. Inc.).

This sequence illustrates the proper way to install insulation on the attic floor (see below). (1) Begin at eaves on one side and work between several rows of joists. (2) Push batts under eaves with long stick. Do not butt insulation tightly against eaves because ventilation there is necessary. (3) Pressing batts down firmly, work toward center of the attic. (4) Use same procedure on opposite end of attic working from eaves to center. (5) When you come to center of attic, cut insulation to fit, saving leftovers for unfinished rows. (6) Start new rows until job is complete. (7) Cut insulation to fit around obstacles. Do not cover vents, recessed lighting fixtures, or exhaust fan motors protruding into attic (Certain-teed Products Corp.).

(1)

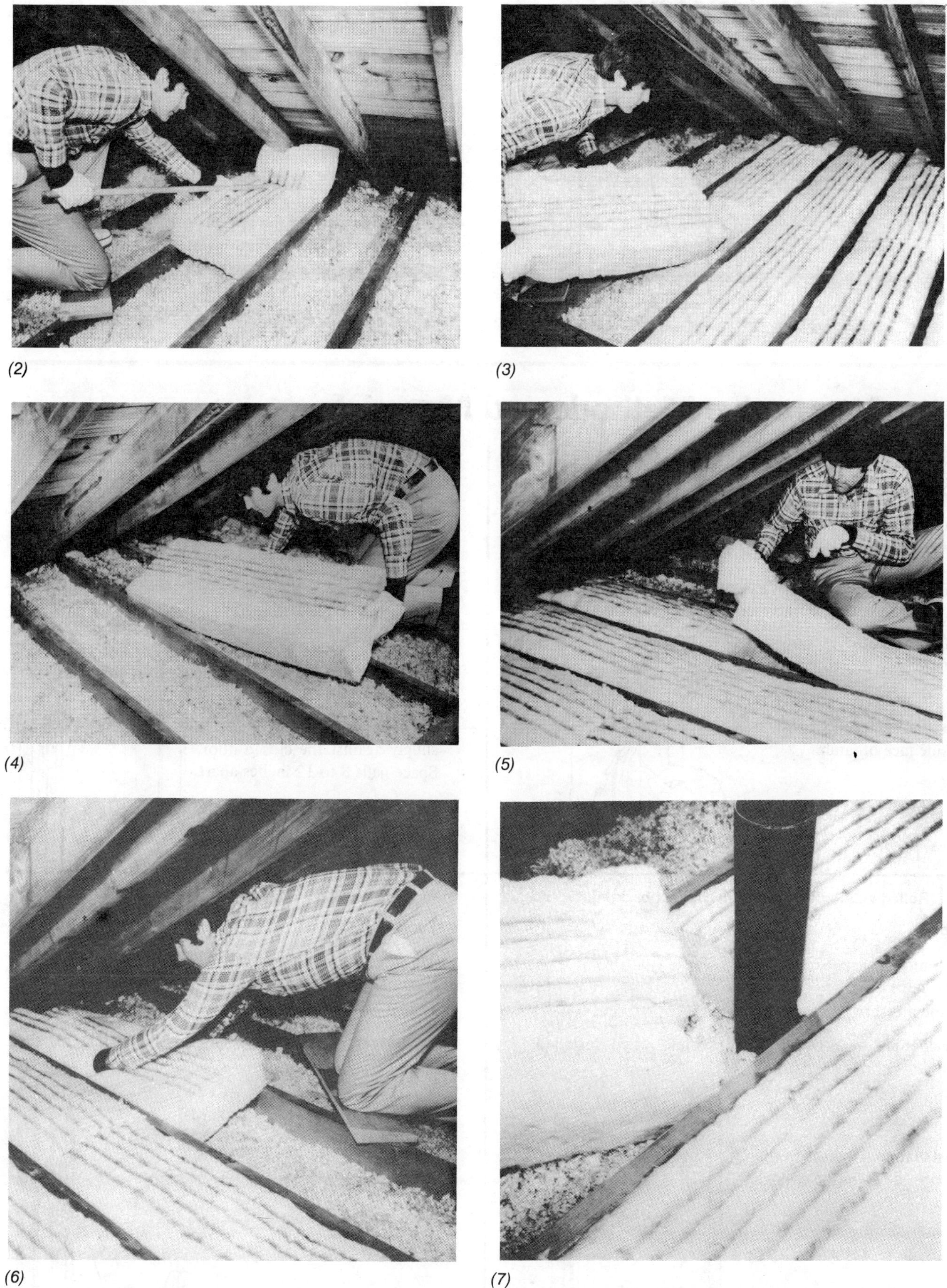

(2) (3) (4) (5) (6) (7)

WEATHERSTRIP YOUR DOORS

AN EASY DO-IT-YOURSELF PROJECT

You can weatherstrip your doors even if you're not an experienced handyman. There are several types of weatherstripping for doors, each with its own level of effectiveness, durability and degree of installation difficulty. Select among the options given the one you feel is best for you. The installations are the same for the two sides and top of a door, with a different, more durable one for the threshold.

The Alternative Methods and Materials

1. Adhesive backed foam:

Tools

Knife or shears,
Tape measure

Evaluation – extremely easy to install, invisible when installed, not very durable, more effective on doors than windows.

Installation – stick foam to inside face of jamb.

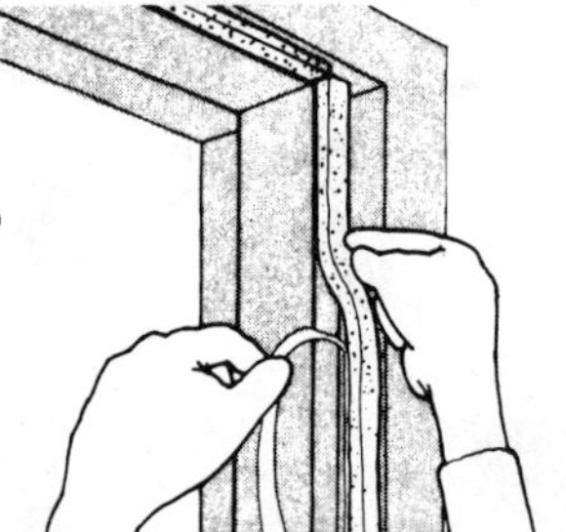

3. Foam rubber with wood backing:

Tools

Hammer, nails,
Hand saw,
Tape measure

Evaluation – easy to install, visible when installed, not very durable.

Installation – nail strip snugly against the closed door. Space nails 8 to 12 inches apart.

2. Rolled vinyl with aluminum channel backing:

Tools

Hammer, nails,
Tin snips
Tape measure

Evaluation – easy to install, visible when installed, durable.

Installation – nail strip snugly against door on the casing

4. Spring metal:

Tools

Tin snips
Hammer, nails,
Tape measure

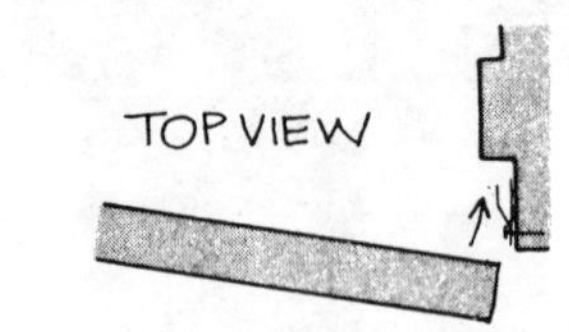

Evaluation – easy to install, invisible when installed, extremely durable.

Installation – cut to length and tack in place. Lift outer edge of strip with screwdriver after tacking, for better seal.

Note: These methods are harder than 1 through 4.

5. Interlocking metal channels:

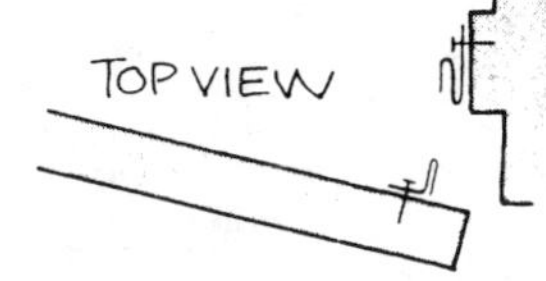

Tools

Hack saw,
Hammer, nails,
Tape measure

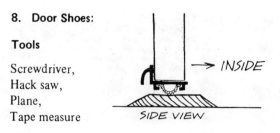

Evaluation – difficult to install (alignment is critical), visible when installed, durable but subject to damage, because they're exposed, excellent seal.

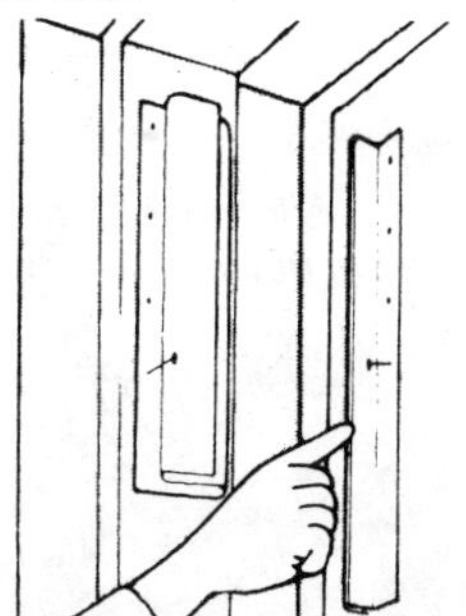

Installation – cut and fit strips to head of door first: male strip on door, female on head; then hinge side of door: male strip on jamb, female on door; finally lock side on door, female on jamb.

8. Door Shoes:

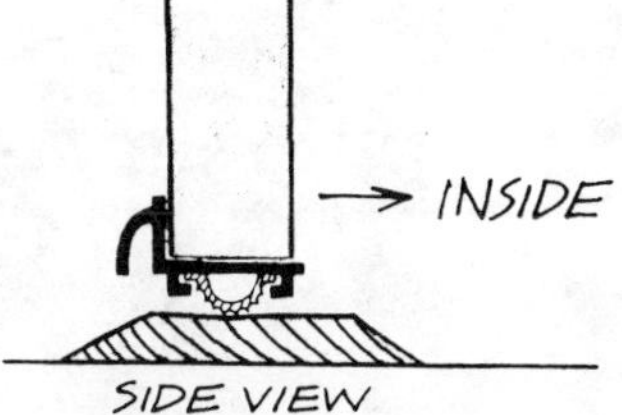

Tools

Screwdriver,
Hack saw,
Plane,
Tape measure

Evaluation – useful with wooden threshhold that is not worn, very durable, difficult to install (must remove door).

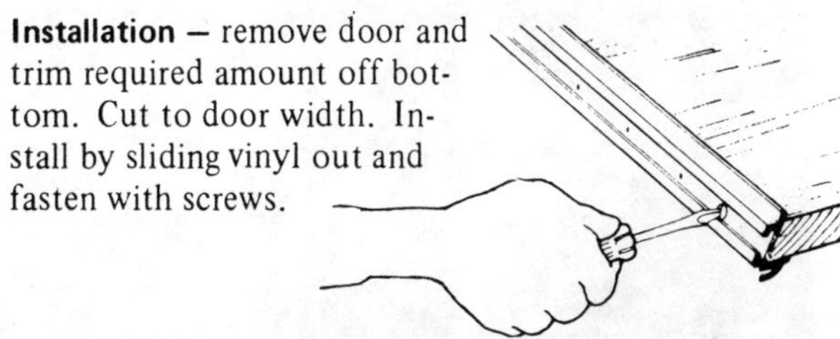

Installation – remove door and trim required amount off bottom. Cut to door width. Install by sliding vinyl out and fasten with screws.

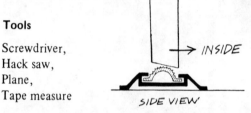

6. Fitted interlocking metal channels: (J-Strips)

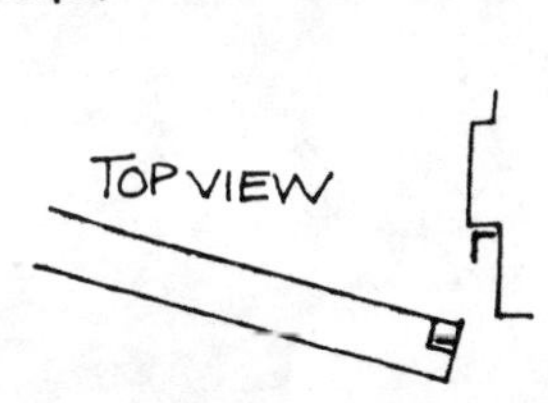

Evaluation – very difficult to install, exceptionally good weather seal, invisible when installed, not exposed to possible damage.

Installation – should be installed by a carpenter. Not appropriate for do-it-yourself installation unless done by an accomplished handyman.

9. Vinyl bulb threshold:

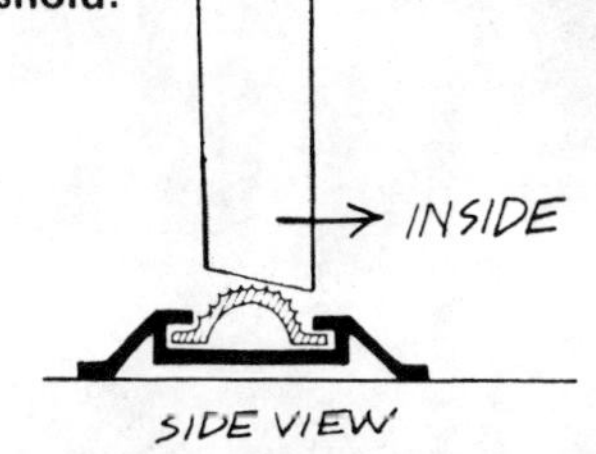

Tools

Screwdriver,
Hack saw,
Plane,
Tape measure

Evaluation – useful where there is no threshhold or wooden one is worn out, difficult to install, vinyl will wear but replacements are available.

Installation – remove door and trim required amount off bottom. Bottom should have about 1/8" bevel to seal against vinyl. Be sure bevel is cut in right direction for opening.

7. Sweeps:

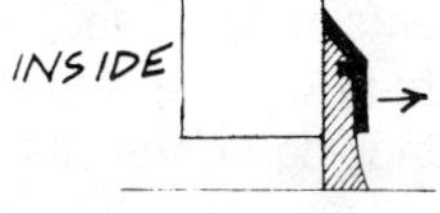

Tools

Screwdriver,
Hack saw,
Tape measure

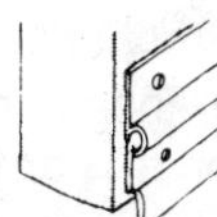

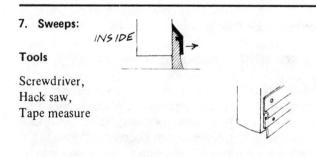

Evaluation – useful for flat threshholds, may drag on carpet or rug.

Installation – cut sweep to fit 1/16 inch in from the edges of the door. Some sweeps are installed on the inside and some outside. Check instructions for your particular type.

Source: Dept. of Housing and Urban Development.

10. Interlocking threshold:

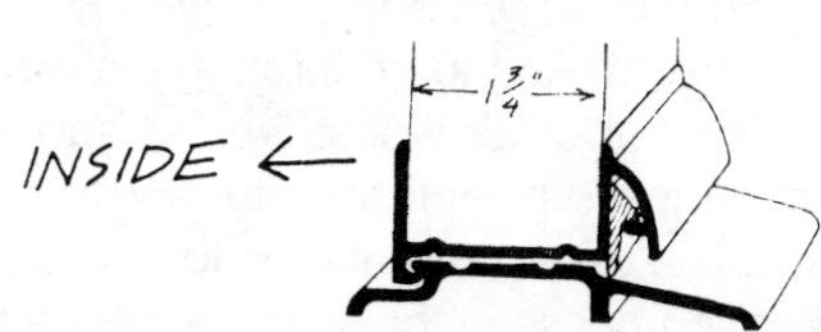

Evaluation – very difficult to install, exceptionally good weather seal.

Installation – should be installed by a skilled carpenter.

Adding plastic sheeting to patio doors or basement windows will greatly reduce heat loss.

Cut off plastic close to the wood strips to keep wind from pulling the edges free.

These decorative materials are not as yet available with the high R factor of the heavier blanket material, and should be used only where necessary.

For wall insulation, the problem is not so simple. If the walls are in very poor condition and you intend to re-do them anyway, you might want to go through the work of removing the plaster or other wall covering and do a thorough insulation job between the studs with rolled blanket insulation. The other alternative is to have a contractor blow insulation between the studs, either by raising the roof to get at the top or by drilling holes in the exterior siding. Get several estimates so you can decide if insulating will be worth the price. For anyone very ambitious, rental blowers are available so it is possible to tackle the project yourself. The ideal time to drill holes in the exterior siding, though, is just before residing. Otherwise you will have holes to fill or cover.

Sometimes an interior door is used as an outside door. This will mean the door has no insulation inside and may even be made of two sheets of thin veneer with only a few support pieces holding them together. You can easily tell if the inside is hollow by tapping or pressing firmly on the facing sides. If this is the case, or if the door is too thin to insulate properly, either replace it with an exterior door or, if appearance is not too important, insulate one side by nailing on a ¾ or 1-inch sheet of foam plastic. The plastic can be painted or covered with decorative fabric to improve the appearance. Check with the paint dealer to be sure any paint you use will not dissolve plastic, as some paints do have that property.

The next part of winterizing is to inspect the building carefully for air leaks. With all storm windows in place, check for windows that fit poorly due to rot or extensive shrinkage. Such areas can be repaired in several ways.

Small wood strips glued or nailed to the edges will restore wooden areas to size. Extensively rotted areas can be rebuilt with any of the automotive body fillers. With these, you can fill in or build up any surface. When the material has hardened, file or sand the new surface down to size and repaint. For other gaps or cracks, foam rubber adhesive-backed strips are available in a variety of sizes. These are effective while they last, but seldom last more than a season or so.

Check carefully around basement windows, since these are small and often overlooked. A surprising amount of heat loss can occur from these. Pretty appearances are often less important than conserving heat. You might consider covering basement windows and some of the other lower windows with plastic sheeting, especially where surfacesare wind-exposed. Sheet plastic covering is also a good idea for screen-enclosed porches and patios, even though they may be unheated. Just shielding a front door from wind can be a real benefit with tenants who are not always careful about closing doors promptly in cold weather.

Check carefully, too, to see all doors close tightly and fit properly at all points. Weather stripping is now available in an astounding array of shapes and materials. Foam rubber, neoprene, brass, felt and aluminum are all offered in rolls or strips to help reduce heat loss from door edges. All of these do help, but they are not all equally effective. Foam rubber is an excellent insulating material, but it is fragile and will not stand up well or stay in place very long unless it is protected. A more effective form of weatherstripping for doors is a roll of foam with a neoprene outer cover and a backing of thin aluminum sheet or thin neoprene with brass wires embedded inside. These are easy to install by nailing the backing to the door casing so the covered foam fits tightly against the door when it is closed. The plastic covered roll is visible, but the appearance is neat and the protection against heat loss is excellent. Brass spring strips are also easy to install and exceptionally long-lasting. While the brass strips may lack the insulating qualities of foam rubber, these can be bent out with a screwdriver to close gaps even in very poorly fitted doors. Nailed to the outside of the door frame, they are invisible when the door is closed and need no attention for many years.

Brass strips, felt strips and foam rubber can all be used effectively to prevent drafts under windows by nailing the strips to the sill. The material used will be very well protected, so the foam or felt stands up for many years. For small gaps around windows, plastic tapes are available to cover the gap with the least effort. Pay attention to even the smallest gaps, since the heat loss over a long winter can add up to many dollars.

Another place where heat loss can occur is ventilators in the basement. If ventilators are open, close them in the

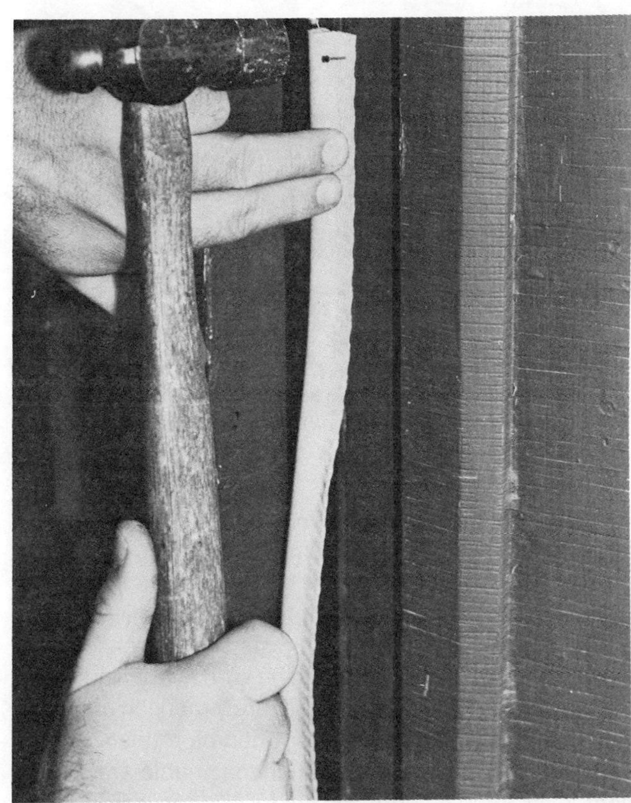

Weatherstrip all doors to seal out drafts.

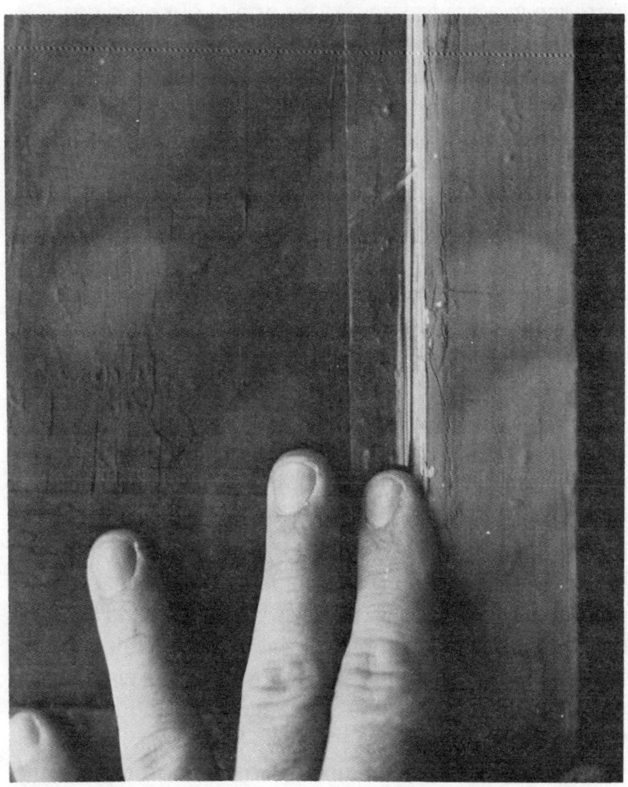

Gaps between storm windows and sill can be sealed with vinyl plastic weatherstripping tape, felt rolls, or foam rubber.

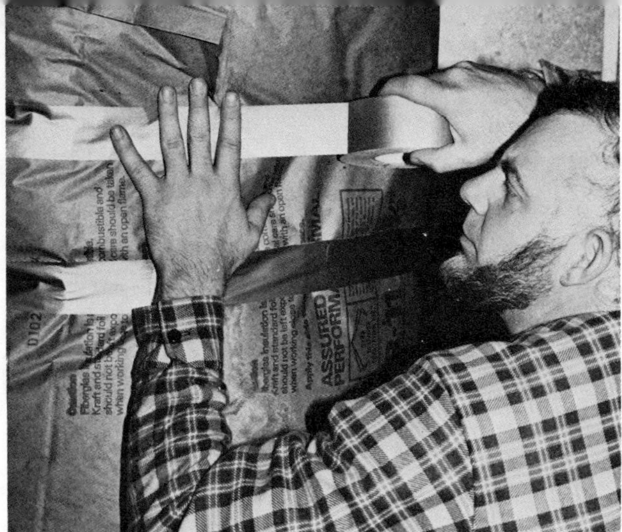

Wrapping a hot water heater with insulation can save up to 20 percent or more on fuel bills.

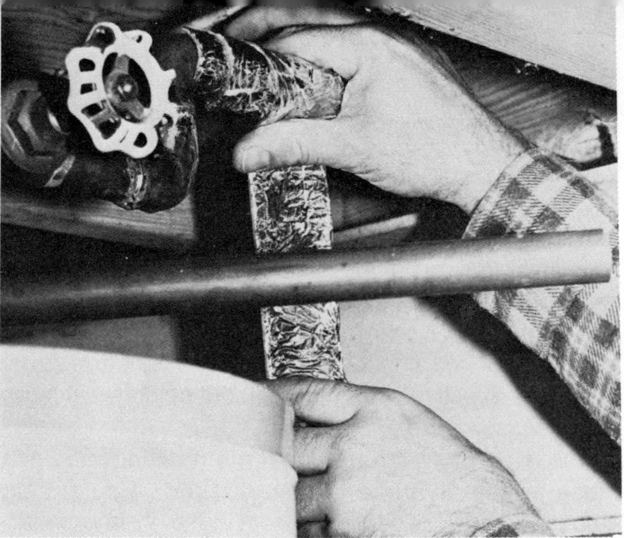

Insulating tape wrapped around hot waterpipes reduces heat loss.

winter. Since they rarely seal well, cut fiberglass roll insulation to fit and cover them from the inside. You can then be sure they are not losing any heat.

Remember you must check for all these things yourself, both when winterizing at the start of the season and at least once during the winter to be sure everything is still satisfactorily sealed. Tenants will rarely mention anything wrong until they are physically uncomfortable. By that time you may have wasted an unimaginable amount of heat. Also, keep a sharp eye out for sudden increases in heating or other utility bills if you are paying for these yourself. Several years ago we noticed an unexplainable increase in a natural gas bill for one of our buildings. On checking the building we discovered an unauthorized and (as it turned out) illegal gas space heater to provide extra heat in a basement. The tenant of a lower unit had connected the heater himself without bothering to mention it to us or even to consider the possible danger to other tenants from an improper installation. Dangerous conditions or wasteful changes can often be detected by comparing utility costs over a period of time.

Another consideration for winterizing is hot water heaters. In older buildings these may easily be 15 years old or more, designed when fuel was far cheaper than it is today. The insulation in these is totally inadequate. Wrap some fiberglass blanket material around the outside of each heater and tape it into place with duct tape. If the basement is unusually damp you may find light nylon or hemp rope will hold better. (If the heater uses gas for fuel, be careful not to wrap the top or bottom to cut off the air supply.) This procedure can reduce the fuel consumption of the heater by 20 to 30 percent. You can add to the savings by turning down the temperature of the water heater. Most are set for 140 degrees, but 140 degree water is not essential. If your heater has an adjustable gauge, reduce the temperature 5 or 10 degrees to save heat.

After completing a number of insulating projects and repairs, watch carefully to see the heating system provides uniform heat to all parts of the building. It may be necessary to re-adjust registers or radiators to distribute heat more evenly.

As a final phase of winterizing, prepare to deal with snow. Make arrangements with a tenant or a private party to shovel walks of larger buildings. Arrange for parking areas to be plowed. Look for roof areas where ice may build up. The investment in electric heat tape for such areas may be well repaid by preventing interior water damage. Insurances seldom cover water damage and the work of re-doing interior walls and ceilings can be very expensive and time-consuming. The heat tapes are easily installed by nailing them in a W pattern along roof edges. You must, however, have an electric outlet in mind where they can be plugged. After the tape has been installed, you can plug it in whenever ice begins to build up along the edges of the roof. They operate continuously, putting out just enough heat to melt the ice above. With all these projects properly completed, you can rest assured you have done everything possible to help conserve energy.

SUMMARY

More than ever before, a landlord must pay attention to conserving energy. Air leaks around windows and doors that might have gone ignored in the past now add up to a significant loss of profit in fuel bills. Check every energy-using device in each building to see if there is any way for the unit to operate more efficiently. Monitor fuel bills of every kind to check for possible changes in a building or to detect unauthorized appliances or hook-ups. Encourage all tenants to report any conditions that may be wasting energy. In most areas power companies offer free energy audits. Take advantage of this to help you find places where insulation may be inadequate or to locate parts of a building where you can save energy. All your efforts will be rewarded with lower energy costs.

7
Remodeling & Redecorating

One of the best ways to quickly realize a substantial profit in real estate investment is to buy a rental property which needs renovating and remodel or redecorate it according to its needs. This has always been a good way to realize a profit through real estate investment and it has received a lot of publicity. "Buy a run-down apartment building, fix it up and make yourself a mint," is a popular theme. Renovating run-down rentals is not as easy as it sounds, however, nor is it always as profitable. A number of pitfalls may trap the unwary investor who buys rental property with the intention of renovating it. Zoning, building codes, current condition of the property and the costs of building materials and labor are a few of these pitfalls. Despite all these problems, the careful investor can make a substantial profit through renovation of rental property. Several times we have remodeled or redecorated rentals and realized a healthy return. We have learned how to select property and how to apply a little creative ingenuity to cut costs. In this chapter we share some of the things we have learned about renovating run-down rentals.

FINDING A BUILDING

The first thing to consider when shopping for a rental to renovate is the zoning. Not every large older home can be converted to a multi-unit rental. In many communities zoning laws are very rigid and virtually unchangeable. We once located an older home that would have converted to an attractive duplex. The neighborhood was predominantly rental. In fact, there was a multi-unit next door to the property. Even then, however, the paper work and committee meetings necessary to request re-zoning of the property in question was prohibitive. Unless you have a great deal of time and patience and can afford to take the financial risk, you should buy a building which is already zoned for the use to which you intend to convert the property.

Also before purchasing the property check the building codes for the neighborhood in which the rental is located. Be sure that you can provide the required number of entrances, exits, hallways and living space for the number of units you plan to establish in the rental. It is better to take some time with the project before you actually buy the building than to purchase the building first and find you have a financial liability on your hands rather than the money-maker you had intended it to be.

When shopping for rental property to convert, you should look for a building with at least one habitable unit. The rent for this unit will help with the mortgage payment while you are remodeling the remainder of the building. A surprising number of buildings zoned for duplex have a remodeled lower unit and a sub-standard upper unit. These buildings were often built as duplexes in the 1930's so married children could live with their parents. Eventually, the children moved into the lower unit and closed off the upstairs unit. The upstairs apartment was used as spare rooms for guests or as playrooms for the third generation. The investor who finds one of these buildings and is willing to do some work on the property should realize a healthy profit when he sells the building. He should also enjoy a good cash flow while he keeps the building.

To insure maximum profit from the investment, the investor should look for several things in the building. The most important factor is plumbing. Putting in one bathroom (if both plumbing and fixtures are needed) will substantially cut into your profit. Units with acceptable bathroom plumbing and fixtures are the most desirable. You may decide to add a vanity to the bathroom, but that cost is minimal compared with the plumbing for toilet and tub or shower. Check the kitchen plumbing too. Almost certainly the kitchen sink and cupboards will have to be replaced to bring top rent for the unit, but if the plumbing is installed you will save several hundred dollars in kitchen remodeling costs.

Often buildings which were built to be occupied by relatives have only a partial bath upstairs. Some of these dwellings may even have shared cooking facilities. If this is true of the building you are considering, make sure there is adequate space for a larger kitchen or bathroom. Sometimes these older buildings have walk-in closets or pantries which can be converted to bathrooms or used to enlarge a kitchen.

Wiring is another important factor. Many of these older buildings do not have adequate wiring for modern tenants. You will almost certainly need to have a line run in for the kitchen range. You may also need new service run into the building. This can be quite expensive, so have an electrician look over the building before you purchase it. If you need to have additional service run into the building, but you still want the property, you can figure your additional cost into the purchase offer. This is better than being surprised by a large bill in the middle of your remodeling project.

REMODELING IDEAS

After you have found the right building, you will want to remodel it in an attractive manner so you can make the greatest amount of profit from the building. One of the simplest remodeling projects is the addition of a wall.

Walls

The addition of a wall can increase your cash flow on the property. One wall, for an example, can convert a one-bedroom apartment into a two-bedroom apartment and increase the amount of rent you can charge for the unit. When adding a wall make sure the partition runs at a 90 degree angle to the ceiling joists so you have something to use as a solid support at the top. Measure the area where you plan to put the wall. Determine the exact height from floor to ceiling. Measure both ends and the middle of the line so you can correct for a variance if there is one. When you know the correct measurements, you can build a frame from 2-by-4's. In a work area large enough to build the entire wall, stretch 2-by-4's along the top and bottom of the frame. Connect these horizontal 2-by-4's with vertical 2-by-4's (studs) at 16-inch intervals along the frame.

When the frame is complete, install it at the proper location. Fit the top into place first. Then hammer the vertical base into place. A heavy mallet or maul works best for this. As you are positioning the frame, make sure to consult your level periodically. This will help you be sure the wall is straight. After the framing is in place, drive nails through the upper and lower frame to anchor it firmly in place.

When the frame is anchored, you should cover it with gypsum board. There are a couple of techniques for installing gypsum board easily. Gypsum board cuts easily with a sharp knife. Score it, then snap it backwards away from the cut surface. Usually the board will remain attached by the paper backing. You will have to cut this paper backing with a knife or scissors. If your wall requires special shaped cut-outs for windows or electrical outlets, you should make them at this time. An old keyhole saw, a coping saw or a cutter blade in an electrical saw will work well for cutting these irregular shapes.

Gypsum board should be held in place on the frame by short nails with cupped heads. Use these nails because they will hold plaster better. When the gypsum board is in place, apply a layer of joint compound over the nailheads. A drywall knife works best for this because it is wide enough to spread the material smoothly. While the joint compound is wet, apply a strip of drywall tape followed by another thin layer of joint compound over the nailheads. Allow this to dry overnight then apply another coat. This coat should be feathered, that is, smoothed out in progressively thinner layers so the gypsum board is covered smoothly around the nail holes. When it dries you can apply a finish coat to the whole wall to create various textured effects. For applying the finish coat use a coarse paint roller, a heavy sponge or a trowel. After thinking about it, you may decide the pre-mixed plaster which can be applied with a paint roller is easier to use than the hand-textured plaster. Whichever you decide, when your last coat is dry your wall is ready to paint.

If you prefer, you may cover the new wall frame with paneling rather than with gypsum board and plaster. Discount suppliers often have paneling at bargain prices, but check to be sure you know what you are buying. Some paneling consists of a particleboard backing with a wood-print plastic or paper facing. The facing peels off easily, making this paneling more difficult to install than those with more substantial construction. Paneling with a plywood base will be much lighter in weight and easier to both transport and cut. Both types, however, are nearly impossible to cut with a handsaw. They cut easily with a circular power saw, as long as the portion you are cutting is properly supported. You will need a large table or a pair of sawhorses to support the sheets for cutting.

The cut panels are nailed into place with panel nails, which have a special gripping shaft and tiny heads. A nail set provides the right seating and the heads will fit flush or slightly lower so they can be covered with a putty stick of a color matching the paneling. Both types of paneling can also be installed with paneling glue, conveniently applied with the same frame you use for caulking windows. Follow the manufacturer's directions with the glue and you will find the panels really do stay in place permanently. Regardless of which type of paneling or means of installation you choose, do not butt the sheets too tightly together. The sheets will expand, with humidity changes causing buckling unless they have some room to move. This is especially true with the particleboard backed materials, so allow plenty of room for them to expand.

When the wall contours are irregular, the easiest way to cut paneling to fit is by using a scriber or compass. Hold a long sheet of shelf paper against the wall surface. With the scriber open part way, run it down the wall with the pointed end held tightly against the irregular contour. The line made by the pencil will be the exact pattern you will need to cut on the edge ot the paneling. Trace this pattern on the paneling. Use a keyhole saw or a coping saw for tricky contours.

When the paneling is all in place, decorative moldings will finish off the joints at ceiling, floor and edges. To splice sections of molding to cover long areas you will need a mitre box. These are available in several grades, but the ones built from solid wood will work fine for cutting a 45 degree angle on moldings. Moldings should be installed with finishing nails. Drive the heads just below the surface with a nail set and fill the hole with a matching putty stick. This gives a finished look that should appeal to the most particular tenant.

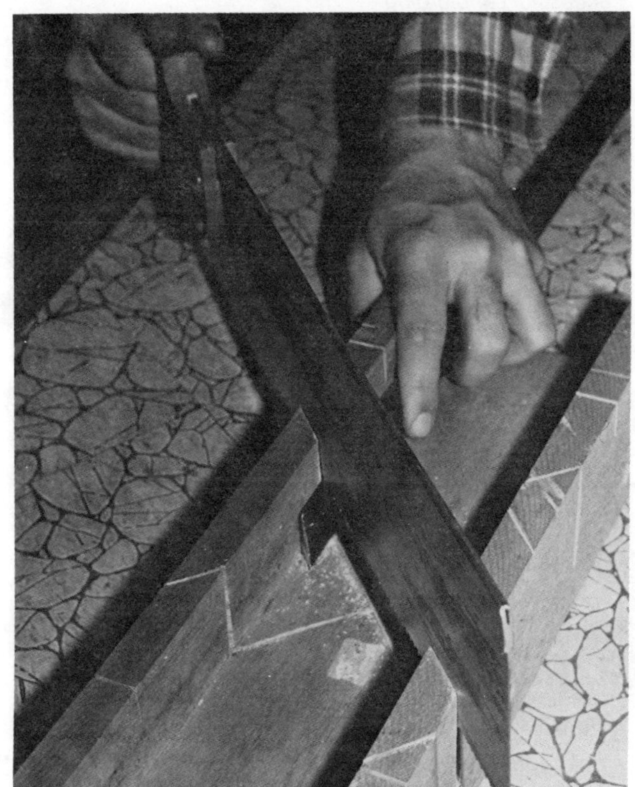

A mitre box holds the saw and molding for precise cuts.

Ceilings

As plaster ceilings age they tend to crack, sag and look unsightly. The problem can be solved by installing a layer of acoustical tile. If the ceiling is reasonably smooth you can install the tile directly over the old ceiling. Remove any loose paint or wallpaper first and install the tiles using an adhesive specially made for that purpose. If the ceiling is uneven or unsound, you will have to nail 1-by-3 inch wood strips (called furring strips) to the ceiling first. They should be installed at right angles to the ceiling joists and held firmly with 2½-inch nails. The tiles can be installed over these using small nails, staples from a staple gun or adhesive.

If the ceiling is badly cracked or buckled or is so high it provides an unpleasant feeling in the apartment, you can solve the problem with a suspended ceiling. These are time-consuming to install, but not too difficult. The approach to your first attempt at a suspended ceiling is to find a building center that carries the metal framing, the suspension wires and the acoustical tiles. Give them the dimensions of the room and they will provide all the materials and explain the technique. Then you will be able to decide if you want to tackle the project yourself.

Floors

By far the easiest of all floor coverings to install is carpet. If you select a carpet with built-in foam backing you can carpet an average size room in about an hour. For a good job you must remove all base moldings so the carpet can fit snugly against the wall. Use an old chisel to pry the moldings loose when they have been painted into

A nail set is used to drive a finish nail below the surface. The hole is then filled with putty stick of a matching color.

Upper apartment before starting remodeling. The unit was a good buy because it needed so much work.

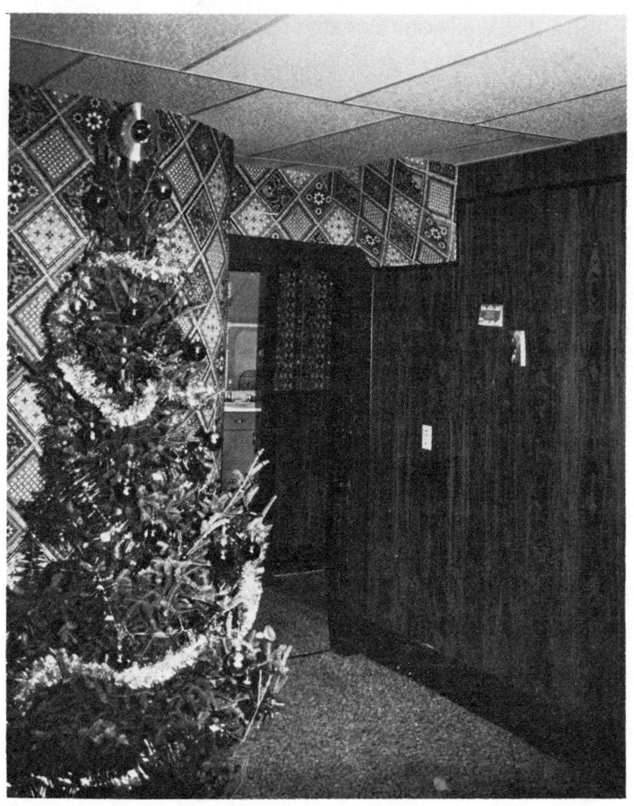

Carpeting, paneling, suspended ceiling and wallpaper have converted this area into a pleasant apartment. A space heater was removed and electric baseboard heaters substituted.

place. Sometimes moldings can be saved intact for reuse. Other times they will have become so brittle and paint-caked they must be replaced.

With the moldings off and the floor clear of all obstructions, roll out the carpet to cover the room, being sure it overlaps on every wall. Once the carpet has been arranged in its approximate position, remove all the wrinkles and stretch it as tightly as you can. Several techniques may prove helpful, depending on the amount of friction between the carpet backing and the floor, and also on the size of the room. If the room is small and the floor below is old linoleum, you may be able to remove all the wrinkles by standing in the center of the room and shuffling your feet as you walk toward each of the walls in turn. If this fails, start at one of the walls and roll the carpet back about two feet from the wall so you can straddle the rolled end with one foot on the floor below and the other on the carpet. Grasp the roll, pulling it toward the wall and slightly upward. Then, with your weight on the outer foot, kick hard against the carpet with the inside of your other foot. You should find the wrinkles disappearing.

If the room is very large or the friction is especially high under the carpet, roll the carpet all the way back to the middle of the room. Then unroll it again, a little at a time. Straddle the roll and walk up and down the length of the roll kicking with your inside foot at the point where the carpet leaves the roll. You will have to repeat the procedure on the other half of the room.

In large areas, you may want to put down several strips of carpet tape to keep the carpet from shifting. Two strips about five feet apart down the center of the room will be enough. Apply the tape to the floor, remove the backing paper and stretch the carpet tightly over it.

The tape can also be used to splice carpet together if the room is larger than standard carpet widths or used with remnants for small areas. Lay one piece of carpet in place. Lift the edge and place a strip of tape under the area so the seam will fall in the center of the tape. Remove the backing paper and fit the other piece of carpet tightly against the first piece. With both halves precisely aligned, walk up and down the seam to bond the joint. If you do make splices, keep them away from areas that will receive heavy traffic. If possible, arrange splices so a sofa or bed will cover the spliced area.

With all splices complete and the carpet held in place with carpet tape, cut off the edge evenly at the wall. A razor knife works fine, but you will probably need to sharpen it on a whetstone several times or change blades be-

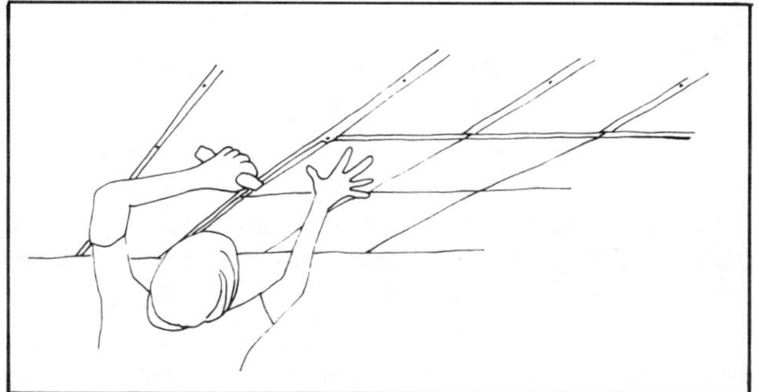

Ceiling tiles can be installed over furring strips or suspended from a metal framework.

fore you are finished. Special carpet edging tools are available, but unless you have a large number of rooms to carpet you can get by without one.

Wherever there are doorways, lock the carpet down securely with a carpet bar. Carpet bars cut easily with a hacksaw. Although the carpet bars come with screws, you will find them impossible to use with most carpets. Instead, use nails about 2 inches long and with heads large enough to absolutely prevent them from pulling through the holes.

When the carpet is trimmed, fasten it down next to the wall using either a series of small carpet tacks or a line of carpet tape around the entire edge. The last step is to replace the moldings. If the old ones are still intact, gently drive the nails back and re-install them. If the old moldings are too damaged to use, you can replace them with either pre-finished or unfinished moldings. If time is a factor, choose the pre-finished ones. Otherwise, you will use a surprising amount of time arranging the unfinished moldings on newspapers, painting them, cleaning paint brushes and waiting for the paint to dry. Moldings should be installed with small finishing nails, set with the nail set, and the holes filled with a matching putty stick.

Although light colors are best for walls, darker colors work out best for carpets. Select dark colors to help prevent dirt and stains from being too conspicuous. For living rooms and bedrooms you will probably have the best luck with either a short shag (¾-inch or less) or a sculptured short-nap. These wear well and are easier to clean than most other styles. For kitchens, special kitchen carpeting is available in a finish that cleans easily. Bathrooms tend to have more water spills than any other room. Thick foam-backed carpets hold water against the flooring. The result can be rot and musty smells that accompany it. The best idea is the acrylic short-nap carpet with a solid latex rubber backing. Cut it to fit and tack it down around the edges. The solid rubber backing helps keep any water from soaking through. If necessary, you can take it out to be machine washed at a laundromat.

You may also install linoleum or tile in kitchens or bathrooms. However, these are much more difficult and time-consuming to install, with linoleum being the most difficult of the group. For the cost difference, you might want to compare the following figures. These represent the very cheapest materials of each type offered by catalog stores. Each price is based on the cost for covering a 9-by-12 foot room.

Vinyl linoleum in roll form	$17.88 (plus adhesive)
Vinyl tile squares	$20.04 (self-stick)
Foam-backed carpet	$21.96 (plus carpet tape)
Carpet squares	$51.84 (self-stick)
Bathroom carpeting	$53.98 (latex-backed)

As you can see, the difference between the linoleum in rolls and carpet in rolls is minimal. When you add the price of the adhesive to the linoleum and the price of the carpet tape for the carpet, you will probably find the carpet a bit cheaper. The carpet squares are strictly out for apartments. Not only are they twice the cost of other floorings but they seldom stand up well under hard use. The bathroom carpeting seems very expensive, but bathrooms are usually far smaller than the room used for comparison. A normal sized bathroom can be carpeted closer to $30. Bathroom carpet does get hard use, though, so the price is justified for carpet that helps prevent bathroom problems. These figures, then, should help you in your selection of floor coverings.

Remodeling Problems

Older buildings, the kind investors often purchase with remodeling in mind, present unique problems for the remodeler. One of these problems is chimneys which jut into the room. One way to make a chimney attractive is to cover it with brick panels. A combination of contact cement and paneling nails, (which are specially hardened for brick or heavy plaster surfaces), make installation of the brick panels a simple matter. Add right angle corner trim to the edges and the finished job provides a very professional brick chimney effect.

Another problem encountered in the remodeling of older apartments, especially lower units, is high ceilings and large rooms. We tried to rent a lower apartment in a building which once had been an elegant home. The apartment consisted of one large room, which had been the front parlor, and the attached sun porch, which had been converted to be the kitchen. The ceilings were the usual 12 feet typical of homes of that period. The people who looked at the apartment said either that it was too huge or that they felt cold standing in the apartment. We could not rent the unit. Since we did not have the time or

Brick paneling gives a real lift to an old chimney.

money to lower the ceilings or to build partitions, we compromised. Short pieces of paneling (available at thrift stores) were used to build a four-foot solid partition between the sunporch-kitchen and the front parlor-living room. Four foot high turned posts were nailed to 1-by-2's to form a railing. This railing was placed on top of the solid partition. Because the posts were four feet short of reaching the ceiling, they were finished off with a 1-by-2 strip across the top. Even though the posts finished off at normal ceiling height (8 feet), it gave the impression of a lowered ceiling. The next couple who saw the apartment rented it. The entire project had cost us $40 and two hours time. The ingenuity of the idea made the difference.

While high ceilings are a problem in the lower apartments of some older buildings, low ceilings are a problem in the upper apartments of some of these buildings. Slanting ceilings may make the apartment seem smaller and more cramped than it actually is. When redecorating an upper apartment with sloping ceilings, be sure to keep the colors light. This will give a feeling of spaciousness to the rooms. Another technique is to panel the walls only half way up. Paint or paper the top half above the paneling. Paneling is often easier to use in redecorating because it will cover just about any imperfection in the walls. In an upper apartment with low ceilings, however, paneling may give the rooms a "closed in" feeling. We have found

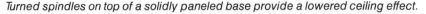

Turned spindles on top of a solidly paneled base provide a lowered ceiling effect.

that by paneling the bottom half of the walls for a wainscot effect, we can use paneling conveniently and prevent the rooms from appearing too small.

Financing Your Materials

One of the biggest problems in remodeling apartments is getting money for these projects. If you must take out a loan for the remodeling costs, the interest rates are often high. Also, the cost of remodeling usually is not recovered in one year, but must be written off over a period of years. The wise investor should look for ways of cutting costs while remodeling without sacrificing appearance or quality.

One of the ways to cut remodeling costs is to purchase materials through classified ads. We learned this the hard way when we compared the costs of our first two remodeling projects. For our first project we purchased all our materials through retail stores. For our second project, we purchased all of our materials through thrift stores and by answering classified ads placed in our local newspaper and shopper. The second project was twice as extensive (we remodeled the entire upper apartment of an older duplex) and it cost us one-third as much.

Paneling and other building materials are available through thrift stores. Although they are often odd sizes or slightly damaged, a little imagination will make them as usable as quality materials purchased retail. Our town has a warehouse for seconds and odds-and-ends left over from one of the major pre-fab contractors in our area. Check in your community to find out if such a center is available to you. Although the hours are not always as convenient as retail stores and you have to load and deliver yourself, the savings are usually worth the extra effort.

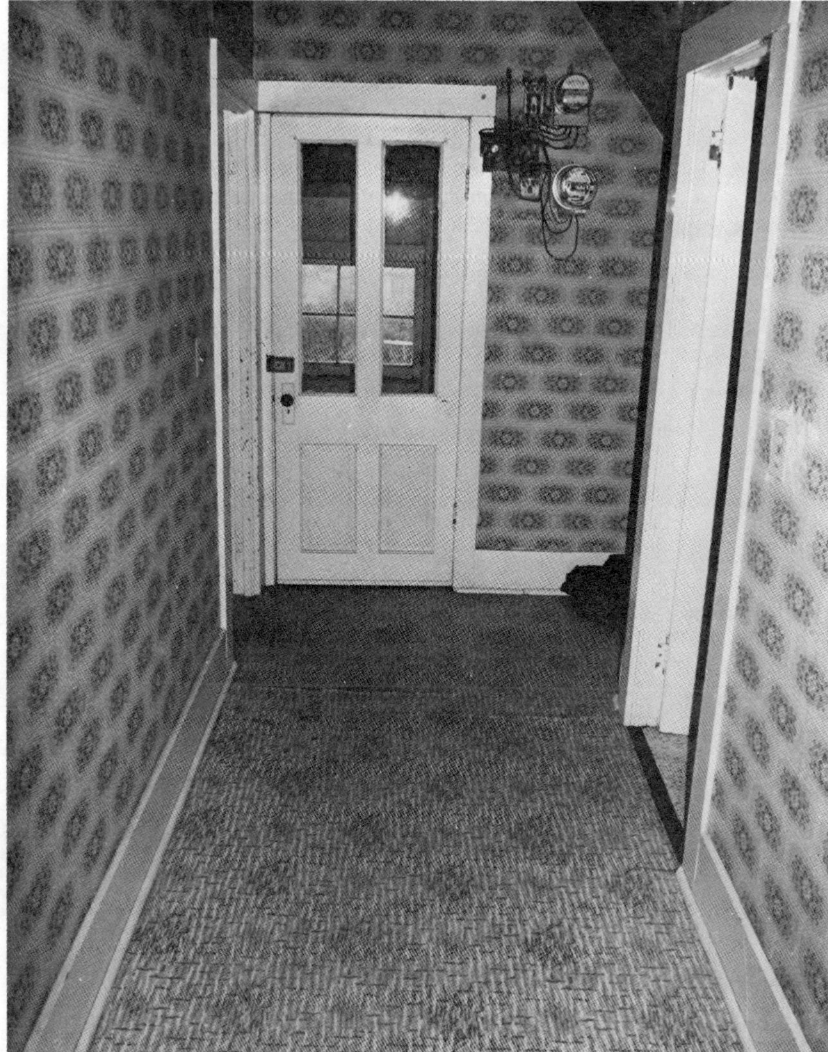

Wallpapered walls and slanted ceilings give a closed-in feeling.

Classified ads are an excellent source for finding building materials. If you are persistent enough you can find almost anything you need through the classifieds. You can often purchase kitchen cupboards and carpeting, two of the most expensive items in a remodeling project when they are purchased retail. You can often cut your costs by 50-75 percent on these items if you purchase them from private individuals. Just one word of advice: if the item is what you want, don't hesitate to buy it. These materials move very rapidly. We have been known to knock at a seller's door at 7 a.m. We purchased 16 feet of cupboards, top and bottom with sink, faucets, countertops and extra closet for $85. When purchased new from a retail store, the similar cupboards sold for more than $600. We thought the savings made our extra effort of shopping at 7 a.m. worthwhile.

Many apartments, especially upper units, rent easier with stoves and refrigerators provided. Appliances are another item which are often available inexpensively through classified ads. We have purchased like-new appliances for next-to-nothing by answering classified ads. This is the exception, however. Often the appliance shows wear. Since new appliances are costly, you should consider purchasing used appliances for some apartments. Try to fit the appliance to the apartment. It makes no sense to put a tiny refrigerator into a three bedroom apartment, for example, nor should you pay for a large refrigerator which will cramp the quarters of an efficiency apartment.

One of the problems with refrigerators has always been the sealing gasket around the door. The factory-installed plastic gaskets eventually dry out and crack off, leaving uninsulated gaps around the refrigerator door. If you can locate an older refrigerator with an operating motor and compressor, but without a good gasket, you can make it a usable refrigerator for very little money. If you check at an appliance center, you can get a new gasket for $15-20 and a two month wait. But for one dollar and

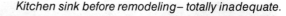

Kitchen sink before remodeling– totally inadequate.

three minutes time, you can replace the gasket with light gray foam weather stripping. Weather stripping is available at numerous stores. Just cut the old gasket off with a sharp knife and run the new weather stripping around the same place. The weather stripping is adhesive-backed so installation is easy. Before we discovered this technique, we turned down many good buys on refrigerators because the original gasket was worn.

Once you have located appliances to install, the trick is to get them into the apartment. Some cities have a delivery service that may be well worth the price they charge. If your city lacks one or you prefer to do it yourself, you will need a vehicle capable of hauling the appliances, usually a van or a pick-up. You may rent a truck, but this is seldom economical unless you have several appliances to deliver at one time.

The key to moving appliances is an appliance dolly. All the one-way truck and trailer rental places carry these for rent. If you have stairs to go down, use the braking system on a dolly. This is a belt stretched loosely on a pair of rollers that can increase the friction against stair edges. To use the brake, just tilt the dolly handles downward until the belts press against the step. This gives you some control, both to keep from banging the appliance around and to make sure the whole unit knows who is boss.

Before attempting to pull a large refrigerator up a long flight of steps be sure you have someone to help in case you run into difficulty. Mid-stairs is not the place to find that you have expended all your energy. You can't just walk away from the unit to take a break.

Taking appliances down a steep flight of stairs can be dangerous. This poses no great difficulty if the stairs are wide enough, but often stairs are so narrow the dolly wheels may not be stopped by the step below. If they bounce off a step it will be unlikely you can stop the unit before it is completely out of control and charging for the bottom. The logical approach is to hire a moving company or furniture store to do it for you. If that proves to be

Just $85 provided this sink and cupboards, found in a classified ad. Definitely an improvement.

impossible, find someone reasonably husky to stand on the top step braced with a rope to the dolly. Most important, make sure no one is on the steps below the unit.

Although you can cut corners in a number of ways, remodeling an apartment is expensive and time-consuming. If you also have other full time employment, the time involved may make you wonder if you are making any real financial gains. On the other hand, it is usually difficult to find someone for short-term remodeling. The expense of hiring cuts into the final profit. An alternative to sacrificing your free time or your profit is to find renters who are willing to help you remodel the unit. If you do decide to make such an arrangement with renters, you should enter into the agreement with caution. Make sure the renters are competent to complete the necessary work. You will probably want to work with the renters on the remodeling. If a reduction in rent is the agreement, you should have a written agreement drawn up to cover the period of remodeling.

SUMMARY

Remodeling an older apartment can be a good means of increasing both the cash flow from the unit and the ease of finding renters for it. Before beginning any remodeling project, however, remember to check on the zoning to be sure your plans are legal. Get a building permit for any major changes to the building. To reduce the high cost of remodeling try to do as much of the work yourself as you can. Compare prices of the materials you select, trying to find as many as possible through classified ads or at thrift stores. By doing this you can keep all material costs to a minimum. Where tenants or independent workmen are to do some or all of the work, be sure you have a written agreement. Be sure, too, that the party doing the work is very clear about where materials are to come from. Are they to be supplied by you or by him? The quality and price can vary enough to cause real problems if these details are left open.

8
Tax Shelter

One of the major advantages usually cited for real estate investment is the tax shelter. The investor is entitled to a number of business deductions. Although some of the tax laws have changed and others are likely to change, the government will probably continue to encourage landlording through tax incentives. The investor who knows tax law and itemizes carefully can shelter a portion of his actual income. The following information is intended as a guide only. Every investor should regularly seek the advice of a competent tax specialist in the area of real estate tax law.

The obvious deduction is, of course, maintenance costs connected with the building. Utilities, gardening fees, and repair costs all should be carefully itemized and claimed against the actual income of the rental. Remodeling costs are also deductible, but they may have to be written off over a period of years.

Also connected to the maintenance of the building are the trips made to the apartment. Any time you answer a tenant complaint, pick up rent or make a repair, you should record the trip. The mileage from your house to the apartment can be deducted at the annual rate allowed by law.

These deductions are all money actually spent. They do not shelter income. (A tax shelter is a deduction which shields income from taxation.) Other deductions which do work to shelter income are deductions of home phone, office space and depreciation of the rental. If you have a number of rentals, you can deduct a portion of your home phone bill because you use the phone in your business. You may also deduct the cost of maintaining a home office for the same reason. Although the home office deduction has been carefully scrutinized in recent years and is not always allowed, you should discuss the possibility of such a deduction with your accountant. You should remember the home office is a place where you conduct your business. The room should not double as a family room or a bedroom.

The deduction that really shelters income is that allowed for the depreciation of property. While the value of your property inflates yearly with the rate of inflation, you can depreciate the property according to a depreciation schedule. You should remember only the improvements on the property are depreciable. The land is not depreciable. Improvements (rental, garage, shed, etc.) can be said to "wear out," thus they lose value. Land does not lose value, and it cannot be depreciated.

Depreciation is usually figured from the cost of the building and the projected financial life of the building. The projected financial life of a building is determined by tax law. In the past, the financial life of the building was figured at 20 to 30 years. Recently that figure has been changed to 30 to 40 years. Depreciation which is figured from the value of the improvements and the projected life of the improvements is called straight-line depreciation. An example of straight-line depreciation follows.

> Investor Smith buys a rental which has improvements valued at $60,000. He depreciates it over a 30 year period. He writes off $2,000 each year as depreciation.

$2,000 (Amount allowed for depreciation yearly)

(Financial life) 30) $60,000 (Value of the improvements)

In some cases, (such as in the case of a new building), the investor may accelerate the depreciation, thus regaining his investment earlier than he would through a normal rate of depreciation. An example of accelerated depreciation is the double declining balance depreciation. (There are also other methods of accelerated depreciation.) With the double declining balance depreciation method, the investor writes off twice the amount he would be allowed if he were to use the straight-line depreciation. The amount of depreciation allowed, however, is figured each year on the balance rather than on the original value. The following is an example of double declining balance depreciation.

> Investor Smith buys a rental which has improvements valued at $60,000. The building is new and he is allowed to use double declining balance to depreciate his property. The first year he divides $60,000

by 30 years for \$2,000—\$2,000 is approximately 3.3 percent of \$60,000. Since he is accelerating his amount of depreciation, he is allowed to write off twice 3.3 percent of \$60,000 or 6.6 percent of \$60,000 the first year.

\$60,000	\$60,000
x.066	−3,960
\$3960	\$56,040

The second year Investor Smith would use the balance \$56,040, as the base for figuring his depreciation rather than the original valuation of \$60,000. He would multiply \$56,040 x .066 and arrive at the sum of \$3698 as the amount he can deduct for depreciation for the second year that he owns the property. Investor Smith continues to figure his depreciation in this way until he has realized the entire value of his property.

If you are allowed to choose an accelerated rate of depreciating your investment property, you should remember you receive the advantage in the early years of your investment. With double declining balance depreciation, you will eventually reach a point where you will be writing off less each year than if you had taken straight-line depreciation. In the case of Investor Smith, after 10 years he begins to write off less than he would if he were taking straight-line depreciation. If you know you will have more income to shelter now than you will have 10 years from now, accelerated depreciation is to your advantage. If you plan to sell the building in a few years and want to receive the maximum shelter of your current income, then accelerated depreciation is to your advantage.

Sheltering current income is not the only factor to consider when you are choosing a method of depreciation for investment property. You must also consider your plans for selling the property. When you sell property you have depreciated according to a straight-line depreciation method, your income from that sale is figured from the depreciated value of the property. That income is subject to the capital gains tax law which says you must pay your regular rate of income tax on 40 percent of the income. The other 60 percent of the income is tax-free. The following example explains this situation.

Investor Smith decided to depreciate his rental valued at \$60,000 using the straight-line method of depreciation. He wrote off \$2,000 each year against the original valuation. At the end of five years he had depreciated the building \$10,000 (\$2,000 each year for five years). This leaves \$50,000 remaining to depreciate. He then sells the building for \$70,000. His profit from the sale is figured from \$50,000 because he has already regained the \$10,000; therefore, he is said to have made a profit of \$20,000. This profit of \$20,000 is subject to the capital gains tax. Sixty percent of it or \$12,000 is tax-free. Forty percent or \$8,000 is taxed at investor Smith's regular rate of income tax.

Let's say instead, that investor Smith is allowed to take the double declining balance method of depreciation. At the end of five years, he has depreciated the building \$17,351. This leaves a balance of \$42,649 remaining to depreciate. He then sells the building for \$70,000. His profit is figured from \$42,649 rather than from the original valuation of the property; therefore, he is said to have made a profit of \$27,351. Part of this profit is subject to capital gains tax. Another part of the profit is taxed at investor Smith's regular rate. In order to figure the tax owing on his profit, investor Smith must subtract \$20,000 (the profit he would have made had he used straight-line depreciation) from \$27,351 (the profit he made because he used double declining balance). He then figures his tax on the \$20,000 according to the capital gains tax law. He figures his tax on the remaining \$7,351 according to his regular rate of income. The additional amount he was able to claim because of accelerated depreciation is taxed when the property is sold.

The wise investor understands tax law and uses it to his advantage when he buys and sells or keeps an investment property. He also takes advantage of all the tax incentives available to him to increase his margin of profit from his investments.

SUMMARY

The wise investor understands tax law and uses it to his advantage. As an investor, you should keep careful books so you have a record of all of your actual expenses (utilities, maintenance, trips to the rentals). These expenses should be deducted from the income of the rentals. You may also be able to deduct the expense of maintaining a home office and a telephone for your rental business. You should consult with your accountant about these deductions. The third kind of deduction the real estate investor is allowed is one for the depreciation of his rental property. Usually this depreciation is written on straight-line depreciation, but in some cases the investor may be able to use double declining balance or another means of accelerated depreciation. The type of depreciation you use depends upon the building and your entire economic picture. Depreciation is the deduction which actually shelters real income, and you should analyze your situation carefully if you are allowed to choose depreciation methods.

9
Tenants' Rights

The tenant-landlord relationship and the concept of tenants' rights dates back to the time of feudal England. During the feudal period, the tenant leased land from the owner. The owner's responsibility ended when he provided the tenant with a specified piece of land in exchange for a specified fee. The tenant's rights included the right to use the property and to pay the rent.

This relationship came to the United States with landlords and tenants. For centuries this landlord-tenant relationship remained unchanged. Then in the 1960's when the rights of many social and consumer groups in the United States were re-evaluated, the relationship between landlord and tenant began to change. Laws regulating terms of occupancy, condition of the building and payment of rent and security deposits were written and enforced. These laws continue to be expanded and modified. They vary from state to state. The wise landlord understands the laws governing the tenant-landlord relationship in his state before he ever rents his first apartment. These regulations are discussed generally in this chapter.

Check the state statutes for the specific laws in your state. These volumes are available in the public library. If you have any questions, you can call the city attorney's office for an explanation of the law. Sometimes the city attorney's office will also have a pamphlet on tenants' rights available. This pamphlet discusses the state laws in layman's language and should clarify any questions. A third alternative is to make an appointment with your attorney and discuss the law with him.

AREAS OF CONCERN

One of the areas where you must be careful in your dealings with tenants is that of evictions. Procedures governing evictions are specifically outlined. Tenants must be duly notified of the eviction according to the state's regulations. The amount of time given the tenant to leave the premises varies with the reason for the eviction. If the tenant should fail to comply with a properly served eviction notice, the landlord must proceed through the courts to complete the eviction. A tenant does not have to leave the premises until the court requires him to do so. Only after a favorable court decision may the landlord regain access to the apartment. Although it is tempting to move the tenant's possessions onto the street and lock the tenant out of the building, this practice is probably prohibited in your state. If the reason for the eviction is nonpayment of rent, an eviction notice will usually result in payment of rent within the specified time. If it does not, you should consult your attorney and proceed with the eviction.

The physical condition of the building is another area of the tenant-landlord relationship governed by law. In many states the property must be maintained in a habitable condition. If repairs are not completed by the landlord after proper notice is given by the tenant, the tenant may assume responsibility for the repairs and deduct the cost of these repairs from the rent.

If the landlord agrees to provide the utilities, he cannot shut them off because the tenant has not paid the rent. He must go through the courts to evict the tenant.

Another area of landlord-tenant relations regulated by law is the security deposit. In some states the amount the landlord can require as a security deposit is restricted. Also, in some states the landlord must pay interest to the tenant while he holds the security deposit. It is a good idea to establish at the time of rental the conditions under which the landlord can use the security deposit. This prevents problems later.

There are also laws regarding discrimination. The Fair Housing Act of 1968 and its amendments state landlords cannot refuse to rent to a person on the basis of his color, religion, sex or national origin. A previous act stated a landlord could not refuse to rent to a person on the basis of his race. The Fair Housing Act does exclude some landlords from these policies, however. Check the law for specific examples.

Landlords do have the right to refuse to rent to tenants for reasons other than race, color, sex, religion or national origin. As a landlord you can decide you will not rent to people with pets or to couples with children. You can set a limit on the number of people who will occupy your apartments. There are numerous reasons you can use to justify your refusal to rent to a particular tenant.

Perhaps future regulations regarding the tenant-landlord relationship will become even more complex with additional truth-in-renting statements, rent controls and discrimination clauses. These restrictions should not deter the landlord from conducting and increasing his business. The wise landlord knows and follows the law and avoids embarrassing encounters with the tenants.

SUMMARY

Although at one time all the landlord was required to guarantee was the right to the "quiet enjoyment" of the rented property, today the landlord-tenant relationship is governed by a number of regulations. The wise landlord is aware of the laws concerning landlord-tenant relationships in his state and abides by them. These laws outline the proper procedure to follow in collecting security deposits and in evicting tenants. These regulations vary from state to state, and you should check with the city attorney's office in your town if you have any questions concerning your rights and responsibilities as a landlord. The Fair Housing Act of 1968 prohibits the landlord from discriminating against prospective tenants on the basis of race, sex, color, religion or national origin.

10
Selling Rental Property

Another aspect of managing rental properties is selling the properties. Effective selling of income property is as important to successful landlording as creative financing or establishing cordial relations with the tenants. Today many landlords buy property with the intention of holding it for a short time before reselling it. They negotiate the purchase of the property with the assumption they will make their profit through the resale of the property rather than the cash flow from the property while they own it. You will often hear the statement, "You really make money when you sell," or "the real money is in the selling not the holding of real estate." Selling property is not the only way to make money on real estate, but it is one way to make a substantial return on your investment. Several factors influence the amount of profit you can expect to make by selling income property. If you consider these factors carefully before you sell and during the negotiations of the sale, you can increase your chances for a healthy return on your investment.

The first thing to consider when you decide to sell a rental property is the timing of the sale. Ask yourself if this is the best time to sell your property. To answer this question, you should ask yourself two other questions:

1. How does the property fit into my overall income picture for the year?
2. What is the market like for the kind of property I have to sell?

To answer the first question, consider the following items:

1. How long have you had the property?
2. What is the equity in your property?
3. What income is the property actually generating?
4. What is your other income or expectations of income for the year?
5. What reinvestment opportunities are available to you?

The best source for the answers to items 1 through 4 is your income tax record. The itemized sheet is a record of your actual and paper losses on the property. It also indicates the way in which the gains and losses on a particular piece of property fit into your entire financial profile.

There are almost as many interpretations of this information as there are investors, but two of the more usual schools of thought are:

1. Offset an actual monetary gain with a paper loss.
2. Sell at a profit when other income is low and sell at a loss when other income is high.

Many investors strive for an actual gain, however slight, coupled with a paper loss on the property. The paper loss usually comes when depreciation of the property is subtracted from the rental income. This loss is then subtracted from the income the investors receive from sources other than the property. The longer an investor owns a property, the greater the net income is because the rents increase while the mortgage payment remains constant. Eventually, he will realize a real profit. When this happens, many investors believe the time is right to sell the property and invest again in something that will show a paper loss.

Many investors find their personal incomes fluctuate. Real estate investments attract families with two incomes, builders and real estate brokers. Fluctuations in the building market and real estate market are expected, so many people in these fields experience fluctuations in their incomes. Two income families often become one income families when they decide to have children, when one partner returns to school, when a family member experiences a serious illness or for a variety of other reasons. Since the investor who sells his property must pay a capital gains tax, he may decide to sell his property during a year when his income is low. Conversely, he may decide to sell his property at a loss when his income is high. Factors which determine the profits or losses of a sale are:

1. The length of time the investor has owned the building.
2. The number of liens on the property.
3. The owner's equity in the property.

When deciding to sell a building, you must also assess your opportunities for reinvestment. To help yourself decide what investment opportunities are available to you ask yourself the following questions:

1. Are there other properties on the market which would be better investments?
2. Is money available for loans on these properties?
3. Will you make enough on a sale for a down payment on a more desirable investment?

If you can answer "yes" to the preceding questions and can justify a sale in view of your total tax situation, you have successfully eliminated one of the hurdles to the questions of timing.

The other factor to consider when choosing the best time to sell is the condition of the market. In recent years the housing market has experienced several noticeable fluctuations. At times money is readily available for loans and interest rates are low. Often at such times rental property is at a premium. This causes buyer interest and prices go up. If, on the other hand, money is tight and interest rates are high, property will not sell as fast as it does in times of ready money. Buildings pile up and glut the market. If you decide to sell at such times, you may find yourself forced to accept a lower price for your property than if you waited six months or a year until the market improved.

LISTING THE PROPERTY

When you decide the time is right for you to sell a property, the next decision you must make is whether you should list the property with a realtor or sell the property yourself. Each of these alternatives has advantages and disadvantages. To make the best choice, you should consider:

1. The condition of the market.
2. Your emotional make-up.
3. Your reasons for selling the building.
4. The type of property you want to sell.

The role the condition of the market plays in the selling of investment property has already been discussed. If the market is healthy, selling property will be easier than if the market is sluggish. If property is in demand, you may decide to sell the property yourself because you will not have to work as hard to find a buyer. If the market is sluggish and much time and energy is required to put a deal together, you may decide to list the property with a realtor.

The second factor is your emotional make-up. Selling a property demands a great deal of attention. It also requires a great deal of patience. If you are already in the rental business, you should have a fair share of these qualities. However, you will probably find that selling a building requires more time and patience than renting units and maintaining rentals. You must have time to describe the property to interested people and to answer their questions. You must have time to show the property, and have the patience and time to negotiate a deal when you find an interested buyer. If you have a number of rentals to manage in addition to a full time job, you may be hard-pressed to find the time to sell a building yourself.

The third factor to consider when deciding whether you should sell the building yourself is your reason for selling the building. Is your decision to sell the building a logical, well thought-out plan to increase your leverage or to add to your string of well-paying rental units? Or is your decision to sell the result of overextending yourself in either time or money? If you feel forced to sell immediately because you cannot manage the number of units you have acquired, you may decide to list the property with a realtor. If you are not in a hurry to sell, you may decide to sell the property yourself before listing it with a realtor. If money is the factor which influenced your decision to sell, you should remember the realtor's commission will take a large percentage of your profit. On the other hand, the realtor may be able to sell the property faster if you are in need of money immediately. As you can see, your reasons for selling the building should be considered carefully and honestly before you list your property with a realtor.

The last factor you should consider is the type of building you have to sell. Will your building be easy to sell because of its location or condition? If so, you may decide to sell the building yourself. How many units are there in the building? If it is a multi-unit, you may find it difficult and time-consuming to arrange showing the building. This may cause you to list with a realtor. You should remember, however, that realtors sometimes ask for increased commissions for multi-units for that very reason. Be sure to inquire about this before you list with any realtor. You may decide the realtor's commission is worth some of your time.

There are some very good reasons for selling a property yourself. The advantage most often cited for selling a property yourself is you can keep the entire profit. Realtors' commissions vary upwards of 6 percent. If you are selling a four-unit for $100,000, you can expect to pay the realtor about $10,000 or 10 percent. This is a substantial amount of money.

Another reason to sell the building yourself is you maintain control of the sale at all times. You always know what interest the property is generating and you can withdraw the property from the market at any time. Let us say, for example, you want to sell one of three rental units. You do not really care which one you sell. They are similar in appearance, location and value. You list all three "For Sale

WB-4 EXCLUSIVE RESIDENTIAL LISTING CONTRACT
Revised 5-18-78 Approved by Wis. Real Estate Examining Board

Wisconsin Legal Blank Co., Inc.
Milwaukee, Wis. (Job 33165)

AGREEMENT made between the undersigned real estate broker and the undersigned seller.

SELLER gives BROKER the sole and exclusive right to procure a purchaser for the Property hereinafter described at the price and on the terms hereinafter set forth.

If a purchaser is procured for the Property by BROKER, by SELLER, or by any other person, at the price and upon the terms hereinafter set forth, or at any other price, or upon any other terms accepted by SELLER, during the term of this contract, or if exchanged or optioned during term of this contract, SELLER agrees to pay BROKER a commission computed as set forth in this contract.

If the Property or any part of it is sold, exchanged or optioned within six months after the expiration of this contract to any person or to anyone acting for said person, with whom BROKER or any of BROKER'S agents negotiated prior to the expiration of this contract, or to whom BROKER or any of BROKER'S agents personally exhibited by showing the Property prior to the expiration of this contract and in either case whose name BROKER has submitted to SELLER in writing by personal delivery or by depositing, postage prepaid, in the U.S. Mails, not later than twenty-four (24) hours after the expiration of this contract, SELLER agrees to pay BROKER the commission set forth in this contract.

If buyer of the Property should fail to carry out buyer's agreement, and SELLER elects to take as liquidated damages all money paid by buyer, then such money shall be applied first to reimburse BROKER for cash advances made by BROKER and one half of the balance, but not in excess of the agreed commission shall be paid to BROKER as BROKER'S full commission in connection with said transaction and the balance shall belong to SELLER; this payment to BROKER shall not, however, terminate this listing contract.

SELLER and BROKER agree that they will not discriminate against any prospective purchaser on account of race, color, sex, handicap, creed or national origin.

SELLER WARRANTS THAT SELLER HAS NO NOTICE OR KNOWLEDGE OF ANY STRUCTURAL OR MECHANICAL DEFECTS, OF MATERIAL SIGNIFICANCE IN PROPERTY, INCLUDING ADEQUACY AND QUALITY OF WELL AND SANITARY DISPOSAL SYSTEMS, EXCEPT THE FOLLOWING: ....

SELLER warrants and represents that SELLER has no notice or knowledge of any planned public improvements which may result in special assessments or otherwise directly and materially affect the property except as hereinafter set forth, and that no governmental agency has served any notice requiring repairs, alterations or correction of any existing conditions except as hereinafter set forth.

Any offer submitted by or through BROKER shall be deemed to comply with the terms of this agreement if it includes, in addition to the terms herein contained, in substance, any or all of the provisions set forth on the REVERSE SIDE HEREOF.

In consideration for SELLER'S agreement as set forth above BROKER agrees to list and use reasonable efforts to procure a purchaser for the Property, including but not limited to the following: ....

Included in the purchase price are such of the following items as may be on the premises, which will be delivered free and clear of encumbrances: all garden bulbs, plants, shrubs and trees; screen doors and windows; storm doors and windows; electric lighting fixtures; window shades, curtain and traverse rods, blinds, and shutters; bathroom accessory fixtures; central heating and cooling units and attached equipment; water heater and softener; linoleum cemented to floors; attached carpeting and fitted rugs; awnings; exterior attached antennas and component parts; garage door opener and remote control; fireplace equipment and accessories.

ADDITIONAL ITEMS INCLUDED IN SALE: ....

ITEMS NOT INCLUDED IN SALE: ....

The listed property is known as (Street Address) ....

in the .... of ...., County of .... Wisconsin,

more particularly described as ....

LISTED PRICE: .... Dollars ($ ....)

MINIMUM EARNEST MONEY TO BE TENDERED WITH OFFER: $ ....

ADDITIONAL EARNEST MONEY $ .... WITHIN .... DAYS OF ACCEPTANCE

TERMS : Cash: ....

OCCUPANCY DATE: ....

USE AND OCCUPANCY CHARGE if SELLER occupies after closing $ .... per day.

ESCROW TO GUARANTEE OCCUPANCY $ ....

CONVEYANCE OTHER THAN WARRANTY DEED, IF ANY: ....

ADDITIONAL EXCEPTIONS TO WARRANTY OF TITLE (AS SET FORTH ON REVERSE SIDE): ....

SPECIAL PROVISIONS: . . . .

. . . .

. . . .

THE BROKER'S COMMISSION SHALL BE . . . . % of:

a. The listed price:
   (1) if a purchaser is procured in accordance with the terms of this agreement, or,
   (2) if the property is exchanged.

b. The sales price if an offer is accepted for the sale of the property or any part thereof.

c. The sales price set forth in an option if the option granted is exercised.

NAMED EXCEPTIONS TO CONTRACT: . . . .

. . . .

TERM OF CONTRACT: FROM THE . . . . DAY OF . . . . , 19 . . . . ;

UP TO AND INCLUDING MIDNIGHT OF THE . . . . DAY OF . . . . , 19 . . . . . but if an offer to purchase is procured prior to said expiration date at the price and upon the terms set forth herein but which provides for a closing subsequent to said expiration date hereof, the term of this contract shall be extended as to such offer up to and including the date of such closing, but in no event beyond three months from said expiration date.

THIS CONTRACT INCLUDES THE BALANCE OF TERMS ON THE REVERSE SIDE.

Dated this . . . . day of . . . . , 19 . . . . .

. . . .	. . . .
Broker	Seller
. . . .	. . . .
By	Seller
. . . .	. . . .
Broker's Address and Phone Number	Seller's Address and Phone Number
. . . .	. . . .

THE FOLLOWING TERMS ARE PART OF THE CONTRACT ON THE REVERSE SIDE.

THE SELLER SHALL, UPON PAYMENT OF THE PURCHASE PRICE, CONVEY THE PROPERTY BY GOOD AND SUFFICIENT WARRANTY DEED, OR OTHER CONVEYANCE PROVIDED HEREIN, FREE AND CLEAR OF ALL LIENS AND ENCUMBRANCES, EXCEPTING: Municipal and Zoning Ordinances, Recorded Easements for Public Utilities located adjacent to side and rear lot lines, Recorded Building and Use Restrictions and Covenants, General taxes levied in year of closing and

. . . .

. . . . provided none of the foregoing prohibit present use.

All funds delivered to BROKER shall be retained by BROKER in BROKER'S authorized trust account.

SELLER agrees to co-operate with BROKER during the term of this contract and will direct all persons making inquiries concerning the Property to BROKER.

Provisions which may be added in substance to any offer to purchase submitted by or through the BROKER in performance by BROKER with the terms of this listing contract on the reverse side hereof.

(General Provisions of Standard Offer to Purchase Form)

BUYER agrees that unless otherwise specified, he will pay all costs of securing any financing to the extent permitted by law, and to perform all acts necessary to expedite such financing.

General taxes levied in the year of closing shall be prorated at the time of closing on the basis of the net general taxes for the preceding year.

CAUTION:

Make special agreement if:

1. Property has not been fully assessed for tax purposes.
2. Area assessments are contemplated.
3. Home-owners Assoc. has assessed or may assess.

Interest, rents, water and sewer use charges shall be prorated as of the date of closing. Accrued income and expenses, including taxes for the day of closing, shall accrue to the Seller.

Special assessments, if any, for work on site actually commenced prior to date of this offer, shall be paid by Seller.

Special assessments, if any, for work on site actually commenced after date of this offer, shall be paid by Buyer.

The Seller shall furnish and deliver to the buyer for examination at least fifteen (15) days prior to the date set for closing, Seller's choice of either:

1. A complete abstract of title made by an abstract company, extended to within thirty (30) days of the closing, said abstract to show the Seller's title to be marketable and in the condition called for by this agreement, except for mortgages, judgments or other liens which will be satisfied out of the proceeds of the sale. The Buyer shall notify the Seller in writing of any valid objection to the title within ten (10) days after the receipt of said abstract and the Seller shall then have a reasonable time but not exceeding sixty (60) days, within which to rectify the title (or furnish a title policy as hereinafter provided) and in such cases the time of closing shall be accordingly extended; or
2. An owner's policy of title insurance in the amount of the full purchase price, naming the Buyer as the assured, as his interest may appear, written by a responsible title insurance company licensed by the State of Wisconsin, which policy shall guarantee the Seller's title to be in condition called for by this agreement, except for mortgages, judgments or other liens which will be satisfied out of the proceeds of the sale. A commitment by such a title company, agreeing to issue such a title policy upon the recording of the proper documents as agreed herein, shall be deemed sufficient performance.

If this offer provides for a land contract, the same evidence of title shall be furnished prior to the execution of the land contract, and Seller shall furnish written proof, at or before closing, that the total underlying indebtedness, if any, is not in excess of the proposed balance of the land contract, and that the payments on this land contract, are sufficient to meet all of the obligations of the Seller on the underlying indebtedness.

If this offer is the result of co-brokerage, then all money paid herewith shall be held in the selling BROKER'S trust account until the acceptance of this offer and shall be transmitted to listing BROKER upon such acceptance. All subsequent payments shall be made to and held by the listing BROKER in the listing BROKER'S trust account.

Should Buyer fail to carry out this agreement, all money paid hereunder, including any additional earnest money, shall, at the option of Seller, be paid to or retained by Seller, as liquidated damages; if such money is held by Broker, Broker is authorized to disburse such money as follows:

1. To Buyer, if Seller has not notified Buyer and Broker in writing of Seller's election to consider all money paid hereunder as liquidated damages or part payment for specific performance within 60 days of closing date set forth in this agreement, or;
2. To Seller as liquidated damages, subject to deductions of Broker's commission and disbursements, if any, if neither party has commenced a law suit on this matter within one (1) year of the closing date set forth in this agreement.

Should the SELLER be unable to carry out this agreement by reason of a valid legal defect in title which the BUYER is unwilling to waive, all money paid hereunder shall be returned to the BUYER forthwith, and this contract shall be void.

In the event the premises shall be damaged by fire or elements prior to time of closing, in an amount of not more than five per cent of the selling price, the SELLER shall be obligated to repair the same. In the event such damage shall exceed such sum, this contract may be cancelled at option of BUYER. Should the BUYER elect to carry out this agreement despite such damage, such BUYER shall be entitled to the insurance proceeds relating to damage to property; however, if this sale is by land contract or a mortgage to the seller, the insurance proceeds shall be held in trust for the sole purpose of restoring the property.

Sample listing contract.

by Owner." When the first one is sold, you can remove the other two from the market. You have not signed any contract which says that you must sell should a buyer be found.

Let us say instead you decide to sell through a realtor. You must then decide which property you should list. You will have to sign a listing contract usually for a period of 90 days, although this may vary from 30 days to six months. If the property is not sold you are not free to withdraw it from the market without first negotiating with the realtor. In the same way, you cannot list all three and withdraw two after the first one sells without making special negotiations with the realtor.

There are equally important reasons for listing your property with a realtor. They are:

1. A realtor saves you time.
2. A realtor has an established clientele.
3. A realtor is an expert in marketing buildings.

A realtor will save you time in appraising, advertising, promoting and showing your property. He will also save you time in negotiating the deal. Real estate is his job. Unlike the landlord, he does not have to work it in around his other responsibilities. He can devote his full attention and expend all his energy on selling your building.

When you hire a realtor, you establish contact with his clientele. A realtor will show your building to many people. This is especially important in the sale of investment property. Many investors do most of their business through one realtor or realty firm. They expect the realtor to do the foot work for them. The realtor finds the property, works out the cash flow sheet and tells them whether or not the investment would be good for them. These investors prefer not to hunt for property themselves. When you list with a realtor, your property is immediately available to them. In addition, a realtor may be able to attract an out-of-town buyer for your property. This is especially helpful if you have a multi-unit to sell.

A realtor is an expert in his field. He knows the market because he studies it daily. He can do a competent appraisal of your building. He has experience in showing properties and will show your property to its best advantage. He also screens clients. This is especially important during times of tight money. The realtor should inquire into the client's financing possibilities before he starts negotiations. When the realtor brings you an offer on the building, he should have made fairly certain the buyer is good for the money.

There are some disadvantages to selling a building yourself. Some disadvantages are:

1. Promoting property is time-consuming.
2. You probably do not have the clientele from which to draw prospective buyers.
3. Promoting your property can be costly.

You will need time to promote a property and negotiate a deal successfully. Preparing an enticing advertisement, answering telephone calls and arranging showings of the property are all time-consuming. Negotiating a deal requires patience and a certain amount of finesse.

Another difficulty owners encounter when selling property themselves is marketing the property. Many investors have limited access to potential clients. A property owner can advertise through local newspapers and shoppers. He can talk the property up among his friends who are also in the rental business, but he probably does not have access to national listings. Especially in the case of multiple units, statewide or nationwide advertising is helpful. You will find advertising is costly. If you decide to promote the property yourself, you should plan to spend a substantial amount of money on advertising.

After carefully considering all the pros and cons, you should be able to decide whether to sell the building yourself or to list the property with a realtor. Whichever you decide, you will need to make a few more decisions.

DETERMINING THE ASKING PRICE

The first thing you should do after you have decided which building to sell is to determine the asking price. This is an extremely important consideration. Of course, you will want to sell the property for the highest possible price. On the other hand, you will not want to list the property at such an inflated price that no one will call or make you an offer on the property. Although at one time you may have been expected to leave room for negotiations on price, today many people price property very close to the price they expect to accept. You should not greatly overprice the property and expect to receive a number of offers.

There are several ways to determine an asking price for your property. Perhaps the easiest way is to do a market analysis. A market analysis requires the use of comparable properties to decide on a price for your rental.

There are several steps you should follow when doing a market analysis:

1. Read through the listings of properties offered by realtors and by owners. Mark those properties which seem similar to the one you want to sell.
2. Call the realtor or the owner who is selling the property. Ask specific questions about the property listed. Be sure to gear these questions to similarities between the property listed and the property you want to sell. Examples of comparables are:
   a. neighborhood
   b. number of bedrooms
   c. garage size
   d. separate utilities
   e. conditions and age of the roof
   f. low maintenance exterior
   g. combination screens
   h. basement
   i. furnace (condition, type and age)
   j. square footage.

   Anyone who puts a property on the market must expect a few of these calls, so do not hesitate to call to help yourself market a property.

Remember, however, this will indicate only the asking price of each property. To find out how much was actually paid for a property, you must go to the courthouse and check the records. You may also call the city assessor's office. Someone there will look up the information for you. When you have thoroughly checked the asking and selling price of comparable property, you should have a fairly good idea of what to charge for your property.

Another way to determine the asking price for a property is to find out how much it would cost to build a comparable property. This may be especially appropriate for a newer building, but it can be used as an effective negotiating tool for selling an older building. For example, if it would cost $60,000 to build a duplex, $40,000 for a well-kept older building seems like a good deal.

The third means of deciding on a price is to do an income evaluation of the property. In the investment business this is called the capitalization approach. Capitalization is a rather complicated calculation based on current net income of the property and the rate at which the investment in the property can be recovered. This method is often used to help price rental properties, although it is not the only method to consider. Most textbooks on real estate will provide you with a detailed explanation of this process.

Lastly, if you want to sell the property yourself but are hesitant to determine the price yourself, you can hire an appraiser. For a fee, he will give you a professional evaluation of your property. You can take the marketing of the property from there.

PREPARING THE PROPERTY FOR THE MARKET

Before you actually advertise your property you should:

1. Prepare an information sheet about the property.
2. Raise the rents to competitive levels.
3. Notify the tenants of your intention to sell.

After you have decided on an asking price, you should prepare an income information sheet. List the rents you are receiving from each unit on the sheet. Add them to show the total income per month for the property. On the other part of the page, list the expenses for maintaining the rental. In expenses include:

1. taxes;
2. utilities;
3. standard maintenance such as snow removal, lawn care and cleaning of common entry ways.

INFORMATION SHEET

Address of investment property:

____

Number of Units:

____

Rent for each unit:

____________________ . . . . ________

____________________ . . . . ________

____________________ . . . . ________

____________________ . . . . ________

Total income . . . . ________

Expenses:

Heat: . . . . ________

Electricity: . . . . ________

Water: . . . . ________

Taxes: . . . . ________

Total expenses . . . . ________

Mortgage payment . . . . ________

Cash flow . . . . ________

Description of the building:

Exterior: ______________________________

Apartment size: ______________________________

____

Furnace: ______________________________

Special features: ______________________________

____

____

____

Sample information sheet (blank).

INFORMATION SHEET

Address of investment property: 212 Grant Street

Number of Units: 4

Rent for each unit:

Apartment #1	200
#2	300
#3	250
#4	250
Total income	1000/month 12,000/year

Expenses:

Heat:	1,100
Electricity:	960
Water:	200
Taxes:	900
Total expenses	3160
Mortgage payment	5400
Cash flow	3,440/yr.

Description of the building:

Exterior: aluminum siding

Apartment size: #1 - 1 bedroom / #2 - 2 bedroom / #3 - 1 bedroom / #4 - 1 bedroom

Furnace: natural gas

Special features: Completely remodeled excellent location

Sample information sheet (completed).

Lastly, estimate the mortgage payment. Books are available for this information. Subtract the expenses and the mortgage payment from the income. This will show the prospective buyer the cash flow—what he can expect from the property. Duplicate this information so you can give it to people who express a real interest in your property.

Do not be overly concerned if the income does not cover the mortgage payment on the asking price plus the expenses in maintaining the building. Many investors are willing to take an actual loss on a rental for the first few years of their investment.

If the loss is substantial, however, you should look carefully at the rent you are receiving. Are your rents competitive with the current market? You should consider raising the rents to the highest rate the rental will bring before you put the property on the market. If the rents are competitive, the property will be more attractive to the prospective buyers. If the rents are low, the buyer can be fairly certain he will have a number of vacancies when he buys the property and raises the rents. He may not be willing to assume the risk and may pass up your property in favor of a similar property with competitive rents.

Before you advertise the property you should also notify the tenants of your intention to sell the building. This can be done either in writing or verbally. The tenants' cooperation is extremely important, so approach them tactfully. Explain you want to sell the building and you hope they will cooperate with you in showing the units. Tell them you will always notify them first and ask them how much advance notice they would like. Also, ask them if you can show the rental when they are not home. Often tenants prefer to be absent when the rental is shown. Tell them they should not allow anyone in the rental unless you accompany the person. Occasionally, prospective buyers attempt to talk their way into rentals without the seller's knowledge. You should protect your tenants against this situation. After all, you do not want the tenants to move. A vacant building does not sell well. Respect your tenants' rights at all times.

Your tenants may also be concerned they will have to move when the property is sold. In a multi-unit you are usually quite safe in assuring them they will not have to move. You should not, however, absolutely promise this since more people are buying multi-units as cooperatives today. In a duplex, the risk is greater that one of the tenants will have to move because the buyer may want to live in part of the rental. The best you can do is to assure the tenants you will notify them as soon as the building is sold and they will be given at least the minimum notice required by law. If possible, try to keep the tenant in the apartment while you attempt to sell the property.

The last factor to consider is the exterior and interior appearance of the building. You should make the building as attractive as possible before you advertise it. A little paint and a few minor repairs will do wonders for sprucing up a building. Do not put the building on the market with the philosophy that if it does not sell, you will fix it up. In the first month you will probably find most of the people interested in the building will go through it. If no one buys it and you then spruce it up, you will probably have to wait until another group of investors begins shopping for property. You may also find that word of mouth has labeled your building as a "bad buy", so even when you do give it a facelift, you will have to wait months until the rumors have faded.

MARKETING THE BUILDING

When you feel the building is ready to be shown and you have notified the tenants, you are ready to advertise the property. Include the rental's best features such as separate utilities, new furnace or maintenance-free exterior in the advertisement. If the property is in a good business area or if it is a multiple unit, you may decide to advertise in out-of-town papers in the hope of attracting investors from other areas. This is especially true if your property is located in a small town with a limited number of local investors, or if you are trying to sell a property with many rentals which would appeal to someone with a large amount of investment capital. For further information on advertising, re-read the section on advertising in "Renting an Apartment."

A successful advertisement will attract numerous calls. Some of these calls will be from realtors who are interested in listing your property with their company. They may tell you they have an interested client. If you have just listed your property, you will probably want to politely postpone any dealings with a realtor. You may, however, keep his offer in mind should you decide later to list with a realtor. Other calls will be from investors who are locating properties comparable to ones they have to sell. Some calls though, will be from serious buyers and you will want to be ready for these people.

To present your property in a favorable light to people who are really interested, you should anticipate all pertinent questions about the property and have answers ready. Many questions, such as taxes, rents and the cost of utilities will be ready on the information sheet you have prepared. All you will have to do is read the information from the sheet. Other questions about the exterior, roof, furnace, amount of insulation and general condition of the units will also be asked. You should be prepared to answer these questions.

Another question which is invariably asked is, "Why are you selling?" This question should be given very careful thought before it is answered. It is a crucial question and the "right" answer is important to the successful marketing of your building. The "wrong" answer to this question may bring a low offer or stifle interest completely. Examples of wrong answers are:

1. "The tenants are giving me a hard time."
2. "The building is too expensive to heat."
3. "The building needs work."

Examples of right answers are:

1. "I sell one building every two years. This is the year I have planned to sell this building." (This shows you are a knowledgeable investor.)
2. "I want to buy a larger building." (This shows the rental business in a favorable light.)

You must remember to answer all questions about the building honestly. Other questions you may be asked are:

1. Are you willing to trade?
2. Will you help finance the building?
3. Will you consider an installment sale?

Answer these questions cautiously. You do not want to commit yourself to an unfavorable deal nor do you want to close the door on a sale. In answering these questions you might say something like:

1. "I'm willing to think about it and to consider any suggestions you make."
2. "I'm open to an offer."
3. "What do you have in mind?"

The most important thing about your answer is that it be positive and definite. Do not say, "I don't know," and expect the prospect to pursue you. Most people do not have the time to prod the seller. They will simply go to another building where the seller is more confident of his purpose.

Usually the conversation will end with something like, "I'll drive by and get back to you if I am interested."

Rather than answering, "Okay," or "Thanks for calling," say something like: "If you want to see the inside after you have driven by, I'll be happy to show it to you."

With this statement you have left the caller with the parting thought the rental is nice inside. You also have indicated he is not to bother the tenants. You want to show him the building. After that all you can do is thank him for calling and wait.

Remember that selling is a waiting game. Do not panic if you have not sold your property the first week. If you are really serious about selling the property yourself, you should have the necessary capital and patience to advertise the rental for several months before you remove it from the market or list it with a realtor.

When someone asks to see the property, take his name and telephone number and ask him to give several times which would be convenient for him to see the building. Check these with your tenants and arrive at a time which is satisfactory for everyone. Call the client with the time for the appointment. Then notify the tenants of the exact time. Arrive at the building early. This allows you time to talk with your tenants. If they have any concerns, they can discuss them with you before the prospective buyer arrives. When the client arrives, show him through the building and draw his attention to the property's good points. Do not exaggerate the property's potential. Also, be sure to point out boundaries and to answer all his questions as completely as you can.

If the client likes the property, he may want to discuss financing with you before he makes an offer. Remember the exact terms of the financing will probably depend on the offer you finally accept from the buyer. Your first discussion of financing will probably be general in nature. The client may also make you an offer at this time, but more likely, he will wait a few days until he has thought about the deal carefully. If his offer is acceptable to you, draw up a formal purchase offer and request earnest money. Earnest money is a payment the buyer makes to the seller to show he seriously intends to follow through on the deal. This payment varies with the price of the property, but it is usually at least $500. Do not be put off by the statement, "We can trust each other." Remember, if you do not have a payment of earnest money, the buyer has nothing to lose should he decide to back out of the deal at a later date. You, on the other hand, have a great deal to lose. Insist on a payment of earnest money. If the buyer should decide he wants out of the deal, he will forfeit his earnest money. The buyer's earnest money is usually refunded if financing is unavailable for the property, however.

After a purchase price has been agreed upon, the buyer must obtain financing. Since most offers are subject to financing, you should do some checking on your client before you accept his offer. Ask him which lender he intends to use. Then check with that lender to see if there is money available for the type of property and the type of loan you are negotiating. This check is especially crucial in times of tight money. You do not want to tie up your property for months while your buyer approaches lender after lender without result. You also do not want to tie up your property while one lender deliberates for months about whether he will offer the loan to your client. While you are waiting for your client to obtain financing, you may lose several other prospects. A few discreet questions will help establish your client's credit and will give you an idea of his possibilities for getting a loan. If you are unsure of your client's credit or if you intend to help him finance the property, you should check his credit rating before you sign the offer to purchase.

If you decide to accept his offer, you will probably turn the matter over to your attorney who will handle the closing for you.

SELLING THROUGH A REALTOR

Selling property yourself is time-consuming. After thinking about all the things you will have to do to promote your property, you may decide to list with a realtor. When you list with a realtor, you still have many of the same responsibilities and decisions you have when you promote the property yourself. First, you must decide how selling fits into your financial profile. Then you must make your property as attractive as possible and notify the tenants you intend to sell. The realtor will probably expect you to prepare an information sheet listing the income and expenses of the rental. Be sure these items are accurate. Utilities are a significant cost today and the owner is held accountable for correct figures. You may even be asked to sign a statement indicating the figures you have listed are accurate.

The realtor prepares and places the advertisements, answers calls about the property, shows the property to prospective buyers and checks the credit references of interested parties. The realtor coordinates the showing times and negotiates the terms of the sale.

When you hire a realtor, you are paying for more than his time. You are also paying for the privilege of using his clientele. For that reason, you should be very careful when choosing a realtor. This is especially true in the sale of investment property. Most people buy one or two primary residences during their stay in a community. They tend to call the realtor who is advertising the property rather than any one specific realtor. Investors, however, buy and sell numerous rentals. They want to develop a good working relationship with one realty firm. When selling a rental property, you should list with a realtor who has established a clientele of real estate investors.

If this is your first or second sale, you may be unfamiliar with the realtors in your area. Before deciding on a particular realtor you should:

1. Talk with other investors you know. Find out who listed their properties and how satisfied they were with the resulting sales.
2. Check the newspaper advertisements. Determine which realtor lists the most rental property. You should also check further to see which realtor sells the most rental property.
3. Call several realtors. Ask them how rental property is moving. Ask them how much rental property they have sold in the last six months. Ask them what their commission rate is and determine whether they will adjust the commission rate according to the amount of the listing. For an example, if you list more than one property at a time, you may be able to negotiate a lower commission rate.

Remember, you want to sell your property with the least amount of inconvenience to yourself and to your tenants. That means you should shop carefully for a realtor. You want to hire a realtor who will immediately draw interested buyers to your property.

A realtor's clientele is especially important in times of recession when money for property is sluggish. He knows who can get the money and he may also have some connections with lenders in the area. He knows which lenders have money available and which lenders are willing to give loans for rental properties. He can also often convince a reluctant buyer to make an offer on the property because he has worked with the buyer before.

You will probably be tempted to choose a realtor who offers you the lowest commission rate. Think carefully before you sign with that realtor, however. He may just be starting in the business and may not have the clientele necessary to sell your property. He may be able to offer you a lower commission rate because he saves money on the promotion of property. On the other hand, he may impress you as a diligent worker. Especially when property is moving well or when you know that your property will be easy to sell, you may decide to give this realtor a chance.

By the same token, do not decide that just because a realtor is expensive, he is good. Other factors should be considered. Do you like the realtor? Remember, you will have to work rather closely with him and you will be paying him a substantial amount of your profit. You should find working with him a pleasant experience.

Will the realtor represent your property well? Pay close attention to what he says about your property the first time he sees it. Does he point out all the undesirable features of your property and neglect the desirable aspects of the building? Perhaps he already has a buyer in mind and wants to list the property at a low price to interest the buyer. If a realtor neglects to mention the good points of your property to you, you will probably wonder how he will present the property to prospective buyers.

You should not feel obligated to list your property with a realtor just because you have talked with him or because you have shown him through your property. However, you

No. WB-1B OFFER TO PURCHASE–With Acceptance
Revised 5-18-78 Approved by Wis. Real Estate Examining Board

Wisconsin Legal Blank Co., Inc.
Milwaukee, Wis. (Job 33163)

. . . . , Wisconsin, ... , 19 . . .

The undersigned Buyer, ... , hereby offers to purchase the property known as . . . .
(Street Address)
in the . . . . of. . . . . , County of. . . . . , Wisconsin, more particularly described as:
. . . .
. . . .
. . . .
having a frontage of about . . . . feet, with a depth of about . . . . feet, at the price of . . . . Dollars ($ . . . .) and on the terms and conditions as follows:

Earnest Money (cash) (check) ($ . . . .) Tendered herewith. Additional Earnest Money (cash) (check) ($ . . . .) to be paid within . . . . days of acceptance of offer (or on . . . .), and the balance in cash at closing or as hereafter set forth.

TIME IS OF THE ESSENCE AS TO ADDITIONAL EARNEST MONEY PAYMENT.

THE BUYER'S OBLIGATION TO CONCLUDE THIS TRANSACTION IS CONDITIONED UPON THE CONSUMMATION OF THE FOLLOWING:

(If this offer is subject to financing, or any other contingency, it must be stated here. If none so state.)
. . . .
. . . .
. . . .
. . . .
. . . .
. . . .
. . . .
. . . .
. . . .

Buyer agrees that unless otherwise specified, he will pay all costs of securing any financing to the extent permitted by law, and to perform all acts necessary to expedite such financing.

THE SELLER SHALL, UPON PAYMENT OF THE PURCHASE PRICE CONVEY THE PROPERTY BY GOOD AND SUFFICIENT WARRANTY DEED, OR OTHER CONVEYANCE PROVIDED HEREIN, FREE AND CLEAR OF ALL LIENS AND ENCUMBRANCES, EXCEPTING: Municipal and Zoning Ordinances, Recorded Easements for Public Utilities located adjacent to side and rear lot lines, Recorded Building and Use Restrictions and Covenants, General taxes levied in the year of closing and . . . . provided none of the foregoing prohibit present use.

Legal possession of premises shall be delivered to Buyer on date of closing.

Physical occupancy of . . . . shall be given to Buyer on . . . .

If Seller shall occupy premises after closing, Seller shall pay use and occupancy charge of $ . . . . per day. Time is of the essence hereto with respect to occupancy. (Strike if not applicable.) It is understood the premises are now occupied by . . . . under (oral lease) (written lease), which terms are: . . . .

The sum of $ . . . . shall be withheld from the purchase price to be escrowed with . . . . to guarantee delivery of possession to the Buyer AND FOR NO OTHER PURPOSE, which sum upon Seller's failure to deliver possession shall be paid to the Buyer as liquidated damages or returned to the Seller if occupancy is delivered to the Buyer on the date of physical occupancy as stated above.

All earnest money paid hereon shall be applied as part payment on the purchase price if this offer is accepted on or before . . . . , 19 . . . . ; otherwise, to be returned to the undersigned Buyer no later than . . . . , 19 . . . . and this offer shall be come null and void.

If this offer is accepted, it shall not become binding upon the Buyer until copy of accepted offer is deposited, postage prepaid, in the United States Mails, addressed to the Buyer at . . . . , or by personal delivery thereof.

The transaction is to be closed at the office of Buyer's mortgagee, if any, or at the office of . . . . , on or before . . . . , 19 . . . . , or at such other time and place as may be agreed to in writing by the Buyer and Seller.

Seller warrants and represents to Buyer that Seller has no notice or knowledge of:

(a) planned or commenced public improvement which may result in special assessments or otherwise directly and materially affect the property except . . . .

(b) any government agency or court order requiring repairs, alterations or correction of any existing conditions except . . . .

(c) ANY STRUCTURAL OR MECHANICAL DEFECTS OF MATERIAL SIGNIFICANCE IN PROPERTY, INCLUDING ADEQUACY AND QUALITY OF WELL AND SANITARY DISPOSAL SYSTEMS, EXCEPT . . . .

The undersigned Buyer has read and fully understands and hereby makes the foregoing Offer to Purchase and acknowledges receipt of a copy of said offer.

THIS CONTRACT INCLUDES THE BALANCE OF TERMS ON REVERSE SIDE. .... (Buyer)

.... (Buyer)

THIS OFFER IS HEREBY ACCEPTED/COUNTERED (Strike One). THE WARRANTY AND REPRESENTATION MADE HEREIN SURVIVE THE CLOSING OF THIS TRANSACTION. THE UNDERSIGNED HEREBY AGREES TO SELL AND CONVEY THE ABOVE MENTIONED PROPERTY ON THE TERMS AND CONDITIONS AS SET FORTH AND ACKNOWLEDGES RECEIPT OF A COPY OF THIS AGREEMENT.

....

.................................., 19 .... (Seller)

.... (If Seller is married, spouse should sign.) (Seller)

EARNEST MONEY RECEIPT

(Cash) (check) received from ....

in the amount of $ .... The undersigned hereby agrees to hold same in an authorized Real Estate Trust Account in .... Bank in .... , Wisconsin. or transmit the same in accordance with the terms of the above offer.

...., Broker

.................................., 19 ....

BY: ....

THE FOLLOWING TERMS ARE PART OF THE CONTRACT ON REVERSE SIDE.

Included in the purchase price are such of the following items as may be on the premises, which will be delivered free and clear of encumbrances: all garden bulbs, plants, shrubs and trees; screen doors and windows; storm doors and windows; electric lighting fixtures; window shades, curtain and traverse rods, blinds, and shutters; bathroom accessory fixtures; central heating and cooling units and attached equipment; water heater and softener; linoleum cemented to floors; attached carpeting and fitted rugs; awnings; exterior attached antennas and component parts; garage door opener and remote control; fireplace equipment and accessories.

ADDITIONAL ITEMS INCLUDED IN SALE: ....

....

....

ITEMS NOT INCLUDED IN SALE: ....

....

....

General taxes levied in the year of closing shall be prorated at the time of closing on the basis of the net general taxes for the preceding year.

CAUTION:

Make special agreement if:

1. Property has not been fully assessed for tax purposes.
2. Area assessments are contemplated.
3. Home-owners Assoc. has assessed or may assess.

Interest, rents, water and sewer use charges shall be prorated as of the date of closing. Accrued income and expenses, including taxes for the day of closing, shall accrue to the Seller.

Special assessments, if any, for work on site actually commenced prior to date of this offer, shall be paid by Seller.

Special assessments, if any, for work on site actually commenced after date of this offer, shall be paid by Buyer.

The Seller shall furnish and deliver to the buyer for examination at least fifteen (15) days prior to the date set for closing, Seller's choice of either:

1. A complete abstract of title made by an abstract company, extended to within thirty (30) days of the closing, said abstract to show the Seller's title to be marketable and in the condition called for by this agreement, except for mortgages, judgments or other liens which will be satisfied out of the proceeds of the sale. The Buyer shall notify the Seller in writing of any valid objection to the title within ten (10) days after the receipt of said abstract and the Seller shall then have a reasonable time but not exceeding sixty (60) days, within which to rectify the title (or furnish a title policy as hereinafter provided) and in such cases the time of closing shall be accordingly extended; or
2. An owner's policy of title insurance, in the amount of the full purchase price, naming the Buyer as the assured, as his interest may appear, written by a responsible title insurance company licensed by the State of Wisconsin, which policy shall guarantee the Seller's title to be in condition called for by this agreement, except for mortgages, judgments, or other liens, which will be satisfied out of the proceeds of the sale. A commitment by such a title company, agreeing to issue such a title policy upon the recording of the proper documents as agreed herein, shall be deemed sufficient performance.

If this offer provides for a land contract, the same evidence of title shall be furnished prior to the execution of the land contract, and Seller shall furnish written proof, at or before closing, that the total underlying indebtedness, if any, is not in excess of the proposed balance of the land contract, and that the payments on this land contract, are sufficient to meet all of the obligations of the Seller on the underlying indebtedness.

If this offer is the result of a co-brokerage, then all money paid herewith shall be held in the selling Broker's trust account until the acceptance of this offer and shall be transmitted to the listing broker upon such acceptance.

All subsequent payments shall be made to the listing broker and held in the listing broker's trust account.

Should Buyer fail to carry out this agreement, all money paid hereunder, including any additional earnest money, shall, at the option of Seller, be paid to or retained by Seller as liquidated damages, if such money is held by Broker, Broker is authorized to disburse such money as follows:

1. To Buyer, if Seller has not notified Buyer and Broker in writing of Seller's election to consider all money paid hereunder as liquidated damages or part payment for specific performance within 60 days of closing date set forth in this agreement, or;
2. To Seller as liquidated damages, subject to deductions of Broker's commission and disbursements, if any, if neither party has commenced a law suit on this matter within one (1) year of the closing date set forth in this agreement.

Should the SELLER be unable to carry out this agreement by reason of a valid legal defect in title which the BUYER is unwilling to waive, all money paid hereunder shall be returned to the BUYER forthwith, and this contract shall be void.

In the event the premises shall be damaged by fire or elements prior to time of closing, in an amount of not more than five per cent of the selling price, the Seller shall be obligated to repair the same. In the event such damage shall exceed such sum, this contract may be cancelled at option of Buyer. Should the Buyer elect to carry out this agreement despite such damage, such Buyer shall be entitled to the insurance proceeds relating to damage to property; however, if this sale is by land contract or a mortgage to the seller, the insurance proceeds shall be held in trust for the sole purpose of restoring the property.

Sample offer to purchase.

should be sure there is no obligation on your part before he appraises your property.

If you decide to list your property with a realtor, read the listing contract carefully. Usually the time the realtor agrees to promote your property is negotiable. Listing contracts vary from 30 days to six months. If you are unsure of the realtor, you will probably want to list the property for a short time, say 30 to 60 days. Ninety days is the most usual time period for a listing contract. Six months opens you to risks. You must be very sure the realtor will promote your property well for the entire six months before you tie up your property with one realtor for half a year. We always think if the realtor cannot sell the property in 90 days, he will not have much more success in 90 more days. A realtor with good contacts will probably be able to bring you an offer on your property within 30 days. Tying up the property for six months is unnecessary unless the property is especially difficult to sell or money is especially tight. If money is tight you will probably decide to wait until a better time to sell anyway.

After listing your property with a realtor do not make the mistake of assuming all is going well. Call the realtor at regular intervals to check on his progress. These calls remind him of your property and your interest.

When the realtor does bring you an offer, be sure you understand all the conditions of the sale. Do not make the mistake of assuming anything that is not expressly stated in the contract. Make sure every condition is spelled out clearly in the contract. For example, a contract which reads:

> This sale is dependent on the buyer being able to secure a loan from a savings and loan at no more that 10 percent interest for a period of not less than 25 years...

does not guarantee you a conventional mortgage. The buyer may secure an FHA loan which meets these conditions and you may have to pay points from your profit. For example, if the buyer borrows $40,000 and the seller is charged six points and each point is equal to 1 percent of the loan, $2,400 may be deducted from the buyer's profit. If you want to sell a building on a conventional loan, make sure the word "conventional" is expressly stated in the contract. If you are willing to sell the property on a loan which requires you to pay points, be sure you know the extent of the amount you could be required to pay. Have this amount mentioned in the offer to purchase because you will probably want to figure it in to the amount you accept for the property.

After you have signed an offer to purchase, do not assume all will go smoothly. Especially in times of tight money, your deal may still run into a number of snares. First, your property's appraisal value has to match the agreed upon purchase price. Finding a time when the appraiser can see the entire building may be a problem, especially in a multi-unit. Check periodically to make sure progress is being made in getting the appraiser into the building. No progress can be made on the sale until the appraisal has been made.

Next, you should find out which bank is handling the deal for the buyer and occasionally check with the lender on the progress of the loan. Remember, in most cases you are the one who cares most about the progress of the sale. Do not hesitate to talk directly with the lender. Hopefully, your offer to purchase has an expiration date so the lender cannot deliberate indefinitely nor can the buyer attempt indefinitely to secure financing.

When you sell a property, you are responsible for having the abstract brought up to date and for having the deed prepared. Your buyer is responsible for paying for the appraisal, a credit check on himself, recording the deed and attorney's opinion on the property. He may also be responsible for a loan initiation fee which today ranges from one to three percent of the mortgage.

Selling a property is a complicated aspect of landlording. The statement "you really make money when you sell" is true only if you correctly gauge the time of your sale and negotiate the sale to your advantage. You must consider both the market and your financial picture in order to sell a property wisely.

SUMMARY

Selling rental property is as important to successful landlording as managing rental units or purchasing rental properties. When you decide to sell a property, you should first consider how the sale of that property fits into your entire financial picture. You should also consider the condition of the market. After you have chosen a property to sell, make it as attractive as possible for potential buyers. Make certain the rents are competitive and the rental looks as presentable as possible.

Your next decision is whether to list the property with a realtor or to sell it yourself. Each alternative has unique advantages. If you should decide to sell the property yourself, you will save yourself the realtor's commission and will retain complete control of the sale. If for some reason you wish to remove the property from the market, you may do so without having to renegotiate with the realtor.

Selling through a realtor also has advantages. A realtor's clientele is especially important to the marketing of rental property. Also, in the case of multi-units, arranging to show the building may be time-consuming. A realtor will relieve you of such tasks.

Whether you decide to sell the property yourself or list the building with a realtor, you should prepare a carefully itemized account of your expenses in maintaining the rental and the income the rental generated during the past year.

11
Are You the Landlord Type?

Since the early years of America's history, landlording has been thought of as an excellent way to make money —lots of money. The stereotype picture of the landlord as the villain who extracts outrageous rents from innocent tenants while he allows their building to deteriorate around them, is an all too usual idea. In addition, some prospective landlords think of themselves as making a healthy profit while they get someone else to do the work necessary to maintain their buildings.

Neither of these extremes is accurate. In truth, the landlord is a hardworking "Jack-of-all-Trades." He is an independent businessman. Like any other owner of a small business, he is vulnerable to outside factors such as overwork and swings in the economy. Almost anyone with perseverance can purchase property, but it takes a special kind of person to be a successful landlord.

First, a successful landlord has good business sense. This means more than adding and subtracting. It means he can feel the shifts in the housing market, sense the best times to buy and sell and know when to raise rents and how much to raise them. It also means he can look at the maintenance costs for a building and determine where the money is being spent. He should be able to spot unnecessary expenditures and correct them. He should be able to account for every penny of income and expense and know each month or each quarter how a particular building is shaping up as an investment. He must like to think about figures and keep accurate books.

This does not mean the landlord must be a financial wizard. A basic knowledge of mathematics and the ability to learn from mistakes is sufficient.

A landlord must also have the time to study the local markets so he knows when to buy and when to sell. Reading the newspapers and talking to other investors and realtors will keep him abreast of local changes. He will also find reading national magazines helpful. Many of these magazines are very readable and geared to the layman. Do not shy away from them because you think they are too technical. Making money is interesting to almost everyone.

A successful landlord needs to be more than a competent bookkeeper, however. At least in the beginning of the business, he needs to be a handyman as well. Repair costs are very high. A clogged drain, a broken window or monthly gardener's wages can seriously cut into the profits of a building. A successful landlord is willing and able to take care of minor repairs in his buildings. He should be able to paint a wall, fix a leaky faucet and repair a roof. Hopefully, he enjoys this work as much as he enjoys bookkeeping and has the time for it. If he can also make major repairs or alterations to the buildings he owns, his margin of profit will be greater.

Some couples find landlording suits them well because one of them is good at bookkeeping and the other is good at repairs. This is how landlording has worked for us.

Successful landlording requires more than good business sense and handyman's skills. A successful landlord must enjoy dealing with people. He must be patient and tolerant of different personalities. He should be diplomatic when solving problems and settling disputes between the tenants or between himself and other tenants.

A landlord must learn to outguess his tenants. Often tenants call the landlord and describe what sounds like a serious problem. The furnace won't work, for example. Often the problem is minor. A blown fuse in the furnace might sound like a major problem, but if you think of checking the fuse box first, you could save yourself the price of a service call.

Then, of course, there is the tenant who calls because the apartment is unheated. You go over to the building to check on the furnace. The furnace sounds normal and the other tenants in the building are warm enough. You begin to worry the furnace is not connected to her apartment or there is a problem requiring expensive repairs. You agree her apartment is very cold. Then you happen to glance at the registers. All of them are closed. The tenant is unaware she must open the registers in order to get heat into her apartment. It pays to think creatively and check everything before you call a repair man.

Of course, the successful landlord knows when to call a repair man. Sometimes a problem requires an expert and the landlord should not attempt such a repair. You would not want a serious problem to result from careless maintenance.

A landlord who manages his own buildings must expect calls early in the morning, late at night and during his mealtimes. He should be agreeable to having his leisure interrupted with both minor and important problems. One of the advantages of landlording is that it can be done in off times away from a regular job. These hours can also be wearing, however. When you have to deal with a tenant complaint just as you are sitting down to a special family dinner, the luster of landlording dims. A successful landlord expects some inconvenience as a means of padding his retirement income, earning his tax break or becoming financially independent. We get what we earn. Landlording is a business conducted during odd hours. If you are not willing to accept this, you will find landlording a burden.

A successful landlord has a sense of humor. When a tenant calls you and asks to have his rent lowered, it is better to laugh than to turn purple with rage at his nerve.

In many ways landlording is a service you provide for your tenants. They pay you to provide them with housing. If you accept your role as a provider of a service, you will be successful in the landlording business.

Landlording is not for everyone because it is not as easy as talk would have it. But a person who is willing to work hard will find landlording a satisfying and fulfilling way to supplement his income.

SUMMARY

A successful landlord combines some sense of the business world with skills in making repairs to the buildings he owns and with skills in dealing with the people who rent from him. He is the proverbial "Jack-of-all-Trades," at least while he is building his business. A successful landlord must have patience in dealing with the varied personalities and problems which he encounters as a landlord. Without patience and a sense of humor, you will probably find landlording a burden.

12 Snares in Real Estate

Advocates of investment in real estate usually stress three advantages real estate offers that other investments lack: leverage, a hedge against inflation, and a tax shelter. It is true wise investments in real estate can shelter your income, keep up with today's inflation rate and give you additional tax free investment dollars. But real estate investments also contain numerous snares for the hasty or naive investor.

LEVERAGE

One of these snares is leverage. Leverage is a two-sided coin. When used wisely leverage can greatly increase your investment potential and put you on the road to financial independence. When used unwisely, leverage can lead to bankruptcy.

Leverage is the use of borrowed money to increase your investments. For example, say you originally bought a building worth $30,000 for $6,000 down. You borrowed $24,000. During the four years you had the building, you paid $4,000 on the loan. During that four year period, the building also increased in value. Today you owe $20,000 on the building which is now worth $40,000. Since the lender with whom you have the loan will allow you to borrow 80 percent of your equity in the building, you can borrow $16,000 toward the purchase of another rental. If you need 20 percent down on the loan, you can purchase a building worth $80,000. You have now acquired $120,000 worth of property for your original $6,000 down and the $4,000 rents helped pay on the first property. Now let's say that property inflates at 10 percent. Your combined property will inflate at $12,000 a year. That means you will be making $12,000 a year on an original $10,000 investment. Now let's say you did not use your leverage to purchase the $80,000 property. You would still have $10,000 invested but you would only be making 10 percent on $40,000 (the price of the original investment) for a total of $4,000 each year. By borrowing as much money as you can you have increased your rate of return.

The problem with using leverage to acquire investment property is you may over-extend yourself. Consider the preceding example from another angle. When you purchased the $80,000 building using your equity in the first property, you had to borrow the entire $80,000. This is maximum leverage. You borrowed the entire amount. Your payments on $80,000 for 25 years at 10 percent interest would be $715.60 each month. Now let's say you had $16,000 cash down on the $80,000 building. That means you would only borrow $64,000. Your payments on $64,000 would be $590.31 each month. This is a difference of $125.29 a month. Before you use the maximum amount of leverage available to you, make sure you can handle the mortgage payments on the borrowed money. The snare some investors fall into is borrowing more money than the income from their investments will support. Eventually, this may lead to the loss of some property purchased with maximum leverage.

INFLATION

Inflation can also work against the investor in real estate. Since the Great Depression of the 1930's the federal government has sought to stabilize the supply of money in an attempt to keep growth and inflation within acceptable boundaries. Their intention is to prevent the bust which typically followed boom periods before the 1930's. As a result, our economy seems to follow a pattern of growth and prosperity countered by a short recession period. During the period of growth, housing starts are up. Immediately preceding the recession money becomes tight and interest rates rise. This brings down the cost of housing and hopefully drops the inflation rate. As the recession reaches a point of low growth coupled with a point of high unemployment, money becomes more available, interest rates drop and the economy is on the upward swing again.

These periodic fluctuations in the money market can snare the unwary investor. Wise investors use inflation as a useful tool to achieve large profits. Naive investors find these fluctuations in the nation's economy often cause them great losses.

The key to avoiding this snare is to watch the money market carefully. Sell when interest rates are lowest. Buyers are much more eager to pay top dollar for a property when interest rates are at 10 percent than they are when interest rates are at 15 percent. Even though they may expect to keep the property for only a few years, the additional percentage points are a psychological deterrent to many investors. In times when money is readily available, banks are willing to give blanket mortgages and second mortgages. When an investor can use his equity in a building, he is more willing to pay top dollar for a property.

On the other hand, when money is tight and banks refuse alternate financing, many investors are unable or unwilling to buy property. This means people who must sell will drop their asking price until they find a buyer who can secure a loan to buy the property. Remember that much of an investor's profit is actually a paper profit rather than cash in hand. That paper profit fluctuates with the times. Sell when your profit on paper is the highest.

By the same token, the wise investor buys when money is tight because this is the time when he can get the best deals. During times of recession there will always be people who cannot hang on through the difficult time or who panic when the market looks grim. These people are willing to take a low price for their property in order to "unload it."

If you buy during these times, be sure you are prepared to hang on for an extended period of economic recession. When property is cheap it is tempting to buy all you can. But during recession periods people lose their jobs. You may find renters are late with rent. You may have to advertise your rentals more often and for longer periods before you find an acceptable tenant. If you extend your credit to its limits you may not have the necessary capital to maintain your newly acquired buildings through a lengthy or especially traumatic recession.

Inflation may also work against the investor during relatively good times. The cost of a building may become so inflated that no one is willing to purchase it. The income from the rental units just does not cover the operating expenses. There is a problem in counting your profit from inflation until you actually have the cash in hand, either through a cash sale or additional financing. Inflation income can give the naive investor a false sense of prosperity.

TAX SHELTER

Even the tax shelter is not the foolproof path to wealth some people make it out to be. The tax shelter on real income usually comes from the depreciation of investment property. A certain amount of money based on the cost and life expectancy of the building is written off each year against actual dollars made on the property or from other income sources. When the building is sold the profit is figured from the depreciated price rather than from the purchase price; therefore, some of that tax sheltered income is eventually taxed when the property is sold.

REMODELING

Other snares also await the unwary investor. Proponents of real estate as the most lucrative investment opportunity usually say the way to make money is to buy a dilapidated building, renovate it and sell it at a profit. There is a lot of truth to this statement, but there are also some snares in this practice.

The first snare is state building codes. Make sure before you buy a rundown property you actually can put additional bathrooms in the closets, close off the hallways for new kitchens or use the basement for another apartment. These building codes change periodically. If you buy a property with the intention of adding bathrooms, furnaces or new units only to discover the state code prevents your doing so, you may find yourself with a property that is an expensive liability rather than the money-maker you had expected it to be.

The cost of building materials is another snare for the unwary investor. The costs of lumber, fixtures and even nails have risen rapidly. Do you know exactly how much it will cost to hire a plumber to install plumbing for an additional bathroom? Do you know exactly how much self-storing storms cost this year and what the price of aluminum siding is? Be sure to pad any estimate you make because remodeling costs are usually more than you expect.

After completely remodeling a building you may find you cannot afford to sell it immediately. People may not be willing or able to pay the price you think your labor and creativity are worth. You may have to keep the building a few years before you feel you can demand a price which adequately pays you for your time.

SALEABILITY

The saleability of real estate is another factor to consider. Real estate is one of the least liquid of all investments. Unlike stocks and bonds which can be traded or sold within a few hours, real estate sometimes takes many months to sell. Finding a buyer and negotiating a sale can be a time consuming process. Unlike art, stamps, coins and other collectibles, buildings cannot be packed up and taken half-way across the United States when you find yourself transferred. If you do have to move away from the community where you own rental property, you will probably have to place your property with a management agency until you can sell it. You may also have to sell quickly and sacrifice much of the profit you expect to make on the building. Real estate has become an expensive investment to acquire. It is also an expensive investment to sell.

TENANTS' RIGHTS

The last major snare for the unwary landlord is the rights of the tenants to whom he rents apartments. Recent court decisions have been favorable toward the tenants. The rights of tenants are protected by both state and federal laws. Most conscientious landlords agree laws are needed to protect tenants from neglectful or ruthless landlords. Most landlords also agree that these laws can sometimes cause the conscientious landlord time, stress and money. Consider, for example, the tenant who does not pay rent. That tenant is protected from eviction by the landlord until a court decides in favor of the landlord. The landlord cannot use his passkey to enter the apartment, and he cannot move the tenant's possessions into the hall or street. He must wait until the court has agreed the tenant has not paid the rent and should be evicted from the premises. If the tenant still does not move, the landlord may seek a writ of restitution which will direct the proper authorities to move the tenant's belongings from the apartment. The authorities may require a deposit from the landlord to cover their costs in moving the tenant. Although the tenant is legally responsible for these expenses, the landlord may wait a long time before he recovers any of the costs in lost rent, court fees and moving expenses from the tenant. If the landlord is unprepared for this eventuality, he may experience a financial and emotional crises.

Landlords should understand the laws governing their business. This understanding will prevent many problems.

SUMMARY

Although real estate is generally thought of as the safest of all investment opportunities, it does contain snares for the unwary investor. Three of those snares (leverage, inflation and tax breaks) can actually work against the naive investor. Others, such as building codes, remodeling costs, the costs of buying and selling property and tenants' rights may also threaten the investor's security.

These snares should not detract from the basic soundness of real estate as an investment. Remember that investment in real estate is like investment in any other commodity. It entails some risks. It is best to know these risks and be prepared for them, rather than ignore them and hope you will not encounter these problems.

13 Tricks of the Trade

If your real estate investments are not doing as well as those of your neighbor perhaps you are not playing the game as successfully as he is. Observing some general rules, called hereafter "tricks of the trade," will help you make real estate investment the financial success you hoped it would be.

Many investors today agree money from real estate investment is made by selling the property rather than by keeping it for a long time. The amount of money you make is dependent to a large extent on when you sell. You must know when your property will bring the most money. Watch the availability of money and the prime rate. Check periodically with loan officers, local banks and savings and loans. Ask them what the interest rate is for conventional mortgages. Ask them if they are lending on investment properties. Ask them if they are giving second mortgages or blanket mortgages. Their answers should give you an idea of the money situation in your community. Read national magazines such as *Business Week, Newsweek, U.S. News and World Report* and *Money* for an idea of the national money market.

When money is available and interest rates are low, alternative mortgage plans are available to buyers. People will be buying and paying top dollar for investment property. Selling at the right time can bring you thousands of additional dollars. It can also save you time and make selling an easy and pleasant experience.

KNOW WHEN TO BUY PROPERTY

Certain tricks of the trade will also make buying property more profitable for you. When buying property use as little of your own cash as possible. Although leverage can be a handicap (see *Snares in Real Estate*), it can also be one of the greatest assets of the real estate investor. Use equity in other properties as a down payment on additional property. The money is tax free. You can build a well-paying string of rental units with careful use of equity and leverage.

Watch the market as carefully when you buy as when you sell. Buy when cost of property is low. This means guarding your credit rating so you can get a loan to buy property when marginal investors cannot secure loans to buy the bargains. Shop for property. Do not buy the first thing on the market because you want to buy a piece of investment property. Shop even when you are not really interested in buying. This way you will know a real bargain when you find one.

SHOP FOR FINANCING

Just as you shop for property, you should also shop for financing. Closing costs are not the same at every lending institution, nor are interest rates always the same. On a loan of $100,000 a one percent initiation fee or an extra one percent in interest amounts to a considerable sum of money. If you can save even a portion of this percent on closing costs or lower interest rates, you have been paid for the time you spend making a few phone calls to shop for money.

Buying on a land contract is another way to save money in financing. If the seller is financing his own property you may be able to negotiate a lower interest rate or down payment as part of the deal. Also, costs on closing a land contract are often less than they are to close a deal financed through a conventional lender.

CONSIDER THE FUTURE OF YOUR PROPERTY

Creative financing is only one of the considerations when buying property. Another thing you should consider is the future of your rental in the community in which it is located. Although you probably cannot make a long term prediction, you can check certain factors before buying. First, check on the number of high rise units under construction in the area of the rental you are considering buying. In a small community with little growth, one high rise or a few new multi-units can seriously affect the occupancy rate of older rentals.

Ask yourself what clientele will be attracted to the building you are planning to buy and compare this with the clientele which will be attracted to the new housing. If the housing under construction will appeal to high income couples with no children and your units will appeal to lower middle class people with children, you need not be too concerned about the competitive housing. If, however, both the new housing and the housing you are considering will appeal to the same kind of tenants, you may have trouble renting your units when the new housing is completed.

Whenever you buy property, you should buy for the clientele you hope to attract. Keep in mind that a two bedroom unfurnished apartment will probably appeal to a long term renter. A one bedroom furnished apartment on the other hand, often appeals to the more transient renter such as a student or single person. Although these are not absolutes, of course, you should keep this in mind when you are choosing property.

Landlords want to own property that rents well. Consequently, many landlords try to buy into very nice property. This is a worthwhile goal for many reasons, but attracting perfect tenants is not one of them. We have known tenants to damage beautiful apartments.

Look for property that can be changed to a better income producing property. Replacing peeling paint with aluminum siding, linoleum with carpeting and cracked walls with paneling are ways to increase the profit of your real estate investment. Attractive units will rent faster and will bring in better rents than unattractive units. An attractive building will also sell better and will command a better price than a rundown building. Many investors are wise to the advantages of giving a building a facelift. In some communities it may be difficult to find rental properties in good locations that need a facelift.

Related to the facelift is the property which lends itself to a complete conversion. Find a building zoned for duplex but presently being used as a single-family. Add a bathroom and a kitchen and either rent or sell it as a duplex. Sometimes the property's potential is an attached lot. You can keep the lot for a few years and build on it, thus increasing your income properties, or you can sell it at a profit.

HANDLE YOUR MONEY WISELY

Americans have always used property as one means of measuring wealth. Even the owner of two or three well-paying buildings may find his gross income from the rentals is greater than the salary from his regular job. If you pay property insurance once a year or figure the cost of heating the rentals into the monthly rent, you may find you still have money remaining after the bills are paid. Do not spend this money for personal expenses. Later in the year you may find you need this money for utility costs or major repairs you did not anticipate. Also, do not spend the equity in your rental properties for personal expenses, such as the cost of remodeling your residence or financing a luxury vacation. Equity should be used to increase your rental properties until you have reached the level of income you desire.

Be sure to keep some cash on hand. As a general rule, you should always keep the equivalent of one month's income from your rentals on hand. This helps tide you over when units are vacant.

Another general rule is to put as little cash into your rentals as you can. Use your equity and negotiate loans with as little down as possible. But remember not to over-extend your leverage. The less cash you put into a building, the less you have to lose should you have to forfeit the building.

You should not put all your available investment money into property. The wise investor keeps some investment money on hand. This cash should not be confused with the equivalent of one month's mortgage payments you have deposited in a separate savings account. This should be money that is free for investment purposes. A few thousand dollars in a savings account gives you security and protects your investments. If you should run into financial problems, this money can tide you over so you do not have to sell a piece of property at a forced sale. You can wait to sell the property for what it is worth.

If your goal is to build a string of well-paying rentals, any profit from your rentals should be used to remodel buildings or purchase additional property. Your profit should not be considered personal income. It should be returned to your business.

PROTECT YOUR INVESTMENTS

Be aware of laws governing foreclosure and keep that possibility in mind whenever you are financing property. This precaution alone will probably prevent a foreclosure from occurring. In a foreclosure settlement the lender is entitled to all properties which are included in the mortgage. If you have mortgaged several properties together, you could lose them all depending upon the extent of your debt and the market value of your property. If there is one property you want to keep at all costs, such as your personal residence, do not include it in other investments which may be marginal.

KNOW YOUR LIMITATIONS

Remember a successful landlord like any other successful businessman knows when to delegate responsibility. Do not think you need to be an expert on law, finance and construction to be a successful landlord. You need to know what you can do well, then delegate the rest of the responsibilities to experts. You need to know how to find and keep experts working for you. The successful landlord also employs a successful attorney, a successful accountant, and a successful carpenter, electrician and plumber. Value the advice and skills of these people and know when to use them to make your landlording successful.

If you know the tricks of the trade, you will be on your way to successful landlording. Employing these tricks to achieve your goal is one of the big plusses of real estate investment. Buying and selling at the right times, finding the right property and fixing it up to increase your income all satisfy the creativity of the ingenious investor.

SUMMARY

Successful landlords observe certain tricks of the trade. They keep up with the country's financial condition so they can buy and sell property according to the constant fluctuation of the money market. You should look for property that has the potential to increase faster than the normal inflation rate, and you should shop for financing so you do not pay more for the mortgage than you need to. You should learn to use leverage to your advantage without over-extending yourself. Although it may seem unlikely or unpleasant, you should also consider the possibility of foreclosure and conduct your business accordingly.

14
Why Real Estate

As you have read this book, you may have asked yourself several times, "Why should I invest in real estate? It is time-consuming, complicated and—to a certain extent—risky."

There are several excellent reasons to choose real estate over other investments. One of the most attractive features of real estate investment is connected with inflation. It is often said real estate is a hedge against inflation because the cost of real estate increases at a rate comparable with the cost of living. Although this is correct, the true appeal of real estate as an investment goes beyond the idea it is keeping pace with inflation. Real estate investments provide the investor with the chance to enjoy the inflation rate on money he does not have.

Consider for example, Joe, who has $10,000 to invest. He may put the $10,000 in a high yield savings account at a current rate of about 9 percent. At the end of the year, he would have earned about $900. He could also use the $10,000 to buy a $50,000 apartment building. If the inflation rate is 9 percent, he has earned 9 percent on $50,000 rather than on $10,000. If he wants to remortgage or sell the property at the end of the year, he can expect to earn $4,500 on his investment. Although there are a number of variables such as maintenance costs for the year and the cost of buying and selling, he still probably does better than he would if he put the money in the savings account. If he keeps the building for more than one year his rate of return will be better because he will have had some time to absorb some of the costs of buying and selling the building. This feature of real estate is an incentive, but it is especially important to the person who does not have enough money to invest in a high yield savings account.

Another advantage of real estate as an investment is its stability. Although art and collectibles are paying high dividends, this investment seems to fluctuate widely and demands a high degree of expertise. Although real estate has experienced some depressed periods, it is a commodity which is in demand and generally produces a stable dividend. According to a recent issue of *Money* (September, 1979) single-family homes increased 38.8 percent in the last recession from November, 1973 to March, 1975. *Money* magazine compared this to several other investments including stocks. Stocks decreased during this same period by 22.6 percent.

Real estate also generates an income while you hold the property. On the other hand, you must sell a painting or a collector's plate before you can enjoy the profit. Real estate offers a shelter to your taxable income. This is a significant advantage over other types of investments. While you may make only a few dollars a month on your rental at first, you will probably find you save a significant amount yearly on your taxable income.

One other advantage real estate has over other investments is the independence of the investor. Landlords can feel they are in control of their investments. They can decide to sell, remortgage or buy as a means of increasing their profit. They are dependent upon their own management of their property to "turn a profit." They do not have to worry about the quality of the management of the company whose stocks they have purchased. They do not have to worry the artist whose paintings they have bought will fall from favor with the critics. That independence and pride of ownership is certainly one of the biggest incentives of real estate as an investment. Real estate offers the man or woman of limited capital a chance, through ingenuity, to increase their wealth.

Experts predict real estate will continue to be a sound investment. According to *U.S. News and World Report* (April 2, 1979) the price of new single-family homes rose nearly 29 percent from the first quarter of 1977 to the fourth quarter of 1978. This means that home ownership is either postponed or put out of reach for many people. Thus the demand for apartments increases. The high cost of building has slowed the construction of new rental units and the demand for existing rentals increases among both investors and tenants. Again, according to *U.S. News and World Report* (April 2, 1979), rental vacancies have dropped to 2 percent in some cities. The present national average is a low 5 percent. Although fluctuations occur, real estate continues to be a sound investment.

If you know the risks and take advantage of the incentives you should be successful with your investment in rental property.

Glossary of Investment Terms

ABSTRACT A written record of the title transactions for a specific property. The abstract records the original title and all subsequent transactions.

ACCELERATED DEPRECIATION Depreciating the value of a property faster than with straight-line depreciation.

APPRAISAL Report of the value of a property.

BLANKET MORTGAGE A mortgage which covers more than one property.

CAPITAL GAINS Profit.

COLLATERAL Security for a mortgage such as interest in a boat, land or house.

CONVENTIONAL MORTGAGE A mortgage that uses the assets of a property and the borrower's credit to guarantee re-payment of the loan. The conventional loan is usually written for 15 to 30 years and is amortized, meaning the payments are equally divided over the life of the mortgage.

DEPRECIATION Decrease in value.

DOUBLE DECLINING BALANCE Method of accelerated depreciation.

DUPLEX A building which houses two families in separate living quarters.

EARNEST MONEY Cash deposited by a prospective buyer when he makes an offer to purchase a property. This deposit shows he is dealing in good faith.

EQUITY The value of a property above the amount of any mortgages on the property.

EVICTION Legal procedure which requires a tenant to move from the apartment where he is living.

FOUR-PLEX A building which houses four families in separate living quarters.

FHA-GUARANTEED LOAN A loan backed by the federal government.

INFLATION Increase in value of material goods.

INTEREST Fee paid on borrowed money.

INVESTMENT A commodity in which money is placed with the hope of realizing a significant cash return.

INVESTOR One who invests.

LAND CONTRACT An agreement entered into by a buyer and seller in which the seller is also the lender.

LANDLORD Person who owns rental property and provides the service of housing to tenants.

LEASE A contract between tenant and landlord which outlines the terms of the agreement to rent the property.

LEVERAGE Borrowed money used to increase an investor's holdings.

LOAN INITIATION FEE A percentage of the mortgage charged by the lender when the borrower is first granted a loan on a property.

MARKET ANALYSIS The use of comparable properties to determine a value for a particular property.

MORTGAGE A contract which outlines the extent and conditions of debt and provides the borrower with a certain amount of money against a piece of real estate.

MULTI-UNIT A building which houses more than four families in separate units.

OFFER TO PURCHASE A written contract offering to purchase real estate. It outlines the terms of the purchase.

OWNER-OCCUPIED A building which is occupied, at least in part, by the owner.

PREPAYMENT CLAUSE Wording in a mortgage contract which allows the lender to charge a percentage of the remaining amount of a mortgage if the property is sold or the loan is otherwise paid before its expiration date.

REAL ESTATE Land and improvements such as houses, garages, and sheds.

REALTOR A person who is licensed to sell real estate.

RENTAL A property which is rented.

SECOND MORTGAGE A mortgage which is secondary to and usually in addition to the primary mortgage.

SECURITY DEPOSIT Money held by the landlord to cover damage to the apartment or delinquent rent payments.

SHARED LOAN Loan given on a savings certificate.

SINGLE -FAMILY Building housing one family.

STRAIGHT-LINE DEPRECIATION A method of recording depreciation of a property in which a certain amount is deducted each year from the value of the property.

TAX SHELTER Legal ways to shield taxable income such as depreciation of property and business expenses.

TENANTS People who rent from the owner of the property.

THREE-PLEX A building which houses three families in separate units.

VA LOAN A loan backed by the Veterans Administration.

Glossary of Maintenance Terms

BUILDING PERMIT Written statement from a zoning commission or town council allowing building or remodeling.

CIRCUIT BREAKER A modern device to limit carrying capacity of an electrical circuit; can be reset.

DOLLY A two-wheeled cart for moving heavy objects.

DRYWALL MUD A pre-mixed plaster compound for all plaster repairs.

EXPANSION-BASE BOLT Bolt designed to anchor firmly in concrete.

FLASHING Sheet metal to provide waterproof joint between chimney and roof.

FURRING STRIPS 1x3-inch wood strips used as a base for ceiling tiles or paneling.

GASKET Any rubber or fiber shape designed to join two sections together without air or water leaks.

GLAZIER'S POINTS Small metal spears used to hold window glass in a wood frame.

GLAZING COMPOUND Putty-like substance that never hardens; used to seal windows and fill cracks in wood.

GYPSUM BOARD A firm, plaster sheet covered with stiff paper; serves as a base for plaster textures.

JOINT COMPOUND A sealing material for joints in water pipes.

JOIST Horizontal floor or ceiling support.

KEYHOLE SAW Small saw for cutting small, irregular openings.

LATH Wood strips formerly used as a base for plaster.

MAUL A five to 12 pound hammer with a long handle.

MITRE BOX A form used to hold a saw for precise angle cuts.

PARTICLEBOARD Man-made board made of wood chips and glue.

R FACTOR Standard measure for comparing insulating efficiency.

RAFTER Sloping roof-support timbers.

STUD Vertical wall support.

SUSPENDED CEILING Metal framework suspended by wires used to hold ceiling tiles.

WAINSCOT Lower part of wall finished with wood or paneling and another material above.

WATER TRAP A U-shaped drain pipe, sometimes circular and set flush with a floor.

WHEAT PASTE The standard adhesive for wallpaper.